margaret mahy
a writer's life

margaret mahy
a writer's life

by tessa duder

a literary portrait of new zealand's
best-loved children's author

Margaret Mahy 15.7.2005

HarperCollins*Publishers*

To Vanessa Hamilton

National Library of New Zealand Cataloguing-in-Publication Data

Duder, Tessa.
Margaret Mahy : a writer's life / Tessa Duder.
Includes bibliographical references.
ISBN 1-86950-485-2
1. Mahy, Margaret. 2. Women authors, New Zealand.
3. Authors, New Zealand. 4. Children's literature — Authorship.
5. Children's literature, New Zealand. I. Title.
NZ823.2 — dc 22

First published 2005
HarperCollinsPublishers (New Zealand) Limited
P.O. Box 1, Auckland

ISBN 1 86950 485 2

Cover design by Sarah Maxey
Cover photo by Alan Knowles
Typesetting by Janine Brougham

Printed by Griffin Press, Australia, on 79 gsm Bulky Paperback

Contents

Acknowledgements

I am indebted to Margaret Mahy's long-time friend and agent, the late Vanessa Hamilton, and her current London agent, Mandy Little, for their help with publishing information and with the bibliography.

My sincere thanks go to: Bill Nagelkerke, of the Christchurch City Libraries for access to the Margaret Mahy Archives and his personal files; Dr Diane Hebley for access to her research material; to librarians Margaret Lindsay (specifically her annotated Mahy bibliography) and Anne Coppell for their assistance in compiling a complete-as-possible bibliography; Julia Wells, commissioning editor of Faber & Faber, London; Fergus Barrowman of Victoria University Press, and editors Drs Elizabeth Hale and Sarah Winters for permission to quote from their forthcoming collection of essays, *Marvellous Codes: the Fiction of Margaret Mahy*; Frances Plumpton for research into Mahy's fictional names; and for their unfailing support Libby Limbrick and other colleagues and friends associated with the Storylines Children's Literature Foundation of New Zealand.

Others who have provided invaluable information and assistance include Jack Lasenby, Brian Cutting, Gavin Bishop, William Taylor, Yvonne Mackay, Sonja de Friez, Veronica McCarthy, John Barr, Joan Gibbons, David Hill, Witi Ihimaera, Anna Jackson, Rose Lovell-Smith, Kathryn Walls, Claudia Marquis, Janice Marriott, Joanna Orwin, Nan Pemberth.

For their editorial encouragement and patience, I wish to thank Lorain Day and the editorial staff of HarperCollins New Zealand in Auckland, along with editor Anna Rogers; also Ian Watt, the commissioning editor at HarperCollins New Zealand when the book was first suggested.

For the pictures, I am especially grateful to the photographer Alan Knowles, Frances Plumpton, *The Press*, Christchurch, *North & South* magazine and Margaret herself.

Thanks must also go to Bill Nagelkerke and Wayne Mills for their comments on early drafts of the manuscript. Every effort has been made to ensure accuracy of sources in the text and of the bibliography, although for an author so prolific, so widely published in many countries and so generous as a speech-maker and interview subject over forty years this has been challenging. In a few cases, efforts made to track down the primary source of clippings or photographs have proved fruitless. Any errors that remain are of course mine, and the publishers and I welcome information from readers for future editions.

Finally, sincere thanks are due to Margaret Mahy, for her unfailing grace and helpfulness in gathering the material for this book, her hospitality at Governors Bay on two occasions during 2004 and others over the years, and her comments on, and acceptance of the manuscript. For her friendship and support over several decades, I and the increasingly wide fellowship of writers and illustrators in New Zealand are profoundly grateful.

Tessa Duder
February 2005

Introduction

It seems remarkable now, when new authors can reasonably expect rapid induction into the heady world of literary festivals, the media and the writers' community, that I did not meet Margaret Mahy for five years after my debut novel was published. Another two years went by before I heard her give a major speech.

There were several reasons for this long wait. The early 1980s had yet to see the spread of the literary festivals — Dunedin, Wellington, Auckland, Christchurch, Whakatane, Waitakere, the Bay of Islands — now securely established on the New Zealand arts calendar and providing, among other things, invaluable opportunities for writers to meet their colleagues. Then, a writer might be individually invited to a more specialised, professional occasion, say a library conference, a children's literature or literacy event, a university seminar or a school's book week. If shortlisted for an award, you might briefly meet other authors, under less than relaxed conditions, at prize-giving ceremonies.

Then surely I, and other up-and-coming writers of the 1980s, would have met one of New Zealand's greatest writers, twice winner (in 1982 and 1984) of Britain's Carnegie Medal, at these occasions, adding New Zealand awards to those she was collecting overseas? No, because her novels, short story collections and picture books, published principally in Britain and the United States, were not then eligible for most New Zealand awards. With the exception of the Esther Glen Medal, which she has won six times since 1970, you will not see most of her great novels of the past 20 years included in New Zealand's book awards.

To me, as a parent, a newish writer and an eager reader of every Margaret Mahy novel as it appeared, the author down in Governors Bay on the shores of Lyttelton Harbour was a distant and Olympian figure.

I finally met her in August 1987, at a screenwriting course being run in Wellington. My novel *Alex*, due for publication in September, was also being adapted for television, so the five trips to Wellington seemed a worthwhile investment in my role as script consultant and coincidentally the opportunity to meet the author I admired above all others. Margaret, by then also recognised as an innovative and successful writer of children's television, with *Cuckooland* and *Strangers* under her belt, was to conduct the last session.

'Oh, Tessa, I'm so pleased to meet you,' she said in that unmistakeable New Zealand small-town voice, smiling broadly under the soft felt Homburg-style hat she often wears in public to cover fine and anxious hair. Holding out mint copies of my first two novels, *Night Race to Kawau* and *Jellybean*, she added, to my astonishment, 'Here, I'd be so pleased if you'd sign your books for me.'

I've since heard that other new writers have had similar experiences of this simple, generous expression of support for the genre and the writers behind the books. Until recently, when she has begun to lament that she simply cannot keep up with all the children's books she wants to read, never mind the adult ones, for decades Margaret followed her dedicated librarian's commitment of reading virtually every New Zealand children's and young adult novel published. And she has happily bought hundreds of them, the picture books too, creating on her living room's high-reaching bookshelves what must be one of the best private collections of New Zealand children's books in the country. Her commitment to 'adult' fiction and non-fiction, local and overseas, is scarcely less.

I remember her session for one other reason. Until then, a good deal of the discussion had been of a defensive nature: how to prevent or at least deflect nasty producers, directors, financiers, script editors and even uppity actors from generally conspiring to ruin your carefully polished script. In the space of a few minutes, Margaret changed all that. Not for her the inevitability of the beleaguered writer, knowing the risk of being called precious but standing firm against the suits and barbarians. Writing for television, she stated then and continues to say, is teamwork with other clever, talented people and for novelists, who normally work in solitude, it's entertaining, surprising, intense, stimulating, full of excitement and thoroughly *enjoyable*. Her session, an informal talk with twelve or so students in a small room, was positive, wise, often very funny, slyly self-mocking, discursive to the point of seeming to tilt the topic off-balance into a lengthy ramble, but also, given a few minutes of often brilliant deviation, bringing her point unfailingly, triumphantly home.

It is Margaret's brilliance as an essayist and speechwriter, her versatility and *completeness* as a writer, together with my belief that, as a novelist, she has been shamefully neglected (in her own country if not elsewhere), that have largely led me to write this book. Even that experience in Wellington was hardly sufficient preparation for the first few occasions I heard her delivering a formal speech to a large and well-informed audience. The first was two years later in New Orleans, where she was a keynote speaker at the American convention of the International Reading Association which, thanks to an Arts Council grant, I was attending on my way to Rome to research the third book in the *Alex* quartet.

In New Orleans, I sat spellbound and proud among a large gathering of equally captivated Americans as, for over an hour, Margaret brought all her wit and eloquence to bear on the subtle, scholarly and subversive nature of her ideas. In 1990, it was Rotorua, a full hall of teachers at the South Pacific Convention of the International Reading Association listening to her talk on censorship in children's literature, and also in Wellington, at the International Festival of the Arts Readers and Writers Week, where I found myself sharing a platform for a children's session with Margaret and the acclaimed British poet Charles Causley. Though comparatively little published as a poet, she was as learned and compelling in the specialist field of children's poetry as he, and able to quote with ease from his widely known, infinitely sad pieces 'My Mother Saw a Dancing Bear' and 'Timothy Winters', among much else. Causley was gratified, respectful, even overawed; I was wise enough to contribute little.

On these and other occasions through the 1990s, the Mahy hallmarks, well honed in more than a decade of constant public speaking were always there: the rich, magical language, the musicality and rhythmic ease of her prose, the provocative and often contrary ideas, the incursions into philosophy and science, architecture and the arts, history and anthropology, the literary quotes and allusions and the social commentary and the psychological insight. Few academics could match her knowledge of children's and adult literature, both historical and contemporary. Along with a lifetime of reading, two decades as a professional librarian and 25 years as a full-time professional writer there is a phenomenal memory that enables her, in any question time or informal gathering, to offer detailed impromptu musings on practically any children's or young adult book you care to name. Characters, storyline, issues, the author's place in the genre under discussion — all are effortlessly, accurately recalled and shared. The same largely applies to 'adult' classic and contemporary fiction or works on a range of science topics, philosophy, popular culture, plays, poetry, horror stories, ghost stories.

In private, she is a creative listener as well as an enthusiastic talker and participant in lively debate. The extent of her reading often astonishes: David Hill, writer and passionate amateur astronomer, once settled down to instruct her on the matter of black holes. Two minutes later, he says, the reverse was happening with 'absolutely no arrogance — she just pays you the tribute of assuming you can participate'. No matter how tired or jet-lagged she is, how currently immersed in work or family affairs, her presentations are invariably delivered with energy, good humour, respect for her audience and skilful timing in a New Zealand accent that she once said sounded more like the sort of voice that should be reading out cake recipes over the radio.

I've come to believe over the years that as a serious novelist, essayist and thinker, Margaret is much underrated in her own country where the general literary establishment persists in seeing writing for children and young adults as outside mainstream literature. Therefore, only serious 'adult' writers (no matter how new or undistinguished) are worthy of their serious critical attention. Margaret's world-acclaimed novels are not widely read for pleasure or academic study because 'Well, she's only a children's writer.' (I've heard those exact words from a quite well-known male short story writer who flared briefly as a 1980s post modernist, among others.) Her speeches, even those on general aspects of literature or culture, attract, in my experience, very few of the literati.

Those of us who work in children's literature, however, or in the associated fields of children's librarianship, literacy education and educational publishing, have had regular, unforgettable reminders since the early 1980s of Margaret as a speech-writer and public speaker without peer.

We have read her internationally award-winning novels, at least five of which, given different book design and covers, could have been published as adult fiction. We're aware of her fairytale arrival on the international scene, in 1969, with simultaneous launches of five picture books in New York and London, and the two Carnegie Medals that she won with her first two major novels. We have some idea of the offshore reputation that she has built up since by sheer brilliance and hard work.

Many of us have experienced on more than one occasion the challenge of her intellectual curiosity, the warmth of her generosity and her extraordinary stamina. Some of us know of literary organisations she has quietly supported with cheques arriving out of the blue, or the occasions when she has insisted that she would pay her own air fares, of the writers who have been offered the use of her book- and video-filled apartment in Cranmer Square in central Christchurch. We have seen on websites — those of several publishers, the New Zealand Book Council, Christchurch City Libraries and others set up overseas — the generous, written responses she has supplied to FAQ (frequently asked questions) pages: long paragraphs, which must have taken hours, about how she writes, her working methods and advice for young writers. Many of us, recipients of occasional emails, notes of congratulations on a new book, long personal Christmas letters or sudden phone calls, count her as a good friend.

Yes, the literary establishment will say, and surely it's true that in 1993 she became the only writer to receive the country's highest civil honour, ordinary membership of the Order of New Zealand. In that year wasn't she also awarded an honorary doctorate by the University of Canterbury? The New Zealand Literary Fund Lifetime Achievement Award earlier, in 1985? The publishing industry's first A.W. Reed Lifetime Achievement Award in 1999? President of Honour of the New Zealand Society of Authors in 1997? If they knew anything at all about children's literature, they might add she has twice been nominated for the Hans Christian Andersen Medal, the world's 'Little Nobel' for children's writers, and a medal bearing her name has been awarded annually since 1991 by the Storylines Children's Literature Foundation of New Zealand for a 'distinguished contribution to children's literature'. Isn't she known to the general public as a 'household name', a beloved National Treasure, as that loveable eccentric from Lyttelton who writes wacky picture books and is often photographed with primary school kids, wearing a penguin suit or a funny multicoloured wig?

These accomplishments, however, comprise the literary establishment's soothing, official mantra; in my opinion, they are only half the story, very often expressed with a sort of condescension and not matched by the sort of recognition and support that would be accorded to an 'adult' novelist of similar international standing.

Where, besides a tiny handful (notably, Claudia Marquis, Kathryn Walls, Rose Lovell-Smith and Anna Smith, all teachers of the country's few university children's literature courses) are the mainstream academic studies? If Margaret Mahy is one of New Zealand's three greatest ever writers, why is she not extensively taught in English literature courses in New Zealand universities, alongside Mansfield, Frame, Mulgan, Hyde, Shadbolt, Ihimaera, Hulme, Gee, Duff and Knox?

Where (besides *A Dissolving Ghost*, a shortish, tantalising collection of speeches published in 2000) are the several substantial books of essays, compilations or edited versions of the best of her many speeches and reviews? Although she occasionally jumps the barrier and makes it as the only children's writer profiled in selections of contemporary New Zealand authors, why does arguably the country's best, most versatile and most original writer not appear in the short story collections, or critical studies or anthologies of New Zealand writing which have been produced since 1980?

As her career as a novelist flowered internationally during the 1980s and 1990s, where were the publishers' launches and nationwide promotions always accorded to, say, Maurice Gee or Fiona Kidman or Patricia Grace or younger writers like Catherine Chidgey? Where, in the book pages of the mainstream media and the literary journals, have been the serious, informed reviews and commentaries accorded to writers of 'adult' fiction? Why do I search in vain for her inclusion in any book of New Zealand quotations, when so much droll, insightful quotable treasure is to be found in her work? As David Hill said in his review of *A Dissolving Ghost*, 'She's eminently quotable: "Pursuing truth in literature is like pursuing a chimera, a dissolving ghost"; "In books for young adults . . . [readers] are looking anxiously for something that's going to make them marvellous"; "It was the year I turned five. I was already a slave to fiction".'

And how has it happened that in Britain Margaret Mahy is known primarily for her novels for young adults, is even, according to a 2005 television documentary, *Made in New Zealand: Margaret Mahy*, 'a household name' there — is often even claimed as one of their own? Why is any mention of these same young adult novels in New Zealand intermediate and high school classrooms met time and again with blank, mystified faces? *The Changeover*? *The Tricksters*? *The Catalogue of the Universe*? *The Other Side of Silence*? Surely they've at least heard of her most recent and better promoted works, both New Zealand award-winners — *24 Hours*? *Alchemy*? There is admittedly a lamentable general lack of teacher and student awareness of locally written young adult novels in our secondary schools, despite many efforts in the past decade, but this is getting close to disgraceful. They are probably being taught Mansfield and Frame and Sargeson and Ihimaera and Duff, but I don't believe they are being taught Mahy.

Until very recently, of course, Margaret was mostly published overseas and her major novels were therefore brought into New Zealand from Britain as pricey imports, without promotional budgets and, through the 1980s, not eligible for awards. But because she has been touched by what Rose Lovell-Smith calls 'the dead hand of children's writing', there is widespread ignorance of the full range of her work, of the unique intellect behind it and of her true international standing.

Within the UK, Margaret Mahy is seen as one of the all-time greats of children's literature, studied by academics alongside Kenneth Graham, C.S. Lewis, Alan Garner and Philip Pullman, says Julia Wells. Editor at Faber & Faber, she is currently working with Margaret on her long-awaited fantasy trilogy begun in the early 1980s. She finds it hard to believe that in New Zealand, a country now being perceived through its film successes as a 'hot-bed of talent', Margaret Mahy is better known for her younger books. 'Margaret is loved here for her picture books, but she is

particularly revered for the quality of her novels for older children
... The characters in Margaret's work engrossed me [as a teenager]
to such a deep level that I didn't at first realise the stories were
set in New Zealand. Not until I read an episode in *The Tricksters*
where the family are having Christmas lunch on the beach ... The
idea of sunbathing on Christmas Day was such an unusual picture
that I instantly had to readjust how I was imagining the story. The
strength of her work is that it can be enjoyed on many levels. For
New Zealand readers, I am sure it is loved for characteristics that
are pure "New Zealand". However, the reason why Margaret has
endured in the UK is because her writing transcends cultural and
environmental differences.'

The literary snobbery which confines children's and young
adults' literature to an invisible ghetto is, however, now much less
fashionable or indeed, inevitable, than it was. Margaret herself
has commented on the attitude that sees children's literature as
'somehow detached from literature . . .', a view totally at odds
with her own conviction that the genre is indisputably 'part of
the literature of a community'. In England, Philip Pullman and
Mark Haddon have famously challenged established notions
of where children's literature stands by winning 'adult' literary
awards with complex, sophisticated novels that defy easy and
condescending categorisation as mere 'children's books'; the Harry
Potter books have won J.K. Rowling a significant adult audience,
as have the superb 'young adult' novels by Australia's Sonya
Hartnett, Gary Crew and Lian Hearn (aka Gillian Rubinstein).
Mahy's *Memory*, runner-up for an unprecedented third Carnegie
Medal, is regarded by many as a compassionate adult study of
Alzheimer's disease; there's enough anecdotal evidence to put in
cross-over claims for William Taylor's *The Blue Lawn* and my own
Alex. The judges for the 1986 Goodman Fielder Wattie award
were open-minded enough to include my novella *Jellybean* in their
shortlist of ten, to some tut-tutting, I have to say. But now, Witi
Ihimaera's *The Whale Rider* and, in Australia, novels like Sonya
Hartnett's *Of a Boy* typify the new enthusiasm for publishing

cross-over books aimed equally at a young and adult audience. Though grumbles about the unwarranted lowly status of children's writers and the lack of review space and critical scrutiny are neither new nor confined to New Zealand, the small, close-knit publishing and literary world here does perhaps mean fewer and more muted challenges to entrenched, outdated or ill-informed attitudes.

Even after more than a decade of strenuous lobbying by the Children's Literature Foundation, the AIM and then New Zealand Post Children's Book Awards, the New Zealand Book Council and a few influential individuals like Greg O'Brien and Professor Terry Sturm, the situation is little better. Consider, for instance, the absence of children's literature, included as a genre like any other, in some of the country's major literary festivals, the lack of regular reviewing and commentary in both the mainstream and literary media. In a small country, one festival director, one publisher, one academic, one buyer for one bookseller, one editor and/or reviewer in one newspaper or magazine can, and very often does, exert disproportionate influence and power — unlike even, say, Australia, where the five-times greater population gives rise to a much broader range of compensating views.

Added to this has been a 'powerful hierarchy of genres' dominating critical discourse about New Zealand literature, 'with poetry and "serious" adult fiction (the novel and the short story) enjoying largely undisputed possession of the field, the genres of non-fiction and drama on the margins, and children's literature and forms of popular writing largely invisible'. Terry Sturm's introduction to the 1991 *Oxford History of New Zealand Literature in English* cited the recent *Penguin History of New Zealand Literature* as therefore capable of relegating 'one of New Zealand's major writers, the children's author Margaret Mahy, to a footnote'. Worse than that, I would add, the footnote includes Mahy not in her own right but only in the context of a book of author interviews by Sue Kedgley.

And Sturm and I are not alone here, nor can I be accused of a bit of nationalistic flag-waving for a local favourite. Overseas

Margaret Mahy is acknowledged as a ground-breaking novelist, one of the 20th century's very greatest fantasy writers and an international leader in the field of writing on family relationships; many another country would be proud to call her their own. Australia, for instance, currently has no real equivalent to Mahy on the world stage. Diane Hebley, whose *Power of Place — Landscape in New Zealand Children's Fiction 1970–1989* has been the only academic trade publication on the genre for nearly two decades, concluded after a detailed survey that 'the amount of useful and extensive critical commentary reserved for New Zealand children's literature is woefully small for a literature that has international standing and excites critical interest in journals overseas'. More specifically, Greg O'Brien asserts in *Moments of Invention, Portraits of 21 New Zealand Writers* that Margaret Mahy is 'in every way, a serious writer, but the fact she writes children's books means she seldom gets the degree of recognition she would receive if she were writing for adults'.

In my research for this book, those comparatively rare occasions where Margaret Mahy has been properly considered within the literary mainstream, and not as a paddler up some distant and unimportant creek, have stood out because of their rarity. Leading academic Mark Williams has shown at least some awareness of Margaret Mahy's standing. Reviewing Bill Manhire's anthology *100 New Zealand Poems* in the literary review journal *New Zealand Books*, he notes Manhire's comment that 'Frame is a poet in all of her work' and adds, 'The same might be said of Margaret Mahy whose books, more than those of any other New Zealand writer, with the possible exception of Janet Frame, derive from the conviction that literature is language that causes us to regard the world with amazement.'

An earlier tribute was a major interview by Murray Edmond which appeared in the literary quarterly *Landfall* in 1987. His introduction states (and what a pity about the coy qualification, 'Although she is a children's writer . . .', which he disowns but still, alas, feels obliged to make):

. . . a great deal [of this taped interview] has been lost in cutting and shaping because Margaret Mahy is an indefatigable and supremely entertaining talker, a genuine intellectual with a mind full of ideas and information as well as a relentless curiosity. What is not lost in this interview is her ability to speak in superbly honed sentences and with great clarity and precision . . . Not until she won prizes in America [*sic*] for *The Haunting* and *The Changeover* did she begin to be acknowledged fully here in New Zealand . . . Although she is a children's writer (and such a qualification should really be unnecessary), Margaret Mahy, along with Katherine Mansfield, Janet Frame and, much more recently, Keri Hulme, is one of our few internationally acclaimed writers. On any level she is a fine stylist, and, as a children's writer, she bears comparison with Kipling for her command over genre and her verbal dexterity.

Yet, in searching through books of New Zealand literary criticism in the past 20 years, I found, besides Sturm, O'Brien, Hebley and Williams, very few references to Margaret Mahy or the country's now well-established literature for children. Ironically, though, in recent years there have been signs that Margaret is being accepted, if not as a novelist, then belatedly as an essayist. O'Brien's generous *New Zealand Books* review of *A Dissolving Ghost* suggested that this rather slim and modestly promoted book should have been bigger, that she should be encouraged, commissioned, to write more major essays on serious topics, not for spoken presentation where the audience is 'sitting so expectantly in front of her' but for the published page where 'she could stretch out more'. Mahy, he concluded, is 'one of a line of New Zealand geniuses that also includes Janet Frame, Rita Angus, Katherine Mansfield and Frances Hodgkins'.

Genius is, or should be, a word used with caution. In a major feature in the *Listener* in 1991, her high school English teacher for three years, Ian McLean, stated that, after 50 years of observing his former student's career, 'I wouldn't be backward in claiming the word *genius* for Margaret.' Many others agree. With the recent death of Janet Frame, is there any other New Zealand writer to whom the word could be applied? Margaret would undoubtedly shy from the thought; she acknowledges sharing with Frame the same idea of myth 'but she's an exquisite writer, and I'm a more plastic, clownish writer. I remember reading her autobiography and feeling it was a story that was true for so many New Zealanders. You get an extraordinary feeling when you suddenly recognise your own story in someone else's; it's a moment of fulfilment.'

Greg O'Brien chose Mahy and Frame to open and close his book *Moments of Invention*:

. . . I imagined these two figures as being like bookends — pillars of both the craft and the imagination; both of them fitting and substantial enough presences to hold in place the nineteen writers who filled the space between them . . . As well as being comparably substantial artists, these two bipolar (in our book plan) figures were remarkably different as writers yet also, as became increasingly apparent, interestingly similar.

If Mahy was the writer of light, of buoyancy and liberation, Frame struck a dark, more restrained note. If Mahy wrote for the child in all of us, then Frame wrote for the adult that exists inside every child. Or so it might appear at first, but — of course — once you dug a little deeper, vistas of redemptive space opened up in Frame. And something darker and more foreboding emerged in the most clearly, brightly voiced of Mahy's tales. In both of them a constant interplay of gravity and levity, light and shade, brilliance and something which is at times heartbreakingly ordinary. This paradoxical quality, I suspect, is at the heart of creative genius.

If Frame tends to present life as a juggernaut we must handle with stealth in order to survive, Mahy sees the world more as a great machine that we can and should tamper with. And while the results might occasionally be disastrous for the individual, such an approach contains the possibility of success and elation. For Frame, language is healing; for Mahy it is more a preventative medicine or, more exactly, a vitamin supplement ensuring, at least, the possibility of health.

While Frame is commonly thought of as a doyen of the inner life, Margaret Mahy is the public speaker, a performer in person as well as on the page. During the 1980s Mahy was often photographed — and existed in the public imagination — wearing a multicoloured wig which she would don, to the delight of all assembled, at readings in libraries and elsewhere (you could almost think of this get-up as a fluorescent revision of the Frame hairdo). This 'persona' drew attention to some of the qualities you find in Mahy's writing; the sense of adventure and risk, and the need for unabashed brilliance up front, a dash of imaginative magic to jump-start commonplace reality.

Further contrasts strike me. If Frame's output, her autobiographies notwithstanding, was almost entirely fiction and poetry, with rare interviews and even fewer public appearances, Mahy's has included, besides her fiction and poetry, an astonishing output of reviews, commentaries, journalism, non-fiction, screenwriting, essays for publication and many as yet unpublished speeches.

If Frame bore no children and lived much of her adult life in Europe, the United States and only intermittently and in the final years in New Zealand, alone and increasingly reclusive, Mahy, though widely travelled on the literary and library circuit, has lived in New Zealand all her life, single-handedly creating a home for herself and her family and frequent visitors. She has been a caregiver for most of her adult life, raising two daughters as a solo parent and for nearly five years looking after an aunt suffering from Alzheimer's, even while her professional literary career took off. In recent years she has devoted substantial daily chunks of time to her six grandchildren.

With Frame, there is the apparent curiosity of this most private of writers producing, in her mid-50s and at what proved to be the peak of her powers, a three-volume autobiography, followed by her agreement to an acclaimed screen version. Some years later, there was Michael King's large, authorised biography.

For Mahy, approaching 70, as productive, adventurous, inventive and generous as ever, the idea of an autobiography, even a memoir, holds no appeal whatsoever; neither does a conventional biography within her lifetime. The reasons were unsurprising. First, there was a genuine scepticism that anyone should find her life — so focused on study, librarianship, providing for her children, travel, visiting schools, always reading and constantly writing — in any way interesting. Equally, family sensibilities were an important consideration; the quest for happiness, honesty, harmony, kindness and love within the dynamics of extended family life is a dominating theme throughout her fiction and emphatically is no less so for her in real life. One of a large family herself, with her own daughters and a new generation of grandchildren, nieces and nephews growing up, she was anxious, she told me, not to have herself cast as any sort of hero in a detailed or intimate history involving the wider family. A writer's statements about self, she believes, are secretly contained in what he or she writes. Meantime, this 'literary history' is offered as a glimpse into the general background, mind and wide-ranging writings of New Zealand's best-known international author.

My original idea was to follow *A Dissolving Ghost* with a bigger compilation of further unpublished speeches, some which I'd fondly remembered from specific occasions and hoped I might gently extricate from Margaret's slightly haphazard filing system. Gradually, however, it seemed she could be better served by placing selections from available writing both by and about her within the broad context of her life and career so far. Much of the material comes from the major, carefully prepared but so far unpublished one-off talks she has been giving all over the world since about 1973 and from some ten hours of interviews recorded in Governors Bay in 2004. Other material has come from various libraries and private collections noted in the acknowledgements.

Thus, on my desk sits probably the most complete collection of Mahy papers yet assembled: photocopies of unpublished and published essays, along with magazine and newspaper interview cuttings, commentaries, academic papers and extracts from books on New Zealand writing and writers. From mostly New Zealand sources, it is impressive for a single writer, yet it is not exhaustive — that huge task remains for a possible future biographer. Despite her librarian training, Margaret is typically somewhat dismissive of the importance of her own archives — 'Who wants all that old stuff?' she said more than once — and in a literary career spanning four decades, two of them more than full-time, she has had no assistant, only infrequent secretarial help to deal with correspondence, filing and other business aspects of a demanding children's writer's life. Some of the speeches, probably from the 1970s, we found on flimsy foolscap paper in boxes possibly not opened for decades, and several could be only tentatively identified by the topic or references to her age or audience. In the absence of a diary or record — 'I'd always assumed I'd remember it all!' — one thing has tended to run into another. Much more so than writers for adults, successful children's writers are frequently called on to speak and write about themselves, their backgrounds, ideas and writing processes, and none has been more generous in this respect than Margaret. For over four decades there has been a constant stream of profiles, author interviews and requests for talks. As Margaret herself has pointed out, over the years she has 'talked a lot and inevitably I have often said the same things in different ways'.

One day there will be a proper Margaret Mahy archive in Christchurch, and it is to be hoped that in time more of her essays, poems, letters and reviews will be published, as Katherine Mansfield has been. For now, though, this volume must suffice. It is neither a biography nor a critical literary study, but in establishing a vehicle for a selection of Margaret's own surprising moments, provocative ideas and energetic, magical language to see the light of day, I hope that it will make an early contribution to the mainstream recognition that this 'children's author' has not yet fully received in her own country and which by every literary measure she so richly deserves.

Part One

The Young Philosopher —
1936 to 1958

A ny narrative about Margaret Mahy, as lifelong and passionate advocate for the power of stories to influence, shape
and structure human experience, should surely begin in the traditional way.

Once upon a time

. . . a first child was born to a couple living in a small, remote
township on the coast of a distant country surrounded by ocean.
The mother and father of this daughter had some standing in
the town: she was a primary schoolteacher, he (somewhat older,
approaching 40) was a bridge-builder, with his own respected
contracting company.

   The child, eventually to be the eldest of five, grew into a solid,
fair and articulate girl who showed an unusually early love for
reading, and, as soon as she was able to hold a pencil and shape
the letters, for writing down her own stories . . .

Or, we could skip the mostly happy middle-class childhood, the
adolescent years of schooling and university study, and move on
to . . .

Once upon a time

. . . there was a young mother who had two daughters, but very
little money. During the day she worked hard as a librarian to
support her young family, but by night, after they were in bed,
she secretly wrote stories that she sent away to get published in a
School Journal and earn her much-needed extra money.

   Gradually, over many years, she became quite well known,
but only in her own country, until one day, a rich and famous
publisher in America happened to read one of her stories.
Immediately she sent a letter offering to be her publisher and
made plans at great cost to fly to that far-off country especially to
meet this writer of unique and unusual talent . . .

Or, we could fast forward to the subsequent simultaneous launch in the United States and Britain and the growing world reputation as a writer of marvellously quirky, funny picture books and start with . . .

Once upon a time

. . . there was a librarian who was also an author. All her life she had written stories for children and many of them had been published as handsome picture books in many countries. To earn extra money, she also took work writing for television, but secretly she yearned to write longer works, serious novels for children and perhaps also for young adults.

One day, when she was in her early 40s and bone-weary after years of working all day and writing many hours into the night, she decided that the time had come; she must try to support herself and her daughters by her writing. Resigning from her job in the library, she began intense work on her first serious novel for children. Imagine her astonishment and pleasure when her book won one of the world's most important prizes for children's writers, and even greater astonishment when her second novel, her first for young adults, won the very same medal two years later . . .

Margaret Mahy's life story always seems to have had something of a fairytale air about it, with herself cast in the persona of the benign, slightly mischievous witch, the weaver of magical or funny or ghostly or powerfully dramatic stories, as it pleases her, or us, her readers.

She lives alone — with her cats and, usually, a dog, and sometimes rabbits and other animals — on the rim of 'a collapsed caldera type of crater, similar to some on the moon, where the sea has come and turned it into a harbour'. In her house of many levels and staircases are the old books, antique toys, masks, pictures, puzzles and countless accumulated treasures a magician might have, while the fruitful garden is a touch tangled and mysterious, with arches and pathways and no clear boundaries. Frequently her house sings with the happy chatter of grandchildren. And though most of her shorter stories and some of her longer ones are set in the land of Anywhere or Somewhere or Elsewhere, and in England (the country where most of her books have been first published), she is often thought to be an English writer and actually claimed there, 20,000 kilometres away, as 'one of ours', Margaret Mahy has never thought of herself as anything other than a New Zealander by birth and by choice, in soul and in spirit.

Storytellers are not always romantic, even about their place of birth. 'I spent thirty-seven years in New Zealand doing the usual things,' she once told an audience in Australia, 'being educated, working, falling in love, having children, pushing cars when they stopped working at traffic lights — before I went overseas for the first time. By then I was certainly what New Zealand had made me.

'Of course in the case of New Zealand the seas are notoriously wide. We're stuck on the outer rim of the great circles of art, science, culture and political and industrial power . . . New Zealand, by contrast [to Australia] is little and twitching, a country of forest and ferns. "Green, green, green," said an early colonist, and he said it in despair. Birds cry out in curious voices full of twangs and gong notes. New Zealand is uneasy because it is volcanic and even when you live far from the active volcanoes, you might find yourself (as I do) living in the ruin of an extinct one, or perhaps on a fault line. [My home town of] Whakatane was built on a fault line, and I think continuation of that fault line runs through me — but then I think it runs through us all. It is just that New Zealand offers its citizens tangible fault lines to observe. Below us the tectonic plates grate against each other, tearing the country in two.' But it was, she added a little later, 'a country of readers'.

More recently, she has described New Zealand as a 'beautiful, damaged country which I love' and has learned over the years to write about it with lack of self-consciousness, 'naturally and passionately', and, more bluntly, as not the 'idyllic country the travel brochures try to suggest. It is part of the world and the damage of the world. Along with its wonderful patches of forest and South Island mountains and its North Island beaches and its programmes for saving endangered birds, it has its share of racial problems — sometimes bitter ones — of crime, broken families, youth suicide. It has its bullies, its abused and ruined people. Its writers describe the beauty, but they want to acknowledge its contentious areas, too . . . These days, we may be concerned with what it is to be New Zealanders, but we are part of the world, the Western world and the Polynesian world, too. We are all world citizens because of books, pictures, films and popular music. We have something to give and receive and something to offer.'

In 2004 it is a country 'looking energetically inwards, defining and redefining its own identity, yet simultaneously longing to be recognised by the wider world. So the recent success of the film *Whale Rider* leads to a curious mood of local self-congratulation. *See! We too, just by being who we are, can be up there with the best* — a mood that is currently encouraged by curiosity from the outside world. *Whale Rider! Amazing! What else is going on in New Zealand?*'

Although she is not known internationally as a writer of distinctively 'New Zealand' stories in the same way as, say, the earlier great Australians Ivan Southall or Patricia Wrightson, and although detailed description of landscape and environment is infrequent in her work, New Zealanders know from subtle but clear evidence where her heart lies. When, as a mature writer, she began setting her novels in and around Christchurch, the descriptive passages in books like *The Tricksters*, contained, in the opinion of academic Tom Fitzgibbon, 'the warmest and most vivid evocation of New Zealand seascape, shore and encircling hills since [Katherine] Mansfield's novella *At the Bay* some seventy years ago'. Here, in the first chapter, is an English visitor discovering Lyttelton Harbour at the start of an antipodean Christmas:

Then, beyond the orchard and the native bush, they came face to face at last with the harbour, held in a circle of craggy hills in the cone of an old volcano. Its grey spaces and reflecting films of water at low tide made it look more like a prehistoric estuary than a commercial port, even though docks and cranes, small as children's toys, could be seen directly opposite. Thin soil lay draped over the bones of the land, in long, curving folds, falling, always falling, down to the sea and ending in a ragged coastline of tiny bays and indentations. Native bush grew darkly in the gullies; the gaunt ridges were freckled with the gold of gorse and broom. The two landscapes ran into each other and made a new countryside altogether (not pretty, but desolate, beautiful and timeless). Towards the eastern end of the beach was the boat house with Charlie's *Sunburst* drawn up on the ramp, and beyond that, just as if the sand and seagrass had worked themselves into a useful shape, was a little cabin propped up by flax bushes and wild yellow lupin.

The landscape of her childhood was also an eastern coast, but North Island rather than South, oceanic, wild and expansive rather than encircled and enclosed. Margaret May, a desired first child, was born on 21 March 1936, in the small coastal township of Whakatane, on the long fertile sweep of the North Island's Bay of Plenty. In pre-European times, it had been a stronghold of Ngati Awa, Tuhoe and Te Whakatoahea iwi. European whalers, sealers and traders began arriving in the 1830s and a small settlement gradually developed into a centre for shipbuilding and a small port for local produce destined for rapidly growing northern settlements. By the mid-1930s some 1800 people lived beside the Rangitaiki rivermouth, servicing a hinterland of productive farmland and looking out seaward to a Pacific horizon dominated by the occasional smoke puffing forth from volcanic White Island. A few kilometres to the south was the glorious long sweep of sand and surf, Ohope Beach. And, sitting right on a major fault line, the people of Whakatane knew about earthquakes. It was not uncommon for families like the Mahys to sit down to a meal and, feeling the floor beneath them tremble and seeing the cutlery and dishes on the table begin to shake, cry 'Earthquake!' and dive under the table or a nearby door lintel. Margaret often had the unsettling experience of seeing 'the ground twist with earthquakes'.

Margaret May was born in the town's small hospital and taken as a baby to the still-existing concrete family home built by her father Frank at 26 Haig Street, across the road from the town cemetery. Six decades later she would remember, for a ghost story she was writing, that 'sometimes you can swim in the river and sometimes you are given the chance to swim in the sea . . . as I wrote I remembered how, when the tide was coming in, it always looked as if the river-ripples were running backwards . . . Twice a day (twice in 24 hours) in that cemetery, the tide would turn and then the light would change and, if you were in that cemetery walking around the old tombstones, those stones would start looking like pages from a book . . . anyone who was walking there at the time when the tide turned looked as if they had been transformed into an angel . . .'

She describes herself as coming from 'good English stock'. Her 'overwhelming memories' of her father's mother are of 'a woman without teeth, leading an almost exclusively gardening life'. Her father was overjoyed to be a parent, and her mother, who had been a teacher, was 'terribly keen to have a clever child'. Margaret was surrounded from the beginning by a large extended family of grandparents, uncles, aunts and cousins. Her paternal grandfather Frank Mahy (with the 'rather peculiar and romantic' history of being unaccountably abandoned at a Bristol orphanage) was a tailor in England who had emigrated to New Zealand in search of a better life for his seven children and settled in Whakatane. He was an unusually domestic man, bottling jam and teaching all his children to sew, the role model for his own children and the model perhaps for the father in *Jam*, the story of a family coping with an overabundant plum tree and one of Margaret's most 'New Zealand' picture books. These paternal grandparents, Margaret was to write, remained enigmatic, feeling 'perhaps with some justice, that bringing up their own seven children had exhausted any interest in childcare'.

The arrival of their son's first child must nevertheless have brought great joy to the Mahy grandparents, and equally to 25-year-old May's parents, teacher Frank Penlington and his wife down in Christchurch. The first Penlingtons had emigrated some generations earlier from Cornwall; it is tempting, reading the poetic, graceful letter to Margaret May written by her grandfather Frank on the night of her birth, to speculate on some powerful genetic Celtic disposition towards language and imaginative storytelling. 'He wrote letters to his other grandchildren too, and none of them became writers. Nevertheless his letter seems to me more than a good wish — it was like a secret instruction.' Though he died when she was about three, Margaret has written that when she reads that letter, 'his voice speaks in my head, and I feel some directive coming to me not only from the actual words on old pages but, it seems, also from in between them'.

Fendalton,
21 March 1936

Dear Little Margaret May

I am informed that you happily arrived this afternoon, quite punctually after a rather long journey. I am sure your mother must have been delighted to meet you for I know she had been looking forward to your coming with much anxious hope. It is probably much too soon to ask how you like your new surroundings and what you think of all the strangers you have met, but what a lucky girl you are to have landed safely on a new planet and to have before you all the new joy and pleasure of the flowers in the field, the sound on the shore, the stream over the stones and the sunshine on the hills. If only I were a fairy Godmother instead of a very common sort of grandfather I might wave a wand and so give to you all rich blessings, and all good graces, but probably your mother and father have arranged these things for you for I am sure that, so far at least they think you just about perfect.

Now, Margaret May, I am going to look forward to seeing you, and tell them, and of course, ever after, you have my best wishes for a very happy life in your new home.

Yours affectionately, Grandfather

So Margaret May arrived today
Not unannounced they seem to say.
She brought no luggage but came to stay.
A doctor went along to greet her,
A kind nurse too was there to treat her,
Of course her mother went to meet her,
Important Margaret May

Perhaps, Margaret has fancifully suggested, this letter is the reason she is now a writer; 'it now seems as receiving a *written* greeting might imprint one, in curious subliminal ways, with the idea of writing back. Certainly my mother's side of the family, when I began inventing poems and stories of my own, did not credit me with my success. "She gets it from Dad," they would say to one another over my head, and perhaps they were right . . .'

Margaret's mother, a third-generation New Zealander, was the youngest of six daughters, with an upbringing that was 'literary in an academic way, and proud of her intellectual background'.

Her father and three of her sisters were teachers; her mother
was frail and 'rather patronised by her children ("Poor mother!"
her daughters would say, before going on to indulge in a little
innocent boasting about their father and his academic abilities.)'
May Penlington had met her future husband when she took a job
as a teacher at a school 12 kilometres out of Whakatane. For a
young woman, marriage in the 1930s 'automatically meant that
she gave up teaching in order to realise her true female destiny by
becoming an utter wife'. But she was nevertheless 'a homemaker
in an interesting way' because she also had the considerable
responsibility of keeping the books for her husband's business and
later became a shareholder in the company, as well as collecting
rent from houses built on land bought by Frank and signed over
to her. So she did have an independent income, a career of sorts;
in Margaret's recollection, her mother considered she had a very
fulfilled and happy life.

By the birth of his first child, Frank Mahy was nearly forty,
the owner of a 'reasonably successful' contracting business in
Whakatane. It was not a huge company, but 'a respectable one,'
which steadily increased in staff and scope of building work as the
family grew up. 'My father's family were all tradesmen, plumbers,
building, cartage contractors . . . men who worked long hours
every day at their chosen trades.' And Frank Mahy's particular
professional speciality was to provide rich metaphors and images
for his observant, thinking eldest child.

'My father actually was a bridge builder. My childhood was
spent picnicing [*sic*] by a variety of bridges, at various stages of
construction. I have written a short story about bridge building.'
This was *The Bridge Builder*, in *The Door in the Air and other stories*,
a reflection on the nature of transformation and death which
is possibly the finest short story she ever wrote; it has been
anthologised in 'adult' collections more than once.

[The bridge] is 'a very lively symbol in my own life. Bridges,
leaping from one place to another, cover a great variety of abysses,
including those between countries, between communities and those

between the inside and the outside world. Probably the adjustment that the imagining individual makes to the complicated real world, is my own obsession. Though I take pleasure, and support the efforts and advances of my country, in developing its own literary identity, this is not why I write and it is only one and possibly not the basic reason, for the existence of literature at all. As well as giving people overseas some insight into what it means to live as a New Zealander, a writer may wish to communicate ideas about the human condition that have nothing whatever to do with geographical situations. The ideas I draw on come from things as random as cracks in the pavement that may appear to presage the break up of material nature, or the reflections of stars whose light may have been travelling many years to reach my telescope, or a daughter exclaiming, "From now on I'm only going to fall in love with really handsome men. It's just not worth it [otherwise]." In the latter case one may find oneself overwhelmed by all sorts of reactions, including the "otherness" of one's children and the vibrations startle all sorts of hidden associations out of the brain. This is an experience that belongs in New Zealand, Australia, Japan — belongs to anywhere in the world. The bridges we build show not only our differences but our sameness, or link us up through the republic of ideas.'

Although the lyrical opening paragraphs of *The Bridge Builder* suggest a greater variety of bridges than was true in real life, Margaret says that the shingle and sand, the steel and cement were an intimate part of her childhood memories. 'I did watch bridges appear and people cross over. If I return to my home town by car I cross at least one of my father's bridges including one I remember from the time of its original construction. We're over it in a second, but of course without that bridge the journey would be more complicated.'

And it was often quite dangerous work. 'We used to travel round the bridges my father was building, and some days he would be away working very long hours, because they were pouring the deck of the bridge, which had to done as a continuous process.

It was dangerous, in a way, because my father could drive a pile down into the bed of the river and find rocks and then, with the next pile he drove, he might find mud. You never quite knew, in small country areas of New Zealand, just what you were going to find under the surface; there was always an element of risk. So, on the one hand, it was nerve-racking; but, on the other hand, he enjoyed the risk.'

As a family man, the bridge builder seems to have been the ideal father for an unusually imaginative first child growing up hungry for stories, the rhythm and sounds of words, music, ideas being expressed and debated, opportunities for laughter, jokes and silly games. He was also a domesticated husband, like his father before him: when he came home in the evening he looked after the family, fixed broken dolls, made jam and read stories. He was, Margaret says, a 'natural philosopher, with imaginative views about right and wrong that weren't typical . . . more of a humanist, essentially, than my mother was'.

As the 1930s drew to their end, the increasing possibility of war in Europe cast its shadow over the young family. In wartime, fewer roads and bridges might be built, and work for a contractor become scarce. Some of Margaret's first few years were spent with her parents in a caravan at the tiny eastern coast settlement of Houhora, in the Far North of New Zealand, where her father had won a contract to rebuild the wharf destroyed by fire. The living near the beach was simple and frugal, with cooking on an oil-burning Primus, and shops distant. The pre-school child started to become aware of talk of war, of a general feeling of alarm, of rationing and even greater frugality, of male relatives going away; her father had had rheumatic fever when young men were being called up for the First World War and by 1939 was too old for active service, though two of his brothers went. Wartime introduced the young Margaret to notions of goodies and baddies, that there were people called enemies to be defeated. She asked, 'Santa won't bring any presents to the German boys and girls, will he?' The war wasn't their fault, mother quickly reassured daughter. It was, Margaret recalls, one of significant little moments of enlightenment in her very early childhood, a moment of alteration when she stopped believing that the Germans or anyone else were baddies, and knew this to be the truth.

For the first few years, it was 'a fairly plain childhood, because war broke out when I was three, but it was a good upbringing from the point of view of being encouraged to do what I wanted and not being defined in any particular way. Whenever I did anything that was in the least bit smart they praised me for it and gave me a lot of positive reinforcement, so I grew up with a good feeling of my own self-worth. When I was about four, for example, I used to make up poems in my head and then recite them to my mother, and she would always praise me and get me to repeat them to my father. I can still remember some of those poems. I couldn't write at that stage, so I learnt them off by heart.'

Given that 'the *told* story or word-game precedes the *read* or printed one', Margaret had stories both told and read to her from infancy, not only at bedtime but during, for example, her mother's frequent stints at the ironing board, when the three-year-old would coerce her into playing a game based on the story of the little red hen. 'I was always the little red hen and my mother was always the fox. "I think I will try to catch the little red hen today," she would have to say, while, in my proto-office under the table, I crawled in and out of a labyrinth of chair legs shouting out to her, telling her what to say. "This is such a nice little hen I don't think I'll eat it. I think I will take it home and we will be friends."'

There was another, similar story based on real life. '"You be Stan Kerr, Mummy, and I'll be the deer," I would cry. My father actually had a friend called Stan Kerr who, dramatically from my point of view, killed deer . . . but in *my* story Stan Kerr, confronted with the little deer, was always touched by its beauty and its endearing ways, and, instead of shooting it, would take it home to be a friend. So, shouting from under the table, I called on both folk tale and everyday life, and used a story to remake reality along more agreeable lines. Invariably

I cast my mother as aggressor and myself as potential victim . . . a victim, however, whose beauty and charming ways always averted disaster . . . I now think I was trying to remake the world along better lines. It must have been fun, because I did it over and over again.'

Her first film, at three or four, provided another moment of understanding. 'At the Regent Theatre in Whakatane — in about 1939 we celebrated Mickey Mouse's birthday party. Children attending the film session were entertained with Disney cartoons and given a slice of birthday cake. I remember the cake, and my astonishment on coming out the theatre to find it was still daylight. And I also remember my distress at one sequence in which Pegleg Pete seized Pluto. "Yes, he is a nice dog," he cried and stretched Pluto out in a way which would have been terribly painful to any of the dogs I knew. All round me people were roaring with laughter, but, believing that Pluto must be suffering, I began to cry. "It is only a joke," my mother whispered, comforting me in the dark. "He can't feel it." It turned out to be a seminal moment for me. Put straight on this point, having been given as it were permission to laugh, laugh I did, making a huge leap towards that future occasion on which I would joke about someone running towards a swimming pool, plunging through a plate glass window and cutting himself severely in the process. I had been authorised to laugh at the contemplation of someone else's discomfort.' Besides, 'I was a child strongly affected by my own theories of animism, to such an extent that many years later, when I was given a new quilt for my bed I rolled the old one up and slept with it in my arms so that it would not feel discarded, though of course it was. I was distressed when our old caravan had to be pulled to pieces but dreamed in the night that its spirit would somehow travel with us, in the pieces of it we salvaged. I am not totally free of such primitive responses to this day, though I think I recognise them for what they are.'

Turning five in Houhora, with a birthday cake thoughtfully posted by her Aunt Frances from Whakatane, and little sister

Helen now welcomed to the family, Margaret was expected to go to the nearest state primary school, Kohukohu. There she vividly remembers seeing books of a kind quite different from her well-used Whitcombe & Tombs classroom readers; these books, new and desirable, were subtly but significantly different, in their print, their margins, the style of illustration. Originating in the United States, they suggested otherness. They came, not from bookshops, the eager children were told, but from the Country Library Service. But this 'rare treat' of school was to be of short duration. The farm milk truck that had provided transport to Kohukohu was taken over by the army, so the six-year-old stayed in the caravan to be taught to read and write by her mother. When the family moved back to their home in Whakatane and enrolled Margaret at the local school, she was an advanced reader for her age, and a competent, if untidy, writer.

She does not, however, remember her primary schooling with much enthusiasm. She was overly talkative and lacked concentration. Her maths was poor, her handwriting worse still. She was often simply bewildered and sometimes found herself being defensive about her reading ability. 'People didn't believe I could read so fast, teachers would say you couldn't read that and they'd question me and I had! Yes, I had a retentive memory, but I also came early to recognise that with certain sorts of reading, where the relationship of one word to another is important, I had to deliberately slow myself down, or I'd miss out.' She was generally considered a slow learner, and 'different'. 'I once got the strap FIVE times, one after the other, for shrugging my shoulders. The funny thing was that I didn't really mean to be rude to the teacher. My shrugging was like a sort of nervous twitch. I will never forget going back to my desk after the fourth strapping and feeling, with horror, my shoulders twitch again and hearing (also with horror) the teacher call me back out in front of the class to be strapped for the fifth time.'

As a solitary child, she lived very much in her own world. 'I used to play by myself, and wander round talking aloud to myself, acting out adventure stories, which I was very keen on. I would try to get other children to join in and act out my fantasies. I couldn't understand why they wouldn't, and why I had problems with other children, because my parents had given me such a strong feeling that I was a worthwhile person and I thought everyone else should see this as plainly as they did. My parents tried to reassure me that I was rather an unusual person, and that it wasn't necessarily a good thing to be like other children when other children laughed at me and refused to play with me. That's probably why I went through primary school in the lowest possible class, even though I read and wrote well. I don't blame those other children now. The misjudgement was mine.'

Her abiding memories of primary school are the conflicts resulting from the 'odd battles with truth' between her seventh and tenth year, and the equal longing for a best friend. 'I didn't have friends for many years; why I'm not sure. I think at times I did seem very different from other children but I don't want to suggest I was unduly sensitive and misunderstood. It might even have been I was understood too well.'

She has frequently written of her yearning to 'become astonishing, not only to myself but to other people as well', and has no doubt that these ambitions sprang 'from the impact of story, for part of the functions of stories is to acknowledge our craving . . . But I wanted stories to be more than entertaining. I wanted them to be true . . . I continually tried to take over the lives of singular fictional identities in such a way that my central wonder would be obvious to everyone in the everyday world.

'In the 1940s when posters outside our local picture theatres tended to be dominated by images from B-grade westerns, boys in particular . . . lived the lives of cowboys in the school playgrounds, shooting with their fingers and arguing incessantly about who had killed whom. Of course I was not included in these adventures. Indeed girls were forbidden, back then, to cross over into the boys' playground, and vice versa, though a sort of flirtation certainly went on along the boundaries. Both boys and girls, but particularly boys, thrilled by possibility, eagerly took on the role that stories alive in the air suggested to them, though they were sensibly aware that real life would never dissolve and make way for the fictions they were assuming.

'However, I tried to tear fictional possibility off the page and fan it to exotic life on the footpaths of Whakatane not as a mere invented flourish, but as something just as real, just as believed in, as the lives of the shopkeeper or the taxi driver. For the day came when Whakatane Primary School was to hold a fancy-dress ball. I wanted to go as a fairy, thinking this would give me the chance to be seen as both pretty and magical. My mother, however, said that a great many girls would dress as fairies and that I should try something different. "You could go as a witch," she said, and then added, speaking to my father over my head, almost as if I would not be able to hear her, "She has the right sort of face for it." I remember very clearly my moment of astonishment at this revelation. My mother — my mother — thought I had the right face for a witch. I was disconcerted rather than hurt, but I accepted her judgement. And this, in due course, probably helped me to take on witch life with spontaneity and conviction.' Subsequently, she refused to abandon it, and laid claim to strange and supernatural functions, including a poisonous bite, chanted spells and physical fights. When unduly goaded, she did bite a child, who for reasons of her own, chose 'to become part of the fantasy, [and] actually confirmed that my bite was poisonous . . . in the end children always knew that I was just another kid from down the road'.

A year or so later the kid from Haig Street moved into 'rather more dangerous territory' after being taken to see Alexander Korda's film of *The Jungle Book*. She became 'instantly and profoundly envious' of Mowgli, and determined to recreate his life in the Whakatane playground. 'I began telling other children that I was an evacuee from Britain . . . but the plane had crashed in the Indian jungle and I was the only survivor. I claimed to have lived there among the animals and learned their language . . . I look back on these allegations with puzzlement. How could I ever have expected any of my contemporaries to believe for a moment in the alternative life I was claiming for myself?'

The story of how she tried in various eccentric ways — eating grass, drinking from puddles, talking gibberish — to live out Mowgli's life is one Margaret has told often in speeches, in comic but rather poignant detail. Her bemused playmates brought her leaves and berries and these offerings she devoured without question, despite how unpleasant they tasted or how risky they might have been. On one occasion, offered a leaf 'with scrupulous care', she was told 'amid screams of pleasure and disgust, that there had been a caterpillar on it'.

Later there were other dramatic lives that she adopted 'obsessively' — 'initially in my head but later by writing them down . . . the life of an 11-year-old girl, Belle Gray (inspired by a film poster featuring the maverick female outlaw Belle Starr), who led an outlaw band in the American Wild West; [later] the life of Edric the Anglo-Saxon boy — a boy so clever and attractive that he won the respect of Norman invaders. Living Edric's limited life, I talked aloud in my own voice for the Normans but in falsetto for Edric, alternately grunting and squeaking, and, as I did so, chopping kindling wood or hitting a tennis ball against a concrete wall to emphasise the obsessive rhythm of my tale . . . for as long as I can remember, being in charge of the story has been a function I proposed for myself, and part of the story was to live the adventurous life.' Edric, the Anglo-Saxon boy with the long golden flowing hair, was with her for over a year. Another favourite, acted out with great intensity, using different voices for the two main characters, was based on the only comic she remembers being allowed to own, *The Adventures of Middy Malone*. Her variations on this story about Middy and the pirate captain with the heart of gold 'placed heavy emphasis on Captain Vice yielding to goodness'.

Now children are encouraged to write or tell their own stories as a valued part of the general acquisition of literacy skills, but then Margaret's unusual talents counted for little. Her concerned mother's success, when Margaret was about eight, in persuading the headmaster to relocate her in the 'top' stream was short-lived: one baffling maths lesson ended with a female teacher angrily telling her to pack her bags and leave the class. 'You're dumb. You're in with the babies,' the children taunted. In *Introducing Margaret Mahy* Betty Gilderdale suggests it is hardly surprising that women teachers, notably headmistresses, often fare badly in Margaret's fiction, portrayed as formidable, if clever, bullies. Her parents reassured her that she was unusual, and special. '"But really, the only thing unusual about me was that I was given such a good opinion of myself that I chose to abide by it when there was a lot of suggestion that I should modify my behaviour . . . Imagination is a wonderful asset, but I do think most people, without doing too much damage to themselves, can learn to adapt and fit in. That immediately sounds as if I'm urging conformity, and I'm not — but I really don't know how useful it was for me to be so unhappy." To have had a bad time at school is, someone once told her, no excuse whatsoever for writing a novel.'

Even before the humiliation of demotion, Margaret had written her first book. As soon as her small hand could control the shapes and the words on the paper to express the ideas in her head, 'when pencil was the only safe thing for a seven-year-old to use', she wrote a story she called 'Harry Is Bad'.

'My mother saved that first book, a series of pages sewed together, so that tells you something of the sort of family I came from. Years later she gave it back to me, and I have it still. I am able to show children that it does not take very much to begin being a writer — it is an activity accessible to anyone who happens to be interested.

'What I remember most about this first book is the way I tried hard to make it look as much like a book as possible. I wrote my name in small print at the top of the pages and then the title of the book . . . underneath the author's name and at the conclusion of the story I wrote THE END in big letters, just in case there was any doubt about it. In those days many books and films finished with the word THE END. To me it was part of the form — part of what made the story authentic. Still compelled by form, I went on to write in notebooks. I thought my stories had to fit exactly into the notebook covers, for stories I had read fitted so neatly in between covers supplied by the publishers. You would never find 20 empty pages at the end or a note saying that in order to read the last chapter of the story you should look in another book. So when I got halfway through my notebook I knew I was halfway through my story and I would celebrate by drawing pictures.'

Reading that first book now, Margaret feels 'on the whole, pleased with my past self because, though there is no great sign of imaginative or significant style, the story does at least have form. It has a beginning, a middle and an end — and a good moral too. The lazy hero, Harry, is whipped by a witch until he learns to love work. Well, who wouldn't! Having achieved this desirable apotheosis, he wakes to find he has been dreaming, but I am sure I intended his moral advance to be a permanent one.'

She now finds it interesting that she wrote this story, not at school, but in her spare time. 'Writing was something that I was choosing to do . . . *what interests me* is that there is a curious little bit of biography in the story. The Hero (a lazy boy, you will be sorry to hear) is lured away from home to the house of a witch . . . The lure that he follows is a pheasant . . . and I remember that, back when I was seven, I thought that pheasants were the most beautiful birds in the world. A short time before my parents had been given a dead cock pheasant which was hung by its legs in our washhouse. I remember how the house seemed glorified by the presence of this beautiful heraldic bird, and I remember my horror and distress when in due course my mother took the dead bird down and began to pluck it. The dismantling of this object of beauty caused me to burst into tears. "Don't worry! It can't feel it!" my mother cried, but my grief was partly at least to do with seeing the beautiful bird reduced, though none of this prevented me from eating part of it with enormous pleasure later in the evening. I don't want to suggest that I was one of those sensitive children. What I want to explain is that real life intruded into my stories even at a time when I felt my real life had nothing to do with anything I read.'

Neither her storytelling nor writing abilities were greatly valued by either teachers or other children. 'I did have one friend called Margaret who wrote stories too, and together we used to make excursions into fantasy, but she really liked other people better than me. We'd go through a day or two when I'd feel she was my friend and I'd be very happy, but then she'd show she really liked someone else better and I'd be miserable and suffer a great deal. I know a lot of people look back on their childhoods as not being particularly happy, but I seemed to experience a lot of that particular angst.'

An ambition to see her work in print was soon evident. 'I published early — when I was seven or eight, sending poems and stories to a children's page in the *Bay of Plenty Beacon* — a paper capable, incidentally, of calling Mary O'Hara Hairy O'Hara, or of advising its readers that Women's World of Prayer will be held in the Whakatane Gospel Hell. I occasionally won writing competitions — thirty shillings for writing the last line of a limerick for example . . .'

The *Beacon* featured a children's column every Friday. 'The Friday after I had posted my story — or perhaps the Friday after that — I ran to our gate to retrieve the paper, opened it, and behold — there it was — a short epic about two kittens successfully catching a mouse — with my name at the end of it. Once again I don't think the printed story had anything like the passion of the stories I was telling myself; it was a trite tale — story reduced to something within my capacity for production. However, standing there, bewitched by seeing myself in print for the first time, I experienced, also for the first time, the strangeness of seeing work that one knows one has written oneself looking as if it had been produced by some other more competent force. Print glorifies but simultaneously displaces the author, moving the story on from writer to reader. Yet there it was — my story and my name given a new authorisation. Screaming with pleasure I ran to show my parents, successfully surprising and gratifying them. I was left in no doubt of their excitement and pleasure.'

There were further enticements available. 'Anyone who had a poem or story or joke published in this column would receive a certain number of points, and when the writer had gained ten points, he or she received a free ticket to the pictures. So in a way, I have always looked for the chance to write for profit. I still have photocopies of a few of those pages. The date on the one at the top of the pile is Friday, September 7th, 1945.' As well as contributing to this newspaper column whenever possible, she used to go in for competitions like those in a small monthly magazine called the *Junior Digest*, and every now and then won a prize. 'I remember opening the issue in which I was first featured in a competition, (one in which I came second) and thinking, "This proves it! I really am going to be a writer."'

Having begun to make books, she was persistent. Between eight and eleven she wrote a series of stories about beautiful wild horses; her notebooks were dominated by versions of *My Friend Flicka* and *Thunderhead*, even though she had not actually read Mary O'Hara's books and was not allowed to see the film. 'The sources of my inspirations were the quiver of discussion at school, the posters advertising the film, and an extensive display of *Thunderhead* in the window of our local bookshop. I will never forget that window made suddenly dynamic by the repeated image of a great white horse galloping towards me. So I continually acted out apprehended stories, trying out bits of conversation by speaking them aloud and rehearsing events that might be, later, transferred in a stilted form to the page. This is something I still do, though rather more knowingly now than then. I don't think, however, I would have played these games with such complexity and conviction if I had not been a word child, encouraged to be susceptible to the stories and to venerate the books that held them.'

The eleven-year-old Margaret's story of 'Belle Gray', based on a film she had never seen, filled three exercise books and was her longest completed book of her primary years. Rereading it a few years afterwards, she was 'filled with agony at an incompetence which had betrayed, on paper, the original vision [of the girl in the film poster] with which I was still essentially involved'. Unable to bear its existence in the inadequate written form, she destroyed the book. But it was the first, she has said, that managed to 'unite two systems that had operated, until then, in uneasy juxtaposition ... story and book, anarchic desire and generalisations of written language, so some sort of beginning had been achieved'.

She believes that quite early her parents recognised her singular writing talent, 'for what that means'. To earn a living as a writer was beyond their imagining, as it would have been for any other New Zealand parents in the 1950s (and to many, even now), but her first appearances in the local paper, school magazine and later the *School Journal* were proudly applauded. 'I can remember my father looking at my first books — by then he was quite stricken with Parkinson's — and holding them in his hands, weeping with pleasure.'

Like many New Zealanders of her generation, Margaret's reading from her earliest days through to adulthood was almost exclusively of books imported from European or American cultures, with the single, notable exception of the localised stories provided in the *School Journal*. Many of today's older New Zealand writers have lamented the lack of indigenous reading in their childhoods, citing instead a staple diet of English children's classics, boarding school and horse stories, theatre and adventure tales, and, to a lesser degree, Americans like Mark Twain and Lousia May Alcott and an Australian or two. Few of the small number of New Zealand books then available are ever mentioned among their best remembered and loved.

For those mid-20th-century children who later became novelists in the flowering of both adult and children's fiction since around 1980, this serious deficiency worked in different ways.

Some writers (like William Taylor, Jack Lasenby, Witi Ihimaera and myself) have been determined to provide their own children's generation with a body of literature that clearly validated and reflected their own country and its culture; others have seen their early introduction to the great classics of the English-speaking world as a sufficient stepping stone to English, American and post-colonial literature, and their lack of indigenous childhood reading as sad, perhaps, but not deeply significant. (Even now, the *School Journal* notwithstanding, educational theory, powerful advocates and governments have not ensured — as they have in varying degrees in Canada and Australia — that New Zealand children read their own country's fiction; yet it is unthinkable that English or American children would, through lack of political will or intellectual laziness or post-colonial cringe or snobbery, be denied deliberate and proud introduction to their own country's literatures.)

In Margaret's case, her childhood reading led to a powerful sense of dislocation and an incentive to create, from the books she read, her own unique, extraordinary and fantastical other worlds deeply rooted in European cultures. As she moved through primary school, being read to and devouring books by the hundreds, she became more and more a 'world citizen'.

Both Margaret's parents were habitual readers who read to her, constantly, from babyhood, even as her four siblings arrived on the scene. Her father, particularly, read widely, 'coming to it in a sort of lower middle-class way, as part of upward mobility'. Margaret's family owned books, bought books for birthdays and borrowed them from local libraries. 'My exposure to these books must suggest the sort of family I came from, a family of school teachers on the one side, and a family of tradesmen on the other, people anxious to be educated, to rise in the world and seeing literacy as a way of rising. I don't wish to suggest that they didn't enjoy the books they read, because they did . . .'

The books that Margaret remembers being read in her

childhood are largely the English/European canon of classic works for children. Initially, via the usual nursery tales such as *The Three Little Pigs* and *Little Red Riding Hood*, she found herself getting involved 'in the drama of who gets to eat who'. When she was a toddler, her mother read her Beatrix Potter and Alison Uttley 'over and over again'; from five onwards she graduated to *Alice in Wonderland*, *Winnie-the-Pooh*, *The Wind in the Willows*, *The Water-Babies* and *The Just-so Stories*, later to *Anne of Green Gables*, and *Seven Little Australians*. Her father read the 'boy's books' by Henry Rider Haggard, R.M. Ballantyne and Captain Marryat. In various speeches she has also mentioned the school stories of Angela Brazil and Bessie Marchant, and coming later to Louisa May Alcott, Arthur Ransome, Elizabeth Goudge and Richmal Crompton, often 'reading them over and over again, for I was, and still am, a quick and greedy reader'. Goudge's *The Little White Horse* was a particular favourite, read with an intensity that she recalls as nearly physical. She missed out on George Macdonald and Edith Nesbit and almost all American writers, whose books were virtually unobtainable. She loved anything that made her laugh, and drove her mother mad following her around the house, determined to share the funny bits. Now, she recognises 'that the stories I enjoyed most showed people in some state of extremity, pitted against death and danger, but managing, in the process of escaping (through courage and good luck of course) to transcend themselves'.

She remembers being 'fairly resilient about fear' in her early reading, though subject to odd particularities. 'Some children like to be scared, like to test themselves, some hate it . . . it must have been about Standard One, around seven, we had a Whitcombe & Tombs reader called *Connie of the Fourth Form*. It was the first story in which I encountered a secret panel. I'd never heard of it before, and I can remember being very frightened by that — just the spooky idea that it was a part of a wall and could be displaced. I can remember trembling and clenching my teeth and my teacher suddenly realising I was terrified of this (no one else in the room was) and she was a bit taken aback . . . it was an odd thing to be scared by, but we don't have panelled wooden walls in New Zealand.' As Margaret told the *Listener* in 1987, 'many of the first stories we tell to children are still basically concerned with "who gets to eat who in life . . . While we could certainly evolve a totally different literature it wouldn't alter the fact that these predatory relationships do exist in nature and that children are sooner or later going to have to come to terms with the fact that their cat is going to eat a baby bird." A lot of children's stories, she says, meet a deep psychological need: like elements of play, there's preparation for survival. Not that Mahy has ever objected to a bit of bloodthirstiness. "There's the story of the little girl who said, 'Sad, I hate sad. But cruel, I love cruel.' I've always been a bit like that. Couldn't take the tragic endings in *The Babes in the Wood*, or *The Little Match Girl*." Many of the Grimm stories, she says, were never in fact intended for children. But Mahy has always loved being frightened. Probably, she says, because she always had a snug domestic security herself. These days the scary stories she writes have that family security written into them.'

As a child she was aware of two New Zealand writers, both from an earlier period. 'There were only a few New Zealand books, some of which I still have, like *Six Little New Zealanders* by Esther Glen and the books by Isabel Maud Peacocke. But not all of these gave any real feeling about what it was like to be a New Zealand child living in a small town, going to school every day and playing or fighting with neighbouring children after school. Almost none of these books featured Maori children although there was one, *The Book of Wiremu* by Stella Morice, that I read when I was at High School. However, before I actually obtained the book I had read a piece from it in guess where? Yes, in the *School Journal*! The chapter I read there made me want to go on and read more. So, when I got a chance to read the book in full, of course I did. Nowadays *The Book of Wiremu* has an odd, rather out-of-date feeling about it, but it was a story set in New Zealand that tried to describe the way we live.'

Very few children's books were published in New Zealand during her crucial upper primary, pre-puberty years — nine in 1945, three in 1946, seven in 1949 — and Margaret recalls 'they were often very modest, even clumsy productions which could not compete in appearance or style with the books from overseas — predominately from England — and they were often imitations of English books anyway, or written by people suffering from the same confusions that I suffered from when my time came. I don't mean that they were all bad, but they were not all that good either. And illustration until recently lagged well behind writing, partly because our art schools looked, I think, beyond representational art and this affected attitudes to illustration which for a long time seem to have been seen as a minor craft, related to graphics and advertising. Anyhow our local booksellers probably did not stock the New Zealand books which were published, and my mother, if she saw them, probably scorned them. There was certainly a strong feeling at this time that things produced in New Zealand were innately inferior to anything produced overseas . . . available reading, and no doubt insidious social reinforcement too, led me to believe that wonder and astonishment were always in some other nameless country.'

Neither did the great stories of Maori mythology appeal as they perhaps should have done, especially to a child living in a community with a large and visible Maori component and thrilled with the folk tales, myths and legends of other countries. In spite of what she once described to an Australian audience as the persistent attempts 'to crush Maori folklore in the terribly strange bed of European culture', Maori stories had nonetheless persisted and continued to stand alongside what else was offered to children by way of the 700 books published between 1833 and 1978, the 'school readers' and the good public library system.

'Since the Maoris had no written language, these stories existed through being remembered, told, acted, carved into wood, and finally through translation into English. As a child I remember having Maori stories read to me. They were reasonably available,

I think. What was not available was the conviction in telling. The voices of the people who read these stories were not Maori voices, and the translations, I now understand, leave a lot to be desired. However, in Whakatane with its large Maori population, I did hear Maori voices singing and chanting and because I heard them in childhood, these voices are part of my heritage even though I am a middle-aged Pakeha. If we had had the true storytellers I am sure the stories would have been part of my childhood too.'

The metaphor of the fault line constantly recurs in Margaret's writings to explain her childhood confusion between the world she lived in and the world of her developing imagination. 'Culturally as well as geographically, we were all on a fault line, and I still feel it pass through me, for my parents did not know, did not feel, the stories of the Pacific as relevant to themselves, and it was many years before I came to feel that they had any real significance for me.'

Even while young, Margaret began to ponder the nature of truth, and the division between the books she was told were true and the stories she knew were not. Reading in Arthur Mee's *Encyclopaedia* that the earth 'had once been a fiery ball that had dropped off the sun', she knew it was true, 'because of the sort of book the information was to be found in. The encyclopaedia was true and Peter Rabbit wasn't. I was thrilled with the fiery ball, and knowing it was true was part of what thrilled me . . . [and] I excited as much resentment for speaking what I did believe to be a literal encyclopaedia truth as I did for acting out fiction . . . although, just to make the situation a little more complicated, nowadays no astronomer believes the earth was ever a fiery ball that fell off the sun. What I learned as truth back then was apparently not truth . . . not even a fact. It was not a story either, though it had some of the dramatic qualities of myth. It was a *mistake*. Still, it fixed my attention, and tied me to the astonishment of non-fiction and to a certain sort of truth as inexorably as if it had indeed been true.'

One novel, perhaps even then an unusual parental choice, she has frequently credited with being the most influential book of her childhood. When the original copy got lost, she haunted second-hand bookshops for some years searching for a replacement: finding a battered copy was something akin to a religious experience.

'When I was eight years old my father read to me from a small, rather unattractive book with a peeling spine, yellowed pages and small print — the very antithesis of all that a child's book should be in appearance. He read to me of an elephant hunt and I was instantly encompassed by incident, drama, excitement and death all acted out against a golden African landscape.

'The book was *King Solomon's Mines* by Sir Henry Rider Haggard, the prototype of many African adventure stories, complete with wild animals, heroic travellers, undiscovered country, a mysterious tribe and fabulous treasure. My father obviously enjoyed the book himself (he was later to introduce me to Ballantyne and Marryat) but I doubt if he expected the story to exercise such a power over me as it did. I read on from where he stopped reading, greedy for the revelation of adventure and mystery it promised. I was sustained beyond my wildest dreams. I begged my mother to read it to me, which she did, though rather unwilling to read me a story I had read already. Then I read it again. And again. In a sense, I have never stopped reading it as I have read it to my own children, the last occasion being in May last year . . .'

Margaret's powerful and thrilled reaction to this book led her to tell other children that it was a true story, 'for I could not bear to think its heady excitement rested on nothing more substantial than one man's imagination, having no more reality than my own games and dramas.

'Adventure is the name of Rider Haggard's game. The story is simple. Brave men set out, a journey is made, a battle is won, a rightful king restored to his throne, a treasure is gained, a brother is found. It is calculable enough — though it wasn't when I was eight. But Haggard invests this basic material with the prodigality of a great imagination and produces the first of a long series of

African romances — a sort of African Gothic — at once real and magical.

'Compared with Stevenson's, Haggard's style has its faults. *King Solomon's Mines* was written in six weeks and has a casual, unpolished quality in its writing. It lacks the excellence and elegance of *Treasure Island*. Yet Haggard's prodigious imagination sweeps the reader along. From the time they hit the desert, after a rather slow beginning, the course of events is breathtaking, the scenes become increasingly remarkable.

'. . . There is much to cause a modern reader to frown in *King Solomon's Mines*. What would a conservationist have to say to the slaughter of the elephants, or the feminist to Quartermain's assertion that there are no petticoats in his story, or the racially sensitive to the patronising attitudes taken to the native servants? These are all points we cannot ignore in reading the story to children. They have to be commented on, put in some sort of historical perspective. But the adventure remains.

'For me, adventure was and still is important, but adventure is only partly an event. It is also a matter of interpretation. The most tremendous happenings, wrongly interpreted, can be uncomfortable, inconvenient or merely boring. A witness of one of Richard Pearce's [*sic*] early flights was asked what he thought when he saw Pearce [*sic*] in his flying machine. "Silly Bugger" the man is quoted as saying and he turned his back on a certain sort of adventure, closed his mind to it. I no longer insist that the events in *King Solomon's Mines* must be true but they have been of as much use to me as if they were. So many of life's uncomfortable passages can be given a new relevance, seen under a new focus, if one is able to see them as part of the adventure encountered on a journey.

'If asked about my own life, I would probably say it was adventurous even though I am involved with a daily job, two children, a garden, cats and chickens — none of which are generally seen as vehicles for adventure.'

But it was Haggard's book and one or two similar novels

that truly turned her young imagination permanently towards the notion that all life, even the most mundane of domesticity, was An Adventure. 'Once, as I was running away with my two children from a burning car, I heard myself shouting as much to myself as the terrified children, "Don't be frightened! Look on this as an adventure!", and as I shouted this an image from *King Solomon's Mines* imposed itself on the bare spare Banks Peninsula around me. There they went, those heroes, tormented by thirst yet struggling on through the desert.'

The desert scenes in Haggard's book held a lasting lesson. 'Back when I was a child and reading this part of the story, I had paused, wondering how it was that one could receive this account of suffering with any sort of pleasure. I stared blankly at the page, and it suddenly came to me that the thrilling adventures in stories (and probably in real life too) came about because something had gone wrong for someone. Heroes, though — true heroes — struggle on through discomfort and pain, and win through.'

In the meantime the adventures of family life at 26 Haig Street were enough to be going on with. Her parents' marriage, says Margaret, was a wonderfully happy one, providing a very secure environment for the five growing children. Her predominant recollection of the house at 26 Haig Street was a happy jumble of laughter, jokes, games, music, stories, books, occasional fights, discussions on politics, religion, ideas; with so many children, and cousins next door, there was rarely very much stillness. She has often spoken publicly of her parents and family with undisguised warmth and enthusiasm, 'though you understand I'm prejudiced in their favour!'

For a glimpse into the subtle, sophisticated and highly individual Mahy 'feminism' that developed early at home and has clearly underpinned her life and her fiction, it is worth reading Margaret's contribution to editor Marilyn Duckworth's *Cherries on a Plate: New Zealand writers talk about their sisters*, published in 1996.

Half of the essay is, it seems, fiction. The 'sisters' (in the feminist sense) come together in a slightly sinister waiting room and find themselves sharing their stories. The narrator is the unmarried writer who begins work at 4 a.m. and is astonished by TV news with more 'edge and variety' than anything she could possibly imagine. The others are an accountant turned solitary pig farmer, a still-married home and quilt maker, and a volunteer official carer. These portraits indicate how she has quietly made feminist theory her own: 'I became myself with them, my present and historical self, in a profound and unspoken way quite impossible with other people more passionately loved. I felt *true* in this company.'

In this memoir Margaret is unequivocal about the true female strength of her family. 'I come from a family dominated by women. Not only am I the oldest of four sisters, but I am the mother of two, and these days I watch my sibling granddaughters with fascination, noting how the younger of the two is entranced by the cleverness and skills of the one above her . . .' The portrait of her Whakatane childhood is pure nostalgia — for her own roaming toddler adventurousness (which drove her busy and anxious mother 'mad'); for the sisterly games, the giggling, the cooking, the tree climbing, the trapezes, the unsupervised swimming in the river, the Ohope Beach visits, the travel on the back of her father's truck; a growing awareness of complicated squabbles, jealousies, manoeuvrings, and the growing up and apart, becoming 'strongly differentiated,' so that they 'have all turned out to be heroines in their own stories'.

Not surprisingly, Margaret disagrees with the often-heard idea that an unhappy and problematic childhood is a useful (maybe even essential) prerequisite for a successful children's writer. In many cases, she allows, such a background would add drama, but generally she believes it to be untrue. She now sympathises with her mother giving her one great wallop because she was late home from school, this being 'a very worrying thing for her — and it never happened again, so did me good in a fashion'. But these strict parental boundaries were established and accepted. An escapade with her cousins of breaking and entering an abandoned bach at Ohope, only to be noticed and told off by a neighbour, had a revealing outcome. Margaret went home feeling very guilty about this misdemeanour, and confessed to her father with some consternation. He went to his brother's house next door, and came back to announce that since her cousins were getting a hiding, to be fair Margaret should get one too. 'So I got a hiding with a bit of stick — I was about nine — but half way through he broke off, saying he'd rather hit himself than hit me, and struck himself over his forearms, which filled me with grief — of course I was in grief because of the pain, but this was a different sort of grief.'

Housework — the assiduous 1940s–1950s model she grew up with and the job she later did at times to earn a living — is something she has often brooded about, very eloquently. Why, as an essential human service, is it regarded as lesser work, 'partly because, being done by wives and mothers, it is largely unpaid, but also because energy is being poured out to achieve results that are not intended to survive'? Pictures get painted, houses and bridges built, but the housewife cleans a home whose 'diligently achieved order tumbles towards chaos . . . I don't think my mother (though she was a well educated woman) ever used the word "entropy" — the measure of the degree of disorder in any system, the study of which tells us that disorder cannot be finally overcome. Entropy is typified not only by the expanding universe but also by housework, which is done in order that it can be intentionally torn apart, sometimes only a matter of minutes later.'

The demands of housework affected relationships. Margaret remembers a mother 'who just had no time for the sort of debate that often takes place between modern parent and child. She had to boil a copper, to wring out clothes by hands or by winding the handle of the washhouse wringer — clothes which included (for we often had a baby in the house during my childhood) whole lines full of napkins.' (In later years, disposable napkins always seemed to her to suggest a sort of flippancy inappropriate to a good parent.) 'My mother had to run a respectable, clean house — had to sweep and mop the floor rather than vacuum it. Even making beds was a very different job from what it is now. Mattresses had to be turned each day. There was nothing as light and warm and informal as a duvet. There wasn't enough time to discuss things with little children. Right and wrong were, on the whole, simply defined, and were imposed rather than argued.'

Music was integral to her childhood. She learned the piano for a while, but was 'never enormously capable' and her mother despaired of the daughter ('of two musical parents') who could not learn to sing in tune. Once, overhearing this pronouncement, she was 'filled with astonishment and dismay. Singing brought me so much pleasure (and indeed still does, I add in a crackling sinister voice) that it was hard to accept the fact that my singing might cause distress to those around me . . . ("Do you have to sing?" my daughter asks me, sometimes plaintively, sometimes irritably and I am seized by an old and furtive guilt, my eyes sliding sideways so that I do not have to look the world in the face and actually see it wincing with pain.)'

But there was singing and family music, nonetheless. Her mother played the piano, her aunt over at Ohope beach the violin, her uncle the saxophone and her father could 'knock out a tune' on a great variety of instruments, mostly by ear: saxophone, banjo, piano (with a 'rather uninspired left hand' as his Parkinson's developed from his early 40s). But, like many of that pre-television generation, he had an enormous repertoire of songs: nigger minstrel tunes, pop songs of the time, old vaudeville and often suggestive music hall numbers. He passed on to his children, too, the rollicking pleasure he derived from singing the songs of the great entertainers of the time: George Formby, Vesta Tilley of 'Burlington Bertie' fame and Arthur Askey, among many others. Margaret may lament her inability to sing in tune, but she too, given an appropriate occasion, can knock out a song — all the verses of *The Lay of the Nancy Belle*, or *The Hippopotamus Song* and other Flanders and Swann classics, many from Tom Lehrer's witty repertoire and just about anything you care to name from Gilbert and Sullivan.

'My connections with music were made in paradoxical ways through language — through sound of course, but through the sound of words . . . Music of a kind is regularly used and misused to announce, to emphasise and to sell . . . and when I was a child musical sound was not quite as ubiquitous. Yet I was, like most children, surrounded by music of a kind that I hesitate to define as music in the more mysterious and profound sense of the word. But having said that I go on to assert that there are strange and indirect connections.

'There are many older people who talk nostalgically about the days when people made their own entertainment and I can certainly remember lying in bed at night and hearing through two closed doors music drifting in on me . . . [the adults in the family] played in their various ways, they sang and, wrapped in darkness, I would listen with pleasure, and more than pleasure. Response to music is part of a primitive and profound human response to the world and though I would never describe myself as musical in the deep sense of the word, yet, paradoxically enough, I have a passionate response to music in ways that sometimes seem to contradict one another.

'My primary response has probably been to the beat of language — to the rhythm and tempo and timbre of it (snatching terms of musical reference from that *World Book Dictionary* definition) and to the joke of the rhyme. Certain lyrics still catch my attention in an inexorable way and the uneasy and rather scornful relationship I have with many current singers is that the words of their songs are so flat . . . and so often inaudible . . . Back then, there were the little printed booklets, readily for sale in bookshops, which contained the words of current songs, and songs, escaping from the radio and from the grooved surface of records into the outer world, were regularly sung and often parodied in the playground . . . my granddaughters currently sing pieces of songs by popular bands, but they don't really know the words in the same way that children used to because the words aren't knowable in the same way. Listeners cannot contain them to anything like the same degree for the words are pins that fix the actual music into us.'

The Mahys were occasional churchgoers, as were many respectable middle-class families of the time. Sometimes Margaret went to the closer Methodist church, against the inclinations of her Anglican mother, 'but,' she adds sympathetically, 'as the mother of five, in the days when you used to handwash nappies, her ideas had crumbled a bit'. The young teenager at Bible class was 'probably extremely irritating, since I used to ask awkward or defiant questions, partly out of teenage curiosity, partly out of personal conceit to show how smart I was. In terms of philosophical belief, I still feel strongly that Christianity isn't necessarily the only system of belief; there's the idea of the need to be kind and think of other people.'

Her intellectual curiosity took her to the local churches of different denominations, most notably to ask the Catholic priest about Catholicism; the idea of 'instruction' was mooted but May, while accepting her daughter going to services with neighbours, angrily vetoed any such suggestion. At one stage, Margaret says, she would have described herself as Christian, but fairly early on began to see herself as agnostic, though she would not have used that particular word. 'If, at the time, I exercised any sort of religious faith it was out of romanticism, but after all, Christianity is a romantic story, one which has affected me deeply at times.'

She has written of childhood spiritual experiences. 'Once, when I was ten or eleven, I found myself separated from my sisters and cousins, wandering along in a block of native bush my father owned. I was not frightened. Although there were no paths I knew this bush very well. At one point I stood still, listening for voices. I heard none. Instead I was engulfed first by silence, and then by a feeling of immanence. I felt something move towards me and contain me. Every leaf, every twig my eye fell on suddenly seemed to have infinite meaning. The world and every familiar thing in it became vast and incredible. I believed I was going to have a vision and looked around wildly into the air, expecting to see the Virgin Mary suspended before me. That was what a vision meant to me back then — the sudden appearance of Mary or of angels of some kind. However I think that I actually had a vision but could not recognise it, because I had no adequate language or image from reading to define it.

'This was a remarkable event in my life, one I remember vividly . . . My own feeling is that somehow I tricked or unintentionally overrode the moment-to-moment insistence of my nervous system that there was nothing around me worth wasting alarm and wonder on. I saw the commonplace world as deserving of amazement, and that experience was welcomed at many levels as part of truth.'

Unusually for a late 1940s girl, she also owned a telescope. She had bought the lens and eyepiece at a camera shop and her father was interested and sympathetic enough to persuade an uncle who was a plumber to make a long metal tin tube of the required length, and assemble all the component parts. That first moment of suddenly focusing on the moons of Jupiter was something she has never forgotten; her delight in seeing the mountains and craters of the moon was an experience she would give Tycho in *The Catalogue of the Universe.*

During the time of making the telescope, he [Tycho] had been close to his father, had watched him adjust it, over and over again, becoming more and more intrigued and serious over the work. Mr Potter had borrowed tools from a friend to help him get it just right. Then they had taken it out into the garden and pointed it at the moon which had been quarter full. Easily caught, it had swung in the object lens, a white fish of night, but for the first second Tycho had been overwhelmed at the imprecision of the image, before remembering that he could focus his telescope and drag shape into what he was seeing. He turned the little screw slowly, the texture of the white fish altered, and suddenly, there was a surface made familiar by many photographs, seen in a flash and then gone again. He turned the screw minutely back — and at last caught it. The moment became the event. There was the Sea of Crises, with the Sea of Fertility below it and the crater Cleomedes above, just as pictures had shown him, but all laid on a surface curving to meet him. There it was — it really was — both outside and inside, a little world hanging in space, a silver apple sliced by a crescent blade of shadow. Tycho, beginning his nightly assignations with this landscape, watched it grow and change, the moon slowly revealing itself, pushing darkness ahead of it, then pulling darkness after it once more . . .

As an unconventional child and teenager, Margaret seems quite early to have decided that she fitted into the 'tomboy' category by which adventurous adolescent girls were then defined. The label was not necessarily a kind or admired one, and nor was the phrase 'career girl' pinned on twenty-somethings who appeared to be giving more thought to their work or study than to the important business of 'settling down'.

Being a writer wasn't the only career option officially and promptly discouraged. 'In Standard Three I once suggested in class (having been told many times by then that being a writer was not a possible career) that I might be a vet, only to have the headmaster (on a fleeting visit to our classroom) declare that girls could not be vets. I distinctly remember his voice, filled with irritation at the stupidity of my suggestion. He made his despotic pronouncement, and yet another possible life dissolved around me.'

This headmaster, she generously allows, was, however, 'probably being less sexist than he seems when I quote him now. Speaking generally, girls left school to become office workers, teachers, nurses or librarians until, with luck, they achieved primary success through marriage. Of course there were old maids, rebels and eccentrics but such lives were not regarded as desirable possibilities.'

Margaret never thought that this traditional path towards marriage, a home and children was for her. 'Even as a child I decided I would like to live a life full of adventures and that I would never get married. There was a brief time as an adolescent when I would have loved to have had a romantic relationship with a boy, but I was incredibly naïve sexually and my mother had told me it was very beautiful when in reality it seemed so rude. When I was about eighteen I suddenly became interested in boys but I wasn't very attractive because I didn't know how to look after myself. I went around in a rather slatternly fashion with straggly hair which is partly why I didn't have much of a social life at university, because then as now people do sell themselves through appearances. Instead of going out I concentrated on writing stories.'

Many years later Margaret wrote about the important transition from a lonely primary school experience to the quite different environment of the local high school:

'At some time during my standard three year, ten children were taken from a lower standard three group and put even further down among the standard twos. I was one of the ten. As, in all modesty, I was a particularly good reader and an effective (though not a neat) writer, I can only assume that my talkativeness (I was often strapped for talking in school) had filled some poor teacher with a desire for revenge. I was in a low ability class for the rest of my primary career.

'It is worth mentioning these circumstances in order to emphasise the transformation brought about in my life by one particular teacher, a teacher of English at what was then Whakatane District High School. On the basis of my English assessment tests Ian McLean campaigned for my inclusion in a group of children designated as "professional". He apparently did this against some strong opposition, partly because of the level of my mathematics assessment paper and partly because the members of my extended family who had preceded me at secondary school had been anything but scholarly. However, Ian McLean persisted.

I was moved into 3P/C and he became my English teacher.

'The first two assignments he gave the class seem improbable exercises these days. Firstly we were asked to parody the first poem in our third form text book and then to write a series of limericks using local place names.'

The thirteen-year-old Margaret came up with:

In the dark little town of Te Whaiti
A fellow put on the wrong nightie
Its owner came in
And made a great din
My Goodness, he did get a frightie!

'These assignments certainly allowed me to display hitherto private skills. Buoyed up by success, I did reasonably well in other subjects, though sewing and mathematics remained enigmatic. (However, during my fifth form year I did put the notable theorem of Pythagoras concerning the right-angled triangles to the music of a song from *The Yeoman of the Guard*.)

'Schooling is a complicated process. I have the memory of one teacher who had a ruinous effect on me, due to no real fault of either of us. But Ian McLean, through what I like to think was true insight and determination, along with genuine idealism, transformed my school life in ways too varied to detail here. He was the magician who gave me something to live up to. I will never forget the fairy tale feeling of being recognised at last for what I felt I was — a writer and reader — and I will never forget the magician who, in transforming my circumstances, gave me, perhaps, the energy to further transform myself.'

This, written in her early 60s, was not the first generous public tribute Margaret had made to the young teacher who for three years taught her English and introduced her to, among other things, the worlds of classical music and the Savoy operettas. According to journalist Celia Dunlop, in an important 1991 feature in the *Listener*, seeing some of her poems had prompted McLean to take a special interest in Margaret's standard third form English test. Having succeeded in having her placed in the top class, he astutely arranged his lesson sequence so that Margaret could excel and find her social feet in the classroom. It was a 'tremendous boost' to the confidence of the physically clumsy girl who had struggled through her early schooling.

Now Margaret found herself being introduced 'to people like T S Eliot, Steinbeck and writers of the classics'. Dickens she had discovered at primary school (her mother was so horrified by finding her reading a comic version of *Oliver Twist* that she rushed out and bought her daughter the proper book) but McLean introduced her to Shakespeare and Edith Sitwell, among many others, and to the encouraging notion that there were poets and writers, notably Frank Sargeson, making a living in New Zealand.

Fiction for early teenagers about her own country, however, was scarce. In 1949, when she was thirteen, Brian Sutton-Smith's stories began to appear in the *School Journal* and were published in 1950 as *Our Street*. These short novels, by an academic who was a world expert on children's play, were something quite new, and disturbing, with tough, young male characters who 'treated their parents as enemies' and were 'both deceitful and cruel'. According to Betty Gilderdale they created something of a furore. Although they were too didactic in intent to stand as credible fiction, Margaret read them with interest. 'For the first time perhaps, I had it suggested to me that my own surroundings and classmates were possible subjects for a story. Some people find this a revelation. There are many people who have recorded their excitement at achieving this sort of identification possible. However, I was not one of them. If anything I was bewildered at recognising my own surroundings and companions and felt rather cheated, for as a reader I was committed to "otherness". I knew all about my life. I didn't need, I thought, to read about it too.'

But Margaret was sufficiently affected by Sutton-Smith's work, and suggestions in English classes that New Zealand needed a great New Zealand novel, to begin deliberately to write stories with New Zealand settings. 'I remember going down to the river and describing exactly what I saw in front of me and working it into a story. All in vain! The description, though no doubt correct enough, brought no conviction. I had a fault line running through me. My inside world did not match the outside one and my imaginative convictions were in terms of a country that existed only in print and images of astonishment . . .'

For three years, McLean encouraged her writing — he lived almost directly opposite, so she often called in with stories, poems and set assignments for comment — and was often astonished by what he read.

By the fourth form, as a result of McLean's urging to sing in the chorus of his annual Gilbert and Sullivan productions, she was producing deadly accurate, authentic parodies and satires of W. S. Gilbert's uniquely rhythmic, comic style. She was fascinated by his 'verbal jazz . . . by his tremendous verbal capacity and his ability to put something into rhyme that sounded inevitable, as though that was the way you'd have said it in real life'. (Much the same could be said of her own work, both the prose and poetry.) These school performances activated a lifelong love affair with patter songs and verse of sophisticated technical dexterity demonstrated three decades later with pieces like her famous performance pieces *Bubble Trouble* and *Down the Back of the Chair*. Many years later, somebody protested when Margaret claimed that she knew Gilbert's songs by heart; and yes, she admits, it is not quite true, 'because I don't know *The Grand Duke* or *Princess Ida* well, but I do most of them extremely well. This is not an exaggerated claim; they always came quite easily to me. I used to irritate my mother, with my ear clapped to the radio series they did of the story of Gilbert and Sullivan's great partnership.' In her enthusiasm, she pursued the programme from station to station, 'a Bay of Plenty listener chasing after such bits and pieces as I could hear in between bursts of static when the series was being broadcast (on 4YA) to listeners in Dunedin'. She badly wanted to learn all those songs by heart, and worked at them very hard. 'Of course, my more profoundly musical friends laugh at me, unable to keep a touch of patronage out of their laughter, when I confess to such populist musical preconceptions, but in the beginning I felt that, through my power over Gilbert and Sullivan, I had become truly cultured.'

Classical music was another area in which she has acknowledged a debt to McLean. She was thrilled by hearing in class composers like Ralph Vaughan Williams for the first time and deciding, as she wrote many years later, 'only partly consciously, to improve myself . . . to become artistic, sensitive and cultured. At the time I had at my disposal a wind-up gramophone and a pile of 78 records . . . including works by Beethoven, as well as selections of well-known operas, *Rigoletto*, *La Traviata* and so on. Winding the handle steadily I listened to these cultural fragments over and over again and certainly grew to enjoy them . . . Round about this time "long playing" records began to appear and everyone, including members of my family, hastened to acquire "radiograms" — record players capable of coping with this astonishingly new technology. Influenced by Lord Peter's musical preference [Lord Peter Wimsey, in Dorothy Sayers' detective novels] I bought records of Bach to which I listened with the self-conscious sense that I was doing the right intellectual thing. However, the day came when I was overwhelmed by a different sort of musical experience. Listening to that music I underwent what I can only describe as transformation. The initial self-consciousness became irrelevant . . . disappeared. The room faded around me. There was nothing beyond my listening ear and that sound. Something was being stated that could be stated in no other way. My whole feeling about music changed forever . . . on my own now I work to the music of Albinoni, Purcell, Vivaldi and Hildegard of Bingen . . . sometimes music is a companion to me — barely heard yet working its way through me and altering me as it does so . . .'

Her growing confidence in her third, fourth and fifth form

years resulted in other kinds of progress. She became a competent tennis player, though this gave her a lasting dislike of competitive and aggressive games, and a better than average swimmer, even winning a school championship. She gained further social acceptance, albeit of an eccentric kind, by not only regularly topping English but also starting a club she remembers now being known as 'The Apolloni Quarto Decimatineo Psycho Phrenologist Junior Society of Genii whose members would study Tautology, Idiosyncrasy, Hugger Mugger and Procrastination'.

To the suggestion that by the end of her secondary schooling she had acquired an exceptionally wide vocabulary and command of language, naturally rich in metaphor, myth and irony, she laughs and says, 'Yes, I was rather self-consciously pleased with myself because of that . . . I suppose it was a talent in the way that another child has for sports or a craft.' The extraordinary freshness of, especially, simile and metaphor noted by so many critics she puts down to her individual response to the world, and her intention to make every story as good as possible, using 'what's going to be the most fertile and interesting ideas that you can'.

Ian McLean remembered Margaret as an 'unusual girl with a zany sense of humour', not so much eccentric, or odd, or peculiar, as 'an individualist who would laugh uproariously at things that no one else would think the slightest bit funny. She didn't go down altogether well with the establishment. Our high school was a very traditional sort of place. And Margaret was certainly not that.' He recalled the talkative fourth former setting the staff room abuzz after an important school rugby game during which 'that Margaret Mahy' on the sidelines had hurled some unprintable lines at the opposition. 'I thought it was vastly funny,' he said, 'but nobody else did!'

And there was the occasion she capered across the road to announce excitedly that she had been reading Christopher Fry's play *A Phoenix Too Frequent*, apparently as a result of studying his better-known *The Lady's Not for Burning* in class. 'That she'd even heard of it amazed me.' She had, he said, cottoned on pretty early to the notion that literature can be interpreted at different levels, 'that if you looked beyond the basic level of the storyline, you would find a level with a meaning about some aspect of life which could be relevant today'. Serious books on ideas, on philosophy and science, were yet to be discovered, 'but of course in a lot of good fiction philosophical notions are implicit'.

Nearing the end of her school days, passing first School Certificate and then University Entrance comfortably, the boisterous student became, in McLean's words, 'quieter and a little more conforming . . . she showed a growth in maturity in what she wrote and did'.

But he has been reluctant in interviews to take any credit for his famous student's later success. 'I think she would have done what she's done whoever had been here,' though according to Dunlop, he admits that Margaret's English class enjoyed a memorable and special rapport between teacher and students.

She continued to astonish him, with poems like *The Burnt Library*, written after a school fire in 1952. With 'an extraordinary breadth and depth of reading for a 16-year-old', she catches the style of Alexander Pope, 'cadences and all . . . The poem could have been written by Pope except that it mentions certain authors that came after him. There are 19 of these, and she obviously knows a lot from the comments she's made. She even refers to [E.M.] Forster's Celestial Omnibus . . . even more astonishing . . . she found these things herself.'

The Burnt Library

Here as they came and all too swiftly went,
The hours of happy solitude I spent;
But for a space I left, and now, returned,
I find my place of silent worship burned.
Here Eliot, Auden, Steinbeck, Lewis, James
Have moved the world, but could not move the flames;
And with them Pope whose shrilly-cutting ire

Has met its master — all-devouring fire.
Mark! Dickens crumbled 'neath the flaming thrust,
And Marlowe's 'mighty line' is in the dust.
Here Shakespeare held his once imperial sway;
Where is his golden thunder then today?
Where are Othello, Hamlet, Lear, Macbeth?
They lie with Shaw in silent ashen death.
And Dante with Defoe and Dekker fell;
No Virgil came to guide him through the Hell;
See how he mingles ashes on the floor
With Homer, Hardy and Sir Thomas More.
And Forster's here; now I shall never know
Where his Celestial Omnibuses go.
See — Shelley's brilliant passion is today
All dull and cold and spent in ashes grey . . .
So shall we be. Wise, foolish, mean and just
Shall sleep together in tomorrow's dust;
The prince and peasant shall appear as one,
As motes of dust seen in a ray of sun.

In her last year at school, two Mahy poems were published in the school's magazine. *Magic* is notable for its prediction of the themes, imagery and freshly minted word play that would later reappear in hundreds of picture books; *Ghosts* impressively anticipates the philosopher.

Magic

Is there no magic in the world?
Is sun just sunshine, raindrops rain?
Are they not fairy gold and pearls?
Is not the wind a fairy train?

Is all the world of magic gone?
Are there no roadways through the grass,

Which mice draw match-box coaches on,
Along which fairy workmen pass?

Is all the world of magic gone?
Are not the roses fairy homes?
Is not the earth beneath our feet
Alive with goblins, elves and gnomes?

If all the world of magic's gone,
And witches do not sail the sea
In eggshells halved, with broomstick oars —
This world is not the place for me.

Ghosts

Two ghosts are walking out today,
And one I cannot see;
The ghost of what I was before,
And what I am to be.

The ghost of what I was before
Is still a friend to me:
The other ghost — the one I fear —
Is what I am to be.

If I could draw the veil aside,
Perhaps I then could see
The face of this, the stranger ghost,
The one I am to be.

Yet I am blessed in this, I feel:
The future's hid from me,
And I must wait and meet the ghost
Of what I am to be.

There are two ghosts abroad today —
And one I cannot see:
The first, a wraith of what I was,
The other is to be.

Freed from school, officially armed with University Entrance in four subjects (English, history, geography and French), Margaret contemplated her future. She hardly bothered telling her parents that she wanted to be a writer: in the early 1950s, middle-class New Zealand girls became teachers, nurses or secretaries before the expected marriage by the national average age of 23. University meant committing money and by now the Mahys, with four younger children to support, were understandably stern about her need to get a job. Margaret was not ready to leave Whakatane but she reacted against the family inevitability of teaching and chose, as something different, nursing.

It proved a short career of less than a year, and 'forced alarming truths' on her. Too young, at sixteen, to be a proper nurse, the nurse aid soon came to recognise that though she enjoyed talking to the patients ('I saw compassion as quite a desirable thing, and I knew I'd be good at that'), she was also physically slow and clumsy to the point of routinely exasperating the other nurses anxious to get through their routines. 'Other nurses and nurse-aids would rally round me to help me finish my duties, partly out of kindness and partly out of self-interest, for no one on the morning's team would leave until everyone was finished.' Girls who had been behind her at school were much more deft and successful in ward work; her younger sister Patricia later did nursing and 'was miles better at it than me'. When she finally went to the matron to say that perhaps she'd be better suited to other work, 'never before or since have I encountered such spontaneous relief in an employer'.

Sometime during this experimental but decisive year, Margaret came across the detective novel *Gaudy Night*, by Dorothy Sayers, set in Oxford. The idealised portrayal of university life affected her profoundly: 'the whole question of academic honesty and ideals starts to come out, the question of truth, the extent to which the university is a sort of fountain and defender of truth. The ideas discussed in that book were ideas that thrilled me a great deal. I thought I wanted to be associated with all this.'

Some hard talking with her parents followed. There were plenty of teachers but few graduates among the wider family: they regarded university as 'a bit of a self-indulgence,' but ultimately agreed to support their bookish eldest daughter during the expected three to four years of study for a BA degree. In February 1953, not quite seventeen, she left the family home in Haig Street, the river and the Pacific coastline to travel north alone, by bus, to New Zealand's biggest city, to enrol at what was then the Auckland College of the University of New Zealand.

After the neighbourly, supportive friendliness of a small, remote township, Auckland was forbidding and lonely, landladies unpredictable, and the boredom of part-time work in a small coffee factory, putting tops on bottles alongside workmates who never read books, mind-numbing.

Margaret enrolled in English, history, education, French and philosophy. This last was not a particularly well-regarded subject: 'Auckland wasn't then a great place to do Philosophy . . . it was the thing you tended to take when you didn't know quite what you wanted to do'. Her mind already awash with an extraordinary range of literature, ideas, questions, ideas for stories, even an ongoing novel, she found herself increasingly interested in the subject. The lecturers seemed rather old and not very articulate, and the Aristotelian syllogisms not particularly interesting, but she managed well enough in her first two years. English meant an introduction to Chaucer, Spenser, more Shakespeare, poetry with Allen Curnow, tutorials with eminent author Professor Michael Joseph; she studied Katherine Mansfield, but not very deeply, and does not remember particularly opting for New Zealand writers. Frank Sargeson, however, came to give a talk she remembers vividly, about living as a writer.

She noted 'a general feeling that when poets and lecturers read their poems aloud a certain degree of drunkenness lent authenticity to the performance. A panel of sober readers somehow felt clerical rather than artistic. There was a certain relish in references to the dissipation of Burns, and rather later the accounts of Dylan Thomas's excesses carried a curious quality of fulfilment about them. James K. Baxter's drunkenness was sometimes quoted as if it proved New Zealand poets belonged to the true literary world. But everyone knows by now that there is more to art than being drunk, and drunkenness is no longer the mandatory feature of artistic utterance in the way it used to be.'

Her university years seem to have remained rather introverted, with little money, hardly any extra-curricular activities and few she came to call friends. 'When I went to university I didn't have much idea about the sort of person I was, and only very general ideas about what I liked and what I thought. I was a slow developing person compared to some.' Children's novelist Jack Lasenby, later to be one of her key *School Journal* editors at School Publications, was a fellow student in English and philosophy lectures. His memory of her is hazy, indicating that the boisterous schoolgirl had been temporarily replaced by another, somewhat lonely and withdrawn, persona. But he recalls a friendly, unusually literate student who 'even then had the whole story thing going, making up stories on the spot especially about the formidable English lecturer Dr Annie Shepherd and icicles forming as she came towards us'.

Without close friends or immersing herself much in activities on the lively fringes of university life, Margaret spent time regularly visiting her Auckland aunt, her mother's sister Dorothy. She was the rebel of the family, the disadvantaged (she claimed) middle one of six girls who had done a degree rather against her family's wishes, then travelled widely at a time when few young women did — and when intelligence in women was not universally valued. Dorothy's travels took her to Canada, Spain, France and Austria, where she became companion to a well-to-do Viennese girl and learned to speak German. In a 1982 speech, Margaret was to describe her as the free-thinking, pro-Nazi aunt she was fortunate to have, 'who suffered terribly during the Second World War, not simply because she was investigated by the secret police who observed a photograph of Hitler on her wall, but because she could not believe the accounts she read in the papers'. She was very intelligent, says Margaret, a natural academic, filled with fascinating ideas, particularly politics and philosophy. Aunt and niece enjoyed lively discussions, frequently disagreeing; philosophy, stated Dorothy, was like a blind man in a dark room looking for a drawer that wasn't there.

Two factors influenced Margaret's decision to move to Christchurch for her final year. One was her struggle with French; at Auckland a foreign language was a compulsory BA requirement. She worked hard, and could translate well enough from French to English, but not, mysteriously, from English to French. After a third failure, she felt she knew the lectures almost word for word. To her great relief, she found by chance that the Canterbury college did not require a language. The other factor was her increasing fascination for philosophical ideas, particularly the philosophy of religion, which was offered at Canterbury.

Moving to Christchurch in 1955, she found her new city made friendlier than Auckland by her Penlington relations, and stage three philosophy at the attractive stone-built Canterbury campus quickly became enthralling. 'I absolutely loved it there. There were good lecturers, Professor Prior and Mike Shorter, and five students: one Buddhist, two young men who were going into the ministry, and me.'

Her enthusiasm for philosophy stems from those years, but Margaret thinks her interest in political and ethical ideas began earlier, at home and in secondary school English and history classes: 'it was always very primitive there, but the whole huge confusion of ideas started to creep in on me in my last years at school, reinforced when we started studying [the English philosopher John] Locke'. Latin had never interested her as a subject, until the day she found a Latin textbook tossed onto the dump in Whakatane. She did not get very far with her intention of studying it, but along with Locke and Sayers, it had been influential in drawing her towards the world of ideas, of the classics. She believes she may have been a different sort of writer had she not discovered philosophy, with its themes of transformation and links to folk tales, myths and legends, when fairly young. 'Classical philosophy underlines my work,' she says, 'with a lot of powerful philosophical ideas unconsciously expressed even in stories for little children. And as you move into older fiction, you get political ideas, ideas about right and wrong expressed much more intricately. If you've done philosophy, that certainly underlines them.'

There was, however, another layer to Margaret's life in her university years. Secretly she 'longed for fantasy and truly amazing things. I was not able to draw that amazement directly out of real life, though it was certainly to be found there if only I had known how to look, and in those days very little fantasy for an adult reader seemed to be available.' She was, though, reading widely: science fiction by John Wyndham, C.S. Lewis, Walter de la Mare, folk tales, horror stories, ghost stories, Henry James and Arthur Machen — and, increasingly, children's books. After the limited resources of a small town, she found shops like Auckland's Minerva Books irresistible, often popping down to Queen Street to spend her free time browsing, 'searching I suppose, for that magical extremity that had been part of my childhood encounters . . . it was in children's books that fantasy had a true and acceptable maturity'. She discovered, among much else, the children's short story collections of English writers Barbara Leonie Pickard and Eleanor Farjeon; the children's books purchased around this time are among the most loved in her extensive collection.

Until this time her own compulsive storytelling had progressed through its various preoccupations with jungle children, swashbuckling heroes and horses, sometimes lasting for anything up to a year and moving in recurring cycles. Later she would assess her earliest attempts harshly. 'When I look with apprehension at my first stories, pencilled words growing very faint now, I am brought low by the singular lack of talent they display. They are, almost without exception, strongly derivative and I am reminded of Tom Lehrer's song *Plagiarize!* Had I the vocabulary or the concept when I was seven I would have called it "writing in a tradition". . . . And yet when my children who have actually owned horses read my early series *Jet the Wonder Horse, Son of Jet* and so on, and laugh derisively, I feel defensive of these raggy little stories written with such earnest satisfaction doomed through the permanence of the written word to perpetually display incompetence and fall so far short of the ideal form Plato thinks all aspects of existence must attain to. The fact is something personal was involved even in these plagiarisms, something which I detect with consternation, some permanent commitment was made to the story . . .'

Her most truly 'original' work had been a consistent output of poetry, and various adolescent attempts at novels, including a prophetic one about a woman who wanted to be Prime Minister of New Zealand. But now aged 18 or 19, while formally studying the world's great writers and philosophers, removed from family life and with no children of her own, she made a conscious, serious decision to develop her talent as a writer of stories for children.

'At the time I was growing up, literature was overwhelmingly realistic. It may have been partly because World War II made magical games, jokes and speculations seem indulgent . . . realism was also allowing New Zealanders both to recognise and to invent themselves.'

Her first encounter with 'magical realism' was probably *Ficciones* by Jorge Luis Borges, 'which generated a very different sort of amazement from that engendered by Lord of the Rings'.

'I have previously speculated as to why British and European adult literature discarded fantasy for a while, and think that in New Zealand's case the necessity of defining a day-to-day New Zealand identity was expressed in defining our relatively new and uncertain identity rather than playing any surrealistic games. It was partly a sort of fidelity to fantasy that made me (I conjecture) a writer for children, since it seemed back in the 1950s and 1960s that fantasy had no place in respected adult writing.'

Fairy tales, folk tales, myth, legend, fantasy — these were the recognised stuff of stories and novels written for children. 'I began to imitate this particular genre myself, knowing for the first time just what I was doing and who my models were.' The nineteen-year-old's degree of confidence in this decision is remarkable. 'I had always known I was part of literature, but at the cost, it now seemed, of some severe displacements. I had chosen fantasy of some kind without being aware that I was choosing anything, and at that time, writing for children was the area in which fantasy attained the easiest acceptance.'

Towards the end of her university years, however, there had been a disturbing experience which stopped her writing for a while and caused her to reflect on the whole nature of ideas and the notion of 'originality'. In September 1987 she described what happened in a celebrated essay, *Joining the Network*, for the British magazine, *Signal*.

'I was writing stories at this time that seemed to me more original than they would sound if I were to describe the plots, all making heavy use of fairy and folktale elements, but not always in ways I recognised. One such story involved a group of people who were travelling through a wonderful imaginary land on some quest, the exact nature of which I forget. I think they were going to save the world from evil or something like that. They had to climb a savage mountain, and one by one they were disabled until only one was left — the one who, through great suffering, would reach the top and do whatever it was he had to to save the world. About this time a lecturer in English at university, listening to me talking about Arthur Machen, who was certainly not on the syllabus, suggested that I read "this new book by J.R.R. Tolkien". I had not read *The Hobbit* and began *The Lord of the Rings* with some impatient reactions to Bilbo and Frodo and the rest. I was soon possessed, read all three volumes, reread them immediately and then reread them for the third time, disconcerted to find things I had somehow imagined were more or less my own ideas in a story which, through 1956 and 1957, completely absorbed me. I read it aloud to my brother and sisters in the Christmas holidays, but in a way it stopped my writing for while, for it seemed to use up every idea I had ever had, or at least it brought me to understand that the ideas were not mine, had never been mine, and were not altogether Mr Tolkien's either, but existed in the network, never exhausted, always capable of revealing themselves in new ways.'

Many years later, she would assess Mr Tolkien's achievement with rather less wonderment. As a student, she had been delighted by *The Lord of the Rings*, 'whereas reading it now [1995] I feel weariness at this great, creaking vehicle of a tale, with its polarised characters, its lack of irony, wit and humour. The invention of the entire imaginary world, complete with a history extending before and beyond the tale, is not the wonder I once thought it was, but a relatively commonplace act of imagination. As such fantasies have proliferated' — and Tolkien, she thinks, 'has a lot to answer for' — 'the predictability of the genre has proliferated too; but part of my weariness is because I have become a more precise reader than I was when I was nineteen.'

Furnished with what she has described as 'a very ordinary degree', Margaret finished her years of formal university study at the end of 1955. There was no serious thought of post-graduate study or overseas travel before marriage. It was understood that she must put her degree to some use, and start earning her living. Nursing had been found unsuitable; she had the wrong skills and no inclination for secretarial work; the very thought of teaching, the most popular avenue for female BA graduates, was unappealing. In what was then an orderly, smug and patriarchal society, young women with basic BAs in the mid-fifties simply did not aspire to climbing career ladders in business, and only rarely to entering word-based professions like law or publishing or political bureaucracies. Most female BAs in arts subjects found themselves teaching, or began travelling to get their obligatory

Overseas Experience before the expected wedding, and Margaret now says she simply didn't see travel as an option.

'The idea of the adventurous life still beckoned me. I thought I might become a police woman, was interviewed, and told at the end of the interview that I was not really suitable. I think I had the idea, a vague amorphous idea, that I might progress rather rapidly through the uniformed ranks to become a detective of a sort . . . someone rather like Lord Peter Wimsey himself, or Ngaio Marsh's Roderick Alleyn, or perhaps their more current counterpart P.D. James's detective Adam Dalgleish — acute, capable of picking up on clues that other people missed, ruthless yet sensitive, and filled with sufficient literary strength not only to recognise quotes from Webster and Ben Jonson but also to complete the quotations. I might have been moderately good at the literary quote side of detective work, but I image the guru who conducted my interview was wise when he closed this particular door for me. The adventurous life retreated yet again.

'In desperation I applied for Library School, was accepted and in due course became a librarian.' It may have seemed like a desperate and possibly even mundane choice at the time, but she must have been one of the better-read 20-year-olds to apply and though occasionally given to sending it up, she was to grow proud of the noble practice of librarianship, and ascribe to it high ideals and status.

'Only a few days ago I saw a picture in which the prim austerity of a female character was emphasised by the fact that she was a librarian. Over the years librarians have been given a repressive image. Time and time again they are shown as humourless women who, being largely sexless, have never escaped into the halcyon work of housekeeping and hanging out napkins. Of course many people are unaware that Casanova was not only sexually prodigious but also progressed to become librarian for Count von Waldstein in Bohemia for 13 years, though admittedly this was towards the end of his career. We have no evidence that he progressed to be an efficient cataloguer. Casanova to one side,

I am here to assert that librarians stand dancing and pivoting on the tenuous ridge that separates chaos from order. That dancing librarian makes so much of the world accessible to others.'

The idea of working with books and bookish people, though, meant another full year of training, another move to yet another major city. After that, she would be qualified to apply for jobs in any library, large or small, in the country.

Despite the five years of hard and mainly solitary study for twin qualifications to make herself employable, independent and secure, Margaret's story was about to enter, as fairy tales do, another and more arduous, testing phase: some fifteen long years of often lonely and relentless struggle towards financial security and the hard-earned beginnings of full recognition as a writer.

Part Two

The Apprentice Writer —
1959 to 1968

With her 1958 diploma in librarianship added to her degree, Margaret began work as 'a dancing librarian' at the Petone Public Library, in the Hutt Valley north of Wellington. Her year in Wellington at Library School had been a much less lonely experience than her university years in Auckland or Christchurch. Now, she found herself enjoying the companionship of the library environment, continuing with her customary, voluminous reading over a huge range of subjects and experimenting with the children's story form which so intellectually fascinated her.

Few of her earliest attempts survive, although there is a large, well-used diary for 1960, in the Christchurch City Libraries Margaret Mahy Archive, that includes not only several of the stories that would later become international picture books ('17 Kings and 42 Elephants', 'Pillycock's Shop' and 'Mrs Discobobulous' — no 'm' at this stage), but a large number of others in fascinating draft form, showing scraps of ideas and dialogue being worked and reworked. The handwriting, never tidy but legible, gives the impression that her writing hand cannot keep up with the prodigious flow of ideas.

Some time in early 1961, to help support herself and the child shortly to be born, Margaret 'sat down and wrote a group of short stories and sent three of them off to School Publications,' publishers of that unique New Zealand institution, the *School Journal*. Since its inception in 1907, the *Journal* had attracted the finest writers to submit stories for the issues that were regularly provided free to New Zealand schools by the Department of Education. Then, as now, writers regarded acceptance as a considerable achievement, no matter how short the story or the poem. The same was true for illustrators: the *School Journal* featured work by such eminent artists as Mervyn Taylor, Russell Clark and Jill McDonald. And shortly after Penny was born and after an anxious, protracted wait for a response, Margaret learned that she was to be published in the *School Journal*. She felt 'intensely thrilled and vindicated, especially when I realised that I could actually earn money from writing'.

'I remember that I had sent the stories in to School Publications and I hadn't heard from them. I happened to be in Wellington and I rang up and asked after my stories and they [School Publications] said ring again that afternoon. I rang back and they said that they were going to print *The Procession* . . . I felt, in a small way I suppose, as God might have felt on the first day of creation . . . and it wasn't much to do with the fact that I would be getting money (though I needed money). It's not something that you ever forget.' She was a little surprised at the story they chose. 'One I wrote for myself and one I wrote not completely for myself. I had a view of the possible market, that is school publications and the use of the story in the school. The story they accepted was the one I had written completely for myself. They turned down the one I had written "for them". This was the opposite way I thought it would be . . . Since then, I continue to do both. People have a special feeling about language, even though it's been so abused. It's a bit like being a minister or teacher. They feel you are dealing with something so special you should do it for free. So the idea of commercialism in writing is a very sensitive area.'

In its understanding of the folk tale genre, its structure, language and metaphors ('a sharp mountain that bites like a tooth at the sky'), the combination of folk tale archetypes with sly, domestic touches ('They toasted muffins on the Dragon'), the underlying idea of transformation and the general air of originality, *The Procession* is strange, poetic, dreamlike, even a touch fey — and unmistakably Mahy.

The Procession

Who came tapping at the door? A wild wandering man, green as Spring! Who came running to open the door? A little girl, eight years old dressed in a filmy, floating, cloudy nightgown!

'Will you dance around the world with me?' said the wandering fellow.

'Yes, of course I'll come,' said the little girl. Off they went together, into a primrose yellow morning. The wanderer played his violin and they danced along the road,

Who was it knocked at the door? A wild wandering man and a little girl wearing a filmy, floating, cloudy gown.

Who came running to open the door? A man with great grey bird wings growing from his shoulders.

'Will you come dancing with us?' they asked him.

'I have been waiting for you,' he told them. 'Why were you so long?'

Off they went together into a blue crystal morning. They danced along the road. The wanderer played his violin, and the little girl sang:

'Honey, honey, dripping from the flower,
Petals, petals, falling from the rose,
Where can I find yesterday's happy hour?
No one knows! Nobody knows!'

Who came tapping at the door? A wild wandering fellow, a little girl in a filmy, flowing gown, and a man with bird wings!

Who came running to open the door? A Fiery Man and his friend the Dragon.

'Will you come with us?' they asked.

'Can my dragon come too?'

'Yes, we need a dragon.'

'Well then, I will come as far as you are going!'

Off they went, and then, suddenly, it was lunchtime.

'Will you have salt in your stew?' the wandering fellow asked politely.

'Will you have honey on your bread, or cheese?' asked the bird-winged man. They toasted muffins on the Dragon, and drank lemonade.

'Do you know what we are?' asked the little girl happily. 'We are a procession.'

'There are no trumpets,' the Dragon pointed out doubtfully.

'The happy feelings inside us are the trumpets for our procession,' the Fiery Man replied peacefully.

The procession went on . . . through a wood, over a bridge, across the sea in little boats (coloured sails like gay wings over the water), over a desert on silent proud camels, up a sharp mountain that was like a tooth biting at the sky.

Who was it clanged on the bell at the gate? The procession! Who came running to peer through the bars? The young King, wild in his crimson velvet robes, shining like a rose red star.

'Take me with you, take me with you!' he cried. 'I want to see, and hear, and smell, and feel the wide world.'

Who came running to pull him away from the bars? Five guards in armour, five wise men in black cloaks, like learned umbrellas, frayed at the edges.

'Come back to your books on law and government,' they cried, 'or you will never learn enough to be king.'

'Law is a fine thing, and government is a fine long word,' said the wandering fellow, 'but what of the song at night by the fire? A King should hear this, once in his life.'

'A King should dance in the moon, and feel the black and silver night around him,' said the little girl.

'Oh,' cried the bird-winged man. 'A King should know poetry that sings, like the soaring of great feathered wings.'

'A King should feel in his heart that life is strong as the music of trumpets, and warm as the flame of a dragon,' added the Fiery Man.

And the Dragon ended: 'But not only a King should know these things. A guard in his armour should know them, and a wise man in a black cloak should know about them, too.'

So the guards opened the gate and the young King ran out. The wise men followed him, flinging off their black cloaks. Underneath they wore patchwork like five pied pipers — all the colours of the rainbow, all the colours of the world.

The guards left their armour to rust. They went out dressed in brown and green, like five sturdy trees.

'Now we are a real procession,' said the little girl.

'But no trumpets!' complained the bird-winged man.

'The happiness that we feel is like trumpets,' the five wise men said.

'Or like kettle drums!' said the five guards.

'It is all sorts of music,' said the young King.

The procession went on and on with singing and dancing and being happy.

Perhaps tomorrow, they will knock at your door.

And a poem, also published in the *School Journal* that year, again signalled the Mahy preoccupations with the images from a thousand folk tales, though sharpened up.

The Witch, my sister

The witch, my sister from over the sea,
Wonderful presents has sent to me.
A whistle to blow, and a bell to ring,
Silken ropes for a shining swing.

A golden lion that will play and purr,
Dancing slippers of silver fur,
And, sharp as a needle, bright as a pin,
A mouse that plays on a violin.

Many primary school teachers around the country used these charming, quirky pieces in their classrooms and must have wondered about their author. One reader who did more than wonder was somehow connected with the New Zealand pop group Blerta, which turned *The Procession* into a song, 'Come Dance All Around the World'. Characteristically, Margaret's quoted comment expressed pleasure while rightly making a point about the business of copyright. 'It's not the sort of thing you expect to happen to a children's story, to have it turned into a song. It's interesting to see how an idea leaves you and goes on to someone else who uses it in a different way. I didn't give my permission to have the story used. I didn't even get a copy of the record. Strictly speaking, someone should have approached the publishers about it, but I felt very pleased to see it used in a different medium.'

Along with the joy of being published 1961 brought the arrival of her daughter Penny. Margaret has described her decision to have a child at 25, as part of a 'romantic and compelling love affair' begun when she was 21, as linking 'very naturally with these ideas I had about adventure'. In those days, adoption was the usual and expected course of action, but despite pressure she never really considered this, confident that she would find a way to support herself and her child. She saw the whole thing very much 'as my own particular adventure and responsibility'. In 1990 she was to reflect that 'at the time I don't think I contemplated the possibility of not succeeding at what I'd done; I never doubted that I was capable of replicating for my own children the sort of marvellous upbringing I had myself as a child'. But in some ways, too, she had a 'rather falsely romantic view of my own role — I saw myself as a woman alone setting out on her adventures. I always assumed that I would be the one to look after them. I think on some unconscious level I had sought to live out the woman-alone-against-the jungle-of-the-world fantasy, otherwise I would have opted for something safer.'

With her baby and very little money, Margaret went to live with a young couple, Belinda and John Rotman, in the Ohariu Valley, north of Wellington. In return for board she would do light housework and help in the garden, tending and picking the tomatoes they grew. Margaret speaks with warmth and gratitude of her three years there, and her long-standing friendship with Belinda Rotman. She was able to fit in caring for her baby and her habitual nocturnal reading and writing around the jobs expected of her. The rural environment was appealing, and the immediate landscape she looked out on really was a 'meadow' with wild flowers, not a paddock. For her part, Belinda Rotman, quoted in a 1984 newspaper feature, looked back 'on the three years of Margaret's stay as the most extraordinary time of her life'. The two women would spend some days 'speaking entirely in rhyming couplets. "It was the most carefree, lovely time. There was never a dull moment. Although she is quite introverted, when you get to know her she has a tremendous wit and sparkle."' In response to a comment about Margaret's vulnerability, Belinda replied, '"Why, she has the strength of forty men. She's one of the strongest characters you are ever likely to meet."'

From the Ohariu Valley, the stories to the *School Journal* started to flow, some with names that would later, as picture books, become world famous: *The Birthday Party, Guy and the Bears* and *The Little Man Who Went to Sea* in 1962; *The Old Bus* in 1964; and in 1965 *The Adventures of Little Mouse, Alone in the House, The Clowns, Once upon an evening* (poem), *A Lion in the Meadow, The Little Wild Woman, The Merry-go-round, Mouse Music* (poem), *Mr Rumfit, Right-Hand Men, Sailor Jack, The Playground, A Witch in the House.*

In 1965, Margaret moved south to Christchurch, which would remain her home. With a modest bequest from her paternal grandfather she was able to buy a small section of land at Governors Bay, on the western shore of Lyttelton Harbour, reached by a spectacular road over the Port Hills from the city. She rented a cottage for a few months, while having the beginnings of a house erected: the most basic two rooms, with, for a good few years, no running water, no inside toilets and no electricity. There was nothing much on the overgrown section except a few fruit trees from an earlier orchard.

There was, however, the spectacular Canterbury landscape, later to become the background to several of her novels: Lyttelton Harbour in *The Tricksters* and *Underrunners*, the Port Hills in *The Catalogue of the Universe*, the city itself in *The Changeover, Aliens in the Family, Memory, The Other Side of Silence, 24 Hours* and *Alchemy*. Descriptive passages in *The Catalogue of the Universe* and, especially,

Underrunners portray a landscape that provided pleasure or challenge almost every day: the Port Hills road rising from the city plain, swooping and curving 'writhing like a desperate serpent pinned down and anxious to be free', until, above a dry creek capable of 'roaring like a beast on a continual, angry note as if the hill side itself had found a throat and was issuing a warning', it 'grew leaner and more treacherous, held at bay on one side by a bank alive with moss and ferns and broom and foxgloves, while on the other it surrendered to the void, a great airy fall on to stony slopes far below. Not only this, the road claimed victims just as if it were a serpent god.'

To the north, from this road, stretch the city plains, the long sweep of misted coastline; to the west the jagged foothills of the Southern Alps, snow-clad for much of the year. When the narrow, winding hillside road to Governors Bay surmounts the saddle and descends, it suddenly offers a framed view of the inner reaches of Lyttelton Harbour, its rim of tawny, barren hills encircling islands and jutting fingers of land lying in water that can be deep turquoise, or green, or a sullen grey, mirror calm or white-capped. Margaret has spoken of the solace of driving down that scenic road to her little home and shutting the door at the end of each daily adventure in the city or beyond, each wearying trip overseas. Governors Bay in 1965 was quite primitive, a place for holiday baches and what would later be called 'alternative lifestylers', but it was her chosen place, her haven.

Like 1961, 1966 brought Margaret two somewhat similar events of equal joy and significance.

First, the *School Journal* editors decided to pay an unprecedented compliment to a single writer and, despite their lack of 'New Zealand' content, devote a whole issue —*The Wind Between the Stars*, Part 3, Number 3 — to stories by Margaret Mahy. They were superbly illustrated by Jill McDonald, a Wellington illustrator, trained as an architect, who was art director of the *School Journal* from 1957 to 1965, then left New Zealand to go on to an outstanding illustrating career in England. Introduced by a strong cover image of animals surrounding a melancholy Harlequin, the seven stories and two poems made up what was, in effect, Margaret's first collection and her first soft-cover book. Five of the stories would later be published in Britain and the United States as hardback picture books: *The Boy who Went Looking for a Friend, Pillycock's Shop, Mrs Discobobulous* (renamed *Mrs Discombobulous*), *The Wind Between the Stars* and *The Princess and the Clown*. Betty Gilderdale has singled out the story *'Small Porks'* as the one tale 'above all others [that] sums up her work by making a wry comment on society within a humorous framework'. Small Porks is the youngest in a litter of ten, and a sensitive chap who responds to teasing and outside criticism of pigs simply by determining to think beautiful thoughts, his own and, after a while, even somebody else's. After three days of intense thinking, Small Porks, singing in a golden voice, wakes his siblings.

> He was still a pig, but he was a new pig — a pig metamorphosed — a pig transmogrified, transformed and utterly resolved — and all that means, simply, he was changed.
>
> He was still pink, but now he shone pink as a rose dipped in the fire of glow worms. His tail was a twist of clematis, white with flowery stars. His spots had changed to the shape of petals and leaves and from his back blossomed two wings, pink and white as shells fresh from the sea.

In what would become a typical Mahy transformation scene and an ironic ending, Small Porks, now 'more myself than I have ever been before', flies off on his adventures ('I always knew that boy would rise in the world,' said his mother) while his family watch amazed and the old pig in the next door pen

> stared at the bright vanishing figure of Small Porks harder than any of the others.
>
> 'Perhaps we're all like that if we want to be,' he said. 'Perhaps Small Porks is the first really truly true pig the

world has seen since we were turned out of the Garden of Eden.'

But the other pigs had heard the clank of the mash and scrap bucket and weren't listening, and after a moment the oldest pig heard the clanking too, and quite forgot his strange thoughts.

The 1966 *School Journal* stories are already remarkable for their range and their command of genre. Even without the editorial support a major commercial publishing house would offer, the confident Margaret Mahy voice rings through work that is poetic, comic, disturbing and lyrical. Take the last W.S. Gilbert-inspired verse of *When the King Rides By*:

> Oh what a fuss when the king rides by —
> Rockets dance in the starry sky,
> Mice in their mouse-holes wonder why,
> The people throw their hats up high,
> The soldiers stamp and the ladies sigh,
> The dogs all bark and the babies cry,
> The puss-cat runs and the pigeons fly,
> And the drum goes rat-a-plan-plan.

Or the opening of the story about an old woman who falls into a washing machine, *Mrs Discobobulous*, which plays with alliteration and words — vixen and virago, tyrant and tartar — very unusual in children's stories of the time:

> There was once a very cross woman called Mrs Discobobulous. Oh she was a scold, a shrew, a vixen and a virago, and a proper tyrant and tartar to her poor husband (whose name was Mr Discobobulous). She niggled and naggled him day and night, from first yawn to last. He was ragged, poor-spirited, uncivil, unkempt and unkind, if you listened to what his wife said about him. Her tongue, people said, was as sharp as

a barber's razor, and three times as long. Mr Discobobulous used to sit in silence, listening to her and staring out hard from under his hat-brim while she scolded him, and then he would stamp out and go and meet his friends, who were all sorry for him, because of Mrs Discobobulous and her scalding, scolding ways.

The second momentous event of 1966 was the arrival of a second daughter, Bridget, when Margaret was just on 30. If being a solo mother was very unconventional in the 1960s, being a solo mother of two was rather more so. Because her daughters had the same father, Margaret was, as she has said, 'very monogamous in those terms'; she was certainly not an early feminist resolving to bear a child with no intention of partnership or marriage. 'As a child I assumed I would never get married, and sometimes I feel that as a child I spoke more truly about what I wanted to do with my life then when I was in my twenties. At university, too, I remember talking in a tutorial about having children without being married, so in a way I suppose I was imaginatively speculating on the possibilities of being an unmarried mother long before I became one.' After the relationship ended, she was 'very conscious of how powerful romantic love can be and how it can take hold of people's lives and make them behave in ways that are irrational and destructive'. Many years later, she said that though there were times when she would love to have been married, recognising that 'a good marriage with shared responsibilities is a wonderful way to bring up children', she doesn't regret not having married. 'I like where I am pretty well and I think for someone like me who has writing as a central passion in life, it's a solitary passion and it tends to exclude other people. You need solitude to be a writer, and although a lot of male writers are married to women who look after the kids and it's taken for granted they're entitled to their solitude, that's not the case with women, who are still on the whole expected to behave like traditional wives. So I suspect I'm better off single.'

She had also long known, well before the feminist 1970s, that the women she admired were those 'who imitated men and lived adventurous lives like men . . . I was always fascinated by women who dressed like men. I have no idea why . . . They had guns and swords which gave them power over life and death and meant they were not natural victims, which women tended to be.

'Perhaps for the same reason my role models in real life were men. I looked to my father and my grandfather as examples, not to my mother. My mother was an excellent and very devoted mother who encouraged me to believe there were no limitations, but deep down what she really wanted for all of her daughters was for them to have a happy marriage and a family since that was what she had had herself. I think that if she had been confronted with somebody who had chosen to have a career rather than a family she would been a little resentful. That may be why I chose male role models rather than female ones. I didn't see reason why I shouldn't be the sort of man that my father and my uncles were — in a way I am, because I have become a hard-working tradesman just like them, someone who earns a living by working hard and never turning down an opportunity to make money.'

With Bridget around a year old and Penny at school, Margaret decided that, after a break of more than five years, she must return to full-time library work. Accepting a job with the School Library Service in Christchurch, she began thirteen years of juggling her maternal role with writing and full-time working, and wrote only short stories and poems because that was all she could do.

She does not look back on this time with any great feeling of complacency. On the whole, she saw it 'as an adventure, and I still see it that way'. There were times when she was 'wonderfully happy,' and times of terrible anxiety and even of suicidal depression; most of the time she looked on depression as something she would get through, hanging onto the thought that, as for Allan Quartermain in *King Solomon's Mines*, real life was bound to have its discomforts too: 'that realisation enabled me to cope with the uncomfortable bits and not get overwhelmed by them'.

CHILDHOOD IN WHAKATANE — the young Margaret, circa 1939, with her father, Frank, outside the family home in Haig Street, Whakatane, and (below) the 'solid, fair' school-child, aged seven.

GRADUATION DAY — Margaret Mahy, BA, 1957.

HATS WERE FAVOURED EARLY — Margaret in her forties.

THE PUBLIC AND THE PRIVATE MARGARETS — during a session for formal publicity pictures, circa 1990 (above), and photographed in Sussex, UK, 1993, by Vanessa Hamilton.

MARGARET MAHY REINVENTED — the slimmer MM at 57, photographed in 1993 by *North & South* magazine.

THE DAILY THINKING TIME — walking Baxter along a solitary beach.

LEFT: Margaret
(middle) with
her mother (right)
and Aunt Dorothy
outside the family
home in Haig
Street, Whakatane.

MARGARET MAHY
PERSONAL COLLECTION

BELOW: Margaret
with her sisters and
brother. Left to
right: Patricia,
Margaret, Helen,
Cecily and Frank.

MARGARET MAHY
PERSONAL COLLECTION

Margaret Mahy, Doctor of Letters, University of Canterbury, 1993.

RIGHT: Margaret
at Callaway Gardens,
Georgia, USA,
October 1995,
with her American
publisher Margaret
McElderry.

LEFT: The famous wig and
scarf — the storyteller
beloved by thousands
of fascinated children.

RIGHT: Ready for
Antarctica, with
mukluks and
name-tag, 1998.

Now attitudes to mothers with jobs are considerably more liberal and compassionate, and childcare more readily available. Then, as a *Listener* journalist wrote in 1987, 'there were the times when she had to leave a 10-month-old baby suffering from pneumonia and go to work "because the idea then of asking for time off to look after a child was just so terrible". Mahy never enjoyed leaving the children: "I'd get off the bus at night and immediately start weeping as I walked toward home." Even when she had begun her career as a librarian — she loved the job — there was still the awful tiredness; of coping with the children and the housework on her own and finally, late at night, sitting down to write. At least one car accident was caused by falling asleep at the wheel.'

Or by small, wayward cars, whose unpredictable tantrums would summon Allan Quartermain to her aid.

'One evening, when my two daughters were small, it became necessary to find some nice stones for a school project, and we drove to a place called Birdlings Flat, which is noted for a strange and rather desolate beach consisting entirely of stones smoothed by the constant churning of short violent waves. As we drove home the sun went down and we were driving into that time of day when one seems to be exactly balanced between day and night without being in either. The sky was colourless, clear as water, and we were suspended between realities. With the going down of the sun it suddenly got colder, and one of the children turned the heater on. There was a spluttering sound and suddenly flames shot out from the dashboard. Combustion was taking place. Material elements were being rejoined into new combinations and as I and my children were material elements in satisfactory combinations already this was a terrifying possibility . . . I decided that the thing to do was to get out of the car and run like mad down the road, and this we proceeded to do. We ran hard, but the distance between us and the smouldering car seemed to diminish very slowly. At the same time I experienced one of those detached moments common to us all . . . feeling that I was really somewhere up around the rocky summits that mark the rim of an old volcano cone watching three people run away from a smoking car. The children were upset, one whingeing with apprehension, the other crying loudly, and in an effort to comfort them I cried aloud in a hoarse voice, running all the time, "Look on this as an adventure." I repeated it two or three times. I know just what I was trying to do. I was trying to change the frame of reference of this uncomfortable incident, to make a different, and no less appropriate sense, of what was going on. I was trying to find a way to make a place for what was happening in my personal framework.

'When I shouted "Look on this as an adventure!" another landscape flowed out of my mind overlying the real one. I could see them both at once . . . the crater walls seen through a desert filled with sand stone and karoo bushes. Crouching under those bushes were five brave men . . . it was while reading about their crossing of the desert in *King Solomon's Mines* when I was quite young, about 8 or 9, that it suddenly came to me that the adventure which I was enjoying so avidly was being achieved at the expense of severe discomfort myself. I am sure there are many other times when I have been in difficulties and have invoked the heroes of childhood reading by shouting "Look on this as an adventure!" But on this occasion I was conscious of calling on that particular story to give me strength and flexibility, and the power even to enjoy what was happening as if I were both a character in a book and the reader of the book at one and the same time. Invocation and the image I chose was from my favourite story of childhood. Through reading, I had access to the imaginative energy the author had stored in his story and linked it up with energy of my own. Allan Quartermain was the code name by which I located that energy and was able to use it . . . Rider Haggard's cautious and resourceful hero has become an emblem of part of my own imagination. It is myself that I am addressing. In *Ways of Telling*, an essay in his book, *Book Talk: occasional writing on literature and children*, Aidan Chambers mentions his personal conviction that we are not changed by our experiences, as common wisdom has it. "What changes us are the stories we tell about our experiences. Until we have formed our lives into story-structured words we cannot find and contemplate the meaning of our lived experiences. Till then they remain in the realm of beastly knowledge. Only by turning the raw material of life into story, but putting it into a pattern of words we call narrative — can beastly knowledge be creatively transformed and given meaning. It is the storying that changes us not the events." I believe this is true, true at least for me and many other people . . .'

As adults, Penny and Bridget have paid public tribute to their mother's dedication to their childhood and teenage years. Penny, whose very earliest memories include her mother house cleaning, tomato picking and (on occasion, because of their poverty) serving porridge three times a day, finds it hard to comprehend just what Margaret was able to achieve in the course of a single day. 'Things became more frantic after Bridget arrived and Margaret went back to work. Mum was in that superwoman era. I actually have a memory of that book sitting on her desk.' A punishing routine of taking children to school, work, early evening home life, bedtime stories — and then about midnight, often until 4 o'clock in the morning, her own writing. This was her life for years, but Penny says 'the important things were never compromised. She was always there for us and we could always talk to her . . .', even when she was almost, or completely, worn out. Because, Penny adds, Margaret 'finds it impossible to say no to people', she would often drive off at night to talk to schools and PTAs, even to the West Coast or south Canterbury. Bridget, too, has spoken of the stability of the gradually developing house and garden in Governors Bay and the closely bonded Mahy family of uncles, aunts and cousins (though none on her father's side). Despite the inevitability of day-time babysitters from the age of about eighteen months, Bridget remembers that her mother always made time for early-evening reading and weekend activities with her daughters. She is 'a workaholic, and probably has been for some years out of a strong desire to support'.

With two daughters, several animals and a mortgage to support, single-handed, Margaret in her mid-30s was creating and experiencing a very different sort of family life from her own. But though such an affectionate, close family life 'is of course a wonderful thing . . . sometimes I think it puts a distortion on the lives of children who grow up thinking that's what their lives will be like. And none of us, for a variety of reasons, including of course social expectations, have had the sort of lives that my parents did.'

With large extended families in both her parents' and her own generation, it is not surprising that Margaret's books contain such a diverse range of possible family combinations. Indeed, as her reputation grew, she began to be recognised internationally, along with writers like Robert Westall, Jan Mark and Anne Fine, for her understanding of and insights into the modern family. The basic nuclear family (sometimes), the extended family (often), the divided family (often), the solo parent family, either as widow or divorced or never married (frequently) — all can be found in both her novels and short fiction, always drawn with compassion and a recognition that both the very young and very old, even old Sophie in *Memory*, are capable of change and growth.

Margaret's handling of the mother-daughter relationship, as between Laura and her mother Kate in *The Changeover*, is noteworthy, given what she has written over the years about her relationships with her own mother and daughters. A real companionship between mother and daughter can, according to Joan Gibbons's reading of Mahy, 'be damaged but is not easily destroyed. It is not that mother and daughter treat each other as equals, because the parent/child difference, the sense of being responsible which Kate feels, is always present, but they do treat each other as women. Such a closeness is rare in children's literature, and indeed, [American academic Marianne] Hirsch suggests, rare in all literature . . . Mahy has, in many of her early stories and in all of her highly acclaimed novels, advanced family themes with sophistication and sincerity, especially as regards casual, friendly relationships between children and parents, whatever their marital status . . . [she] has also developed the relationship between mother and child, showing not only the process of the child growing towards adulthood, but also the continued development of the adult.'

Once accused that her families 'were a bit like psychic battle grounds', Margaret replied that 'Family life is where you get your greatest blessings, but it's also the area where a lot of people sustain their greatest damage. People who speak about the survival of the family often overlook the terrible damage people receive from families. Things can often depend on something as random as a person's place in the family. I was the oldest. My experience of my father sounds quite different to my sister, who's third in the family.'

Margaret's deeply felt but subtle feminism (as subversive and influential as any from those who have claimed to be 'feminist' writers in the past two decades) has also given her international standing as 'a leader amongst writers who have broken from tradition in their treatment of females and children'. But traditionalists should take heart from Margaret's overall treatment of her 'ambitious, courageous and determined' female heroes, whose 'focus for their activities is their family . . . Many books with strong, adventurous girls have been accused of backing off as these girls become young women, allowing domestic responsibilities and need to care for others to replace their sense of adventure and of fun. In children's literature, growing up as a girl has largely meant being diminished as a person so as to allow, altruistically, for the growth of others. This does not happen to Mahy's young women . . . they learn that the family is the true centre of what goes on in the world, the place where truly important things happen . . . Being associated with their families does not rob them of holding other important positions in the world. Fulfilling oneself is as important as helping others; it may even be a prerequisite. Neither need mothers be self-denying.'

There were fewer Mahy appearances in the *School Journal* after the dedicated 1966 issue, only one story a year between

1967 and 1969. Returning to full-time work, juggling children and babysitters and neighbours, gardening, food shopping with no car and living in a quite primitive little house with a view and hundreds of books but no running water and no time for housework or ironing uniforms took their toll, even on Margaret's legendary stamina. The final years of the tumultuous 1960s were among the hardest of her life. Later novels such as *Underrunners* and *The Catalogue of the Universe* would deal powerfully with the scrimping realities of solo motherhood.

Margaret had been writing stories seriously now for around fifteen years; apart from the *School Journal*, no publisher had responded with any positive enthusiasm to the collections she had begun to submit. 'They wrote me notes back saying, we don't think they're sufficiently New Zealand in their content to enable us to publish them.' She had no agent to push her work, because in the New Zealand of the 1960s, with local publishing in its infancy, there were no such people; and unworldly New Zealand children's authors did not go looking for overseas literary agents or consider the glittering possibilities of overseas markets.

Neither could she find any satisfaction in self-consciously attempting to give her work more New Zealand content, as she once had at high school. 'I was enthusiastic about the idea, and I certainly tried but I never enjoyed writing them; I would go out and look at the landscape and try to write about it, but the stories didn't seem to work.' Friends confirmed her fears. 'I'm still puzzled as to why that should be, except that I know writing isn't just sitting down and looking at something and describing it. It involves a whole lot of subtle and mysterious things like the ability to give landscape a mythical quality and for some reason I wasn't able to give the New Zealand landscape that quality . . . I was made the inhabitant of a country that didn't exist.'

Sometime in 1968, a letter from New York was to 'transmogrify, transform and utterly resolve' her own life, in a fairytale fashion gifted to few writers with long-held ambitions to get published. But around this time, there was also another mentor poised to play a similarly crucial, if less dramatic, supporting role in Margaret's career. In 1969 Jack Lasenby, her former fellow student at university in Auckland, joined the editorial staff at School Publications, taking over editorship of the *School Journal* from Wellington poet Louis Johnson. (Margaret's very first editor of her earliest stories was probably John Kelly, who had preceded Johnson.)

A noted children's writer now in his early seventies and the only one of her early editors still alive, Lasenby knew of Margaret's work from his seven preceding years as a primary classroom teacher. 'I knew her stories pretty well: *A Lion in the Meadow*, *Pillycock's Shop*, that extraordinary issue in 1966 . . . They were just so extraordinarily fresh and profligate of language. My God, nobody had written like that, certainly no one in New Zealand. Elsie Locke's lovely *Runaway Settlers* had come out — and that was a huge milestone — but here was someone flinging words around like Kipling. There's a sort of genius to her. That abundant generosity, the extraordinary stamina. She learnt early the secret of unlocking energy from tiredness itself — and that funny old Kiwi voice of hers, it's all part of the wonderful whole.'

Until he left in 1975 to teach at the Wellington Teachers' College, Lasenby was regularly selecting and editing 'as many as we could get out of her. Her stories were sometimes handwritten, and needed very little editing. She wrote some beautiful poems at that time, too. Her particular genius was that lovely ability with language and the released imagination. Occasionally, she'd miss a beat, descend into lushness . . . but the best of them were simply wonderful. In her writing I see little bits all through, of things that I know about her personal life, that she used as all writers do. Some children's writers go out with their little notebooks and consciously record young people, their speech and behaviour, but they don't come within a bull's roar of what Margaret does imaginatively.

'She once said to me, with a searching look, "You know, before you went to School Pubs they weren't very reliable." On arrival as editor, I'd got a big hard-backed exercise book to begin a register in which all arriving material, voluntary contributions and commissioned, had to be entered. Until then they just relied on memory. Margaret told me she actually had a story lost by School Pubs. I've never dared ask her about that again. I don't know if it turned up later, but the thought of having one of her stories just disappear like that — I said to her, you've got a copy of course, knowing she possibly hadn't — just gave me the cold shakes.'

Lasenby was dismayed to find that some Mahy stories had been accepted but never used. 'One thing I was delighted to do for her: I found, set in print in galleys, somewhere over there at the Government Printer, her series of stories about Tai Taylor, a Maori-Pakeha kid. I was just swept off my feet by them. Although too difficult for the junior *Journal*, they had been bought for Alistair Campbell's Part 3 and 4 some years before and unused for some reason. I could never get the reason out of Alistair, nor anybody else.'

Encouraged by his boss, Lasenby proposed that the Tai Taylor stories should be dusted off and used. All School Publications material was then vetted by a senior inspector. 'I was knocked back on Tai Taylor, because there were things in the story such as Tai Taylor portrayed as being "the sort of hero who could pick up a headmaster and press him in a book like a wild flower". I was rapturous about it. I remember saying to this rather dry inspector, "Can't you *see* the enjoyment this will give kids in all those happy classes where the teachers *do* get on with the kids, and they'll grin at each other knowingly?" And he said, "But it's the others I'm worried about." The world has shifted since then.'

Undaunted, Lasenby circumvented the senior inspector and went to see Brian Pinder, 'the driest Director of Education ever appointed in New Zealand, one of those with lights on up in his office with his senior inspectors until nine or ten o'clock every night, Monday to Friday. I told him, "I think this is a brilliant story and deserves publication."' Pinder, though displeased by the breach of protocol, agreed to read the manuscript after Lasenby pleaded that it should be published — for the sake of the kids.

'He rang me first thing the next morning and said of course it must be published, as is. I was delighted, for Margaret and for the story, but it also gave me a certain strength after that with any of her other work. She would have had a widespread reputation among New Zealand teachers and inspectors by the early 70s; her sudden publication abroad came as no surprise.'

Lasenby says that the School Publications editors had many long talks about Margaret Mahy, wondering about her, how far she would go. Towards the end of his editorship, he got her to write a story that would teach children how to use a library. Instead of an instructional pamphlet, who better than this 'writer, mother, librarian' to come up with something more interesting to children? To his delight, it was supported, and was published in 1977 as *Look Under V*. One day, he says, it should be reprinted.

Margaret was not without her critics within the School Publications offices, as Jack Lasenby recalls. 'Pat Earl, the chief editor when I first went there, was an admirer of writing that comes from direct experience. He finally said that you must realise that Margaret's experience is her imagination itself. There's a deep truth in that; she has a truth of the imagination that most people would never achieve. I remember one of the editors being suspicious of her witches, though not on any religious grounds. Interestingly, over the years the crank religionists haven't had a go at Margaret, to my knowledge, and yet a lot of writers have kept off that very topic for years. And what I've always thought of as the first women's movement story from Margaret was that lovely little thing with the long long title, *Concerning a Little Woman and how she won herself a house and a servant and lived happily every after* —about a little woman who's the servant to a slobbish green-backed beetle. She has to rub his back with handfuls of moss each day and he says, "Rub harder, little woman." He's a thorough-going joker-prick. But at the end of the story she's got herself a house and he's had to become her servant. Margaret is far too subtle a person to be given to feminist writing as such, but that had something of it in it to great effect.'

Lasenby remembers Margaret attending a course that School Publications ran for writers in Christchurch. After a full day's work, they had agreed to write a story that night; Margaret apparently intended to call in at the library and do a couple of hours' work before driving over the hill to Governors Bay. 'She turns up first thing the next morning with not one but two stories, and one of them was the most spooky thing about a kid whose brother pretends to be turning into a robot — Margaret had put her own imaginative slip on it, so the younger boy begins to actually be a robot and scares the shit out of his older brother.' This story, which Lasenby considered chilling and superb, was later published as *The Mad Puppet*, in a 1982 *School Journal*.

Later, according to Lasenby, 'when Margaret signed up with Helen Hoke Watts, it took some hard learning for the authorities [at the Department of Education] to accept that somebody such as Margaret Mahy couldn't be constrained by having had first publication in the *School Journal*. Her new offshore publishers generously agreed to send so many copies of the books to the Department. I remember these great parcels arriving, our *Journal* stories now as individual printed books. We'd go through discussing the illustrations and designs, delighted, of course. But while I'm very fond of those stories in the *Journal* because they are part of my earliest reading of her, the fullest enjoyment I got from Margaret's writing was from *The Haunting* onwards, the great novels. Suddenly she strode off into the older "young adult" stage — from every point of view those novels have got structure, characterisation, development, they're just perfect of their kind. That image in *The Catalogue of the Universe* of the mother scything the long grass by moonlight — it's unforgettable.'

But the novels were still ten or more years away. Even before Lasenby arrived at School Publications and embarked on his enthusiastic support for Margaret's work, an event had taken place on the other side of the world. Involving just one very short story of 26 lines published some years earlier in the *School Journal*, it would set in motion events which would completely transform her life.

Part Three

The Picture Book Writer —
1969 to 1980

A Lion in the Meadow first appeared in the *School Journal* (Part One, Number 3) in 1965. Essentially a profound statement about the power of the imagination to alter reality, it was the story that, more than any other, altered the reality of its impecunious but determined writer's long struggle towards publication and recognition.

The transformation begins in a public library on Long Island, New York, where Sarah Chockla Gross, an editor with a respected New York publisher, Franklin Watts, is browsing one day. Mrs Helen Hoke Watts, the owner's wife, looks after the children's list and has an internationally known eye for outstanding picture books, and the artists and writers whose talents make them memorable. Among her protégées are the hugely popular illustrators Brian Wildsmith, Charles Keeping and Jan Pienkowski. In the Long Island library Mrs Gross sees a touring printing exhibition that includes some *School Journals* from New Zealand's Department of Education. Perhaps someone has chosen to display the small book in a glass case, open at a particular page; perhaps she is leisurely thumbing through one issue.

The little boy said, 'Mother, there is a lion in the meadow.'

The mother said, 'Nonsense, little boy.'

The little boy said, 'Mother, there is a big yellow lion in the meadow.'

The mother said, 'Nonsense, little boy.'

The little boy said, 'Mother, there is a big, roaring, yellow, whiskery lion in the meadow!'

The mother said, 'Little boy, you are making up stories again. There is nothing in the meadow but grass and trees. Go into the meadow and see for yourself.'

The little boy said, 'Mother, I'm scared to go into the meadow, because of the lion which is there.'

The mother said, 'Little boy, you are making up stories — so I will make up a story, too . . .'

It is a moment all editors yearn for, hope to have at least once in their careers. Sarah Gross, elated, seeing the picture book potential of the story, immediately rings Mrs Helen Hoke Watts — long-distance, because she happens to be in London at the time. She has barely finished reading the story before Mrs Watts asks: 'Who wrote that? Where did you find it? It's absolutely perfect for a picture book, I wouldn't want to change a word!' Most authors wait a few anxious months, some even years, for decisions like that — and may find their carefully polished text ruthlessly cut or altered by an editor — yet Mrs Watts, clearly a woman of action, writes a prompt letter to Margaret Mahy, care of School Publications, Department of Education, Wellington, to say that her story will make an ideal picture book, and has she got any more like that. She sends a cheque for US$1,000 in advance royalties ('Too much money always works — people can't resist money — pay plenty!' she is quoted by Betty Gilderdale as saying, and in 1968 that is serious money) and briskly begins the process of finding English co-publishers like Heinemann, Dent and Dobson and first-rate illustrators like Helen Oxenbury, Charles Mozley and Jenny Williams for no fewer than five Mahy books to be published simultaneously in New York and London, and before the end of 1969.

In publishing terms, this was unusually speedy, heady stuff — and canny, since, only a few months later, Margaret received another, independent inquiry from the United States, which later caused a typical smile: 'No one likes to think that their success has been totally due to something as random as good luck.' With the advance, she was able to get water piped into her small house and buy a car, which was an overdue necessity.

She has described reading Helen Hoke Watts's letter as feeling 'like Cinderella entering the ballroom and being seen at last in her true beauty', and that 'within seconds a heavenly choir had begun to serenade me'.

'I opened it — read it — and felt I was dissolving. The idea of actually having a book published was overwhelming, though it was one that had been with me for many years. Of course in the first few seconds, I knew I was going to write back and say, "Yes I would love to have the story published as a picture book. Please take it."'

In fact, she wrote back a letter 'servile in its enthusiasm, knowing myself to be lucky, but unaware just how lucky I was. I had no idea that at this time picture books in the USA were profitable, for apparently many schools libraries in those halcyon days received a federal grant which they were to spend only on books. I had an opportunity which I had done nothing to deserve, and had not sought.'

There was a certain sense of both utter disbelief and a destiny fulfilled, '. . . a transmutation that I had imagined so often that, when it came about, it seemed like the inevitable fulfilment of a prophesy, and yet a fulfilment so frail, so contingent, I could hardly believe it had ever been achieved.' From the age of about nine, when she was second in that essay competition, 'I always had that feeling in the back of my mind and when I had my first book published, part of me remembered that childhood fantasy and said, of course, I always knew this was going to happen! When I was a child and people said, what are you going to do when you grow up, I started out by saying, be a writer, but people kept saying you can't earn your living as a writer, so after a while I said instead, I want to be a writer but I suppose I'll be a librarian or a teacher to earn my living. When I went to university, I said to myself, I'll get a degree even though what I really want to do is write stories. So I didn't give up on the idea, I just postponed it.'

But this approach from New York was not, astonishingly, just about one story.'When she first got in touch, Mrs Watts said rather foolishly, have you got anything else you'd like to show us, and I sent her practically everything I had. She wrote back and said, "Are you aware that you've sent us over a *hundred* stories and poems?" I suppose the interesting thing is that I had just kept on writing, even though I didn't think there was ever any strong prospect of getting anything published, other than the *School Journal.'*

In the light of this New York enthusiasm, it may reasonably be asked why no New Zealand publisher other than School Publications had recognised her potential? Margaret had made some efforts on her own behalf, making up a collection from the *School Journals* and submitting them to various local publishers, such as Blackwood and Janet Paul, A.H. & A.W. Reed and Whitcombe & Tombs, because she felt she would be 'less lost and anonymous in New Zealand than I would be in either the USA or Britain . . . They were always returned, sometimes with the usual terse rejection slips, but sometimes with rather fuller comments, so that I formed a picture of a publishing industry catering for a small population and restricted to very small print runs. My stories were not "local", were set, indeed, in an area where, if published, they would be competing with a similar genre of book coming into the country from overseas, and available much more cheaply than indigenous productions. On the whole I don't think New Zealand publishers were very cosmopolitan, which isn't to say they weren't involved in some very creative publishing at times.' They 'made it plain that their only commercial option was to publish books with a New Zealand voice' but 'I was a determined and assiduous writer of poetic tales and tall stories. I wrote on and on and on.'

To publishers who wanted a self-consciously New Zealand voice, telling stories of farm life, bush adventures, tui, pohutukawa, Maori pals and Maori artefacts, Margaret's settings, metaphorical language, archetypal characters and images were too firmly rooted in European traditions, and possibly, in the women's storytelling tradition for editors in a male-dominated profession to take their own imaginative leap outside a perceived need for only 'New Zealand' stories. Unlike Jack Lasenby at School Publications, there were evidently no editors reading unsolicited manuscripts for the trade publishers similarly able to recognise that here was a writer with a unique, universal voice and so demonstrably of world class that she could be profitably published towards an international future. International co-editions, where publishers share costs, were virtually unheard of. Picture book publishing, in full colour, was, and still is, costly, and the New Zealand market notably small. Through the 1960s fewer than 20 children's books by New Zealand authors were published annually, and many of these were produced by London and New York publishers. In 1969 there were 23, including Margaret's five: fifteen were published overseas. They included books by Anne de Roo and Ruth Dallas, Janet Frame's only children's book *Mona Minim and the Smell of the Sun*, and *The Duck in the Gun*, the first major picture book by another future international star of similar age, Joy Cowley.

As Margaret has written, overseas publication still commanded disproportionate respect. Even now, 'it is hard for a book with a Kiwi idiom to find a place in Britain, which produces 7000 children's books a year, many of which are probably not as good as the best that New Zealand can offer, but have the advantage of local voices and local reference . . . While New Zealand *needs* stories with local content and local idiom to help its children become New Zealanders, local content may disadvantage the story when international sales are explored. New Zealanders are great bridge crossers. They have had to be. The food has often been on the other side of the bridge. Publishers, however, are cautious bridge builders, for, given the choice, many people do not want to cross over. Publishers need the international sales, and so do authors and illustrators, if they are to buy the time it takes to produce the next book.'

With the Franklin Watts contracts signed, the production process under way, and a long-term relationship with the young author in mind, Mrs Watts plans a trip to New Zealand. She is an indefatigable trans-Atlantic traveller, with apartments in New York, London and Rome, but New Zealand is another matter altogether before the jumbo jet era has arrived. It is also highly unusual: even today, publishers do not generally go chasing halfway round the world after authors. But Margaret's stories have star quality written all over them, so Mrs Watts packs her bags.

In fact, this tall, 'notably well-dressed', larger-than-life New York grandmother packs no fewer than thirteen of them, and her arrival at Christchurch's small airport does not pass unnoticed by the press. Two taxis have to be hired to cope with $1,000 worth of excess luggage and follow Margaret's battered second-hand Mini over the Port Hills. At the modest Governors Bay Ocean View Hotel a second bedroom has hurriedly to be taken for the luggage. (Just what was in those bags? Margaret believes clothes, though it was January, summertime. There were also books and many gifts; 'she was carrying quite a lot of whisky and gin. She drank a lot, which naturally I enjoyed sharing with her.')

'On the one hand I found her intimidating because she was very tall, rich and had the power to publish my books. On the other there was something oddly naïve about her romantic view of herself and her world. She saw herself as being powerful through riches and glamour and talked freely about her lovers and men who had admired her, including D.H. Lawrence and Dylan Thomas.'

Moments of high comedy occur all through the visit. Her first words to Margaret, waiting nervously at the airport, had been 'My God, this really is the end of the world — they don't recognise American Express.' Ice for drinks proved difficult even at the hotel. In Margaret's two-roomed house in Merlincote Crescent, just below the hotel, she likes the idea of a Scotch on the rocks, but Margaret has no running water, let alone ice: 'I was carrying water in plastic containers from the library over the hill to my home.' The house has no electricity and the outside toilet is a little hut housing a can with a lid; a hole is dug and the contents buried about once a week. A septic tank is not allowed because of the house below. What a sophisticated New Yorker who keeps a permanent suite at the Savoy makes of all this can only be guessed at. Inside, there are books everywhere, but as yet no bookshelves; when she returns to the United States Mrs Watts will begin to construct a compelling legend that Margaret Mahy is building her own home herself, conjuring up images of the writer in a builder's apron hammering in nails. Margaret says this was never quite true: she was having the house built in stages and was simply waiting until she could afford a builder, though she did help to dig the foundations. But there is ample treasure for Helen Hoke Watts to justify her rather surprising week in New Zealand: within the house she finds more Mahy handwritten stories, dozens of them, in suitcases, in files, even (reported the *Woman's Weekly*) one stuck to congealed plaster in a bucket. A few months later Margaret tells the local newspaper that Mrs Watts 'went over a lot of material I had written, did a bit of editing and wanted certain changes, and took more material away with her'.

'She stayed at the local hotel for a few days, and then shifted to a hotel out by the airport,' recalls Margaret. 'The children were sometimes there, and though she was nice to the girls, and bought them presents, she wasn't really interested in them. She took us all out to dinner, which we all regarded as hugely sophisticated, and she took a great deal of pleasure in seeing our pleasure, since she was operating in such a beneficent way. Her purpose was to sign me up, yes, but she was a romantic in many ways, an incessant traveller who loved travelling and being rich and able to do it all first class. She knew a lot of publishers and editors and exercised a certain amount of power.' Helen Hoke Watts died in 1991.

Margaret has always remembered her extraordinary publishing debut with gratitude. 'Helen was to launch my books in the USA with a generosity that I did not appreciate at the time, simply I did not understand it . . . [and] didn't altogether realise how unusual it was . . . I remember her enthusiasm vividly . . . and her strong approval that nobody could tell my books were New Zealand books. I was not upset or insulted. I was too glad to be getting published. However, it did give me a tremble of self-doubt, because, after all, I was a New Zealander and the books were constructed out of what New Zealand had offered me . . . the idea that though we were good at producing butter and wool, our own artistic ideas had no authority — that it was overseas that Imagination with a capital "I" flourished most richly, and that what we did in Auckland or Christchurch was bound to be inferior in both skill and essence.'

Margaret now looks at those first five books with some incredulity. The number of words on the page and the size of the print would not, she says, be acceptable today.

'I would describe *The Procession* as a poetic progress, *A Lion in the Meadow* and *The Dragon of an Ordinary Family* as touched with elements of amused fantasy. *Pillycock's Shop* as a sort of horror story. *Mrs Discombobulous* seems to me now the story in which I most closely move towards humour, though it would be unpublishable today, not only because of its length but because of its subject. The nagging woman, a basic character of past folktales and jokes, is no longer a politically acceptable subject in spite of her presence in folk tale though . . . in defence of *Mrs Discombobulous* I would like to make the following points. She is a woman who loves language . . . and who uses it, dramatically, to rescue the gypsy princess from the Baron. *Mrs Discombobulous* isn't witty or epigrammatic but there is a joyous element of release in her flowing abuse . . . these days I would not write this story in the way I wrote it thirty-five years ago . . . after all if I did I am sure that Learning Media might hesitate to publish it whereas School Publications, back then, did not . . . but I quote it because it seems to mark for me a move towards assertive and even flamboyant language and to embody the suggestion that words, juggled and exaggerated, have the power to make us laugh, that laughter not only reinforces our necessary bond with language, but signals release.'

Even the most prolific authors can become permanently (and sometimes unfairly) associated in the public consciousness with one book, often the first, but sometimes the 'take-off' book or novel adapted for the screen. For Janet Frame, it is probably *Owls Do Cry* that comes to mind; for Maurice Gee, *Plumb*; for Elizabeth Knox, *The Vintner's Luck*; for Maurice Shadbolt, *Strangers and Journeys*; for Fiona Kidman, *A Breed of Women*; for Sherryl Jordan, *Rocco*; for William Taylor, *Agnes the Sheep*; for Paula Boock, *Out Walked Mel*. With Margaret Mahy, the sheer body of notable titles has made it much more difficult. In Britain, where she is equally or better known as a novelist, Margaret is probably most associated with her two Carnegie winners still in print, *The Haunting* or *The Changeover*. In New Zealand, of all the picture books, notwithstanding the claims of *The Wind Between the Stars*, *The Great White Man-Eating Shark* or *The Man Whose Mother was a Pirate*, *A Lion in the Meadow* is still probably the first that springs most readily to mind.

Considered within the body of Mahy picture books and stories published during the 1970s, it is also a somewhat unusual story. As Betty Gilderdale points out, 'for the most part [Mahy's] characters are adult, like their predecessors in myth and fairy tale. Where she does take a child for a central character it is usually alone or in a close, secure relationship with an adult, not with another child. The child alone is more likely to be sensitive to the world of the imagination, to see things at the edge of vision, and perhaps for this reason needs domestic security, such as that enjoyed by the boy who could run to his mother to tell her he had seen a lion in the meadow.'

The publishing history of the book is also unusual: it has been twice illustrated by the same illustrator, and the second time given a different ending.

'*A Lion in the Meadow* is a very simple story. It looks as if it would take five minutes to write. However, it took longer than that, because in the beginning it was really two stories.

'I began by working on a story about two people writing letters to each other on behalf of two other people After working on this tale for about a week I finished it early one evening, and found I had pushed myself it into a particularly excited mood. I wanted to go on writing, as after a few restless minutes I immediately began another story — an extremely short story. It needed very little correcting. I got it right almost at once.

'When I read the two stories a week later I found it was the second one, *A Lion in the Meadow*, which I liked best. Nevertheless I'm sure I could not have written it if I hadn't written the other story first. Somehow writing these stories had been a bit like pole vaulting. When people are pole vaulting they need to take a long run before hoisting themselves up in the air. The long run is part of the vault, part of the act. I think writing the first story was like taking the long run, and *A Lion in the Meadow* was like the leap into the air.

'I don't want to make what is after all a slight playful story bear the burden of too much interpretation but I think I can say that, from my point of view, *A Lion in the Meadow* was disguised biography and in a way more complex that I could even have imagined at the time I was so impulsively writing it. Writing is a vain profession and writers, particularly writers who are asked to talk about their books, often think intently about what they have written . . . however, it also seems to me significant that *A Lion in the Meadow* concerns a struggle between reality and the power of the imagination. The child in the story successfully does what I had never been able to do, pulls an image from imagination into pragmatic everyday life where it achieves an established reality. The boy in the story fulfils the misplaced attempts and longings of my own childhood, succeeding where I failed. The lion materialises and hides in the broom cupboard. It is real . . . well, real enough. His mother has to recognise it and change her own behaviour to accommodate it.'

For Margaret, *A Lion in the Meadow* and her most complex novel, *The Tricksters* (1986), are 'basically about the same thing — which is, someone whose imaginative extremity actually produces an alteration in reality'. As to the mystery of where that archetypal *lion* came from, a children's literature gathering in Auckland in 1975 provided probably the first published account of the source of her famous 'great big black-maned Abyssinian lion'. Twenty-one years and many retellings later Margaret told a dinner audience at Harvard University:

'Sometime after I had become used to the idea that I was actually the author of a book, I was suddenly seized with a great curiosity to know what it would be like to read this story for the first time. It is a curiosity impossible for the writer to satisfy. The story he or she has written has probably been revised and written out again and again, and can never return to the state of being totally unknown. Nevertheless I decided to trick myself, as far as was possible, into reading my own story as if I were a casual reader, picking the book off a library shelf, making an accidental contact, and accepting or rejecting it accordingly. After all, this is the moment to which the story has been directed . . . the moment when it springs out of a book and becomes the reader's story.

'I knew just where *A Lion in the Meadow* was on my bookshelf. I walked past the bookshelf, not looking at the books on it, and then, pretending I was really interested in something else, trailed my fingers over the backs of the books until I found the one I knew so well. I pulled it off the shelf, and carried it in to my bedroom, whistling and glancing to left and right, still pretending to think of other things, and deliberately refusing to glance down at the cover in case I was jolted into a state of familiarity too soon. The moment of truth had come. Opening the book at random, I looked down, quickly and ruthlessly, and read the first words I saw. "The little boy said to his mother, 'Mother, there is a big, roaring, yellow, whiskery lion in the meadow'."

'Then, overwhelmingly, I remembered something I had not thought about for many years . . . certainly not at the time when I was writing the story. I remembered myself as a small child, three years old, sitting on my father's knee and listening to a series of stories he invented evening after evening, all unrecallable now, except for the opening line, which was always the same. "Once upon a time, there was a great big black-maned Abyssinian lion." I stood transfixed, staring down at the page.

'I remember that beginning, only the beginning, repeated night after night, and it suddenly seemed to me that the lion in my story was the same lion my father had given me all those years ago, and my own story, the one I had written, had been packed into a millionth of an inch . . . inside its own opening line. I had not been inventing at all. I had been pushed by the energy of the moment into a secret remembering and reconstruction. A big, roaring, yellow, whiskery lion and the great big, black-maned Abyssinian lion certainly move to the same beat. So, by now, it seems that the first story I remember hearing was in some way the story of the first book I had ever published. In contemplating an ending, the achievement of an ambition I had entertained since I was seven, I had been returned to a beginning.'

The original 1969 *A Lion in the Meadow*, in landscape format, featured strongly symbolic, strongly coloured illustrations by the London-trained and well-established British illustrator Jenny Williams. In 1986 a second version appeared, in a square format, with the new illustrations requested after the loss of the original film in an Austrian printing house. The colour palette used by the artist is softer, the landscape and farmhouse clearly English, or at least northern European, the interiors with their pine furniture and children's felt tips and toys clearly comfortable middle class. And now there is a younger child, a baby sister in pink baby-gro, who quite clearly is seeing (as the mother still does not) the lion too; a very different, cosier ending replaces one Margaret described as 'a bit of a stark ending, a bit implacable and enigmatic for children, and it also isn't quite what I meant. What I meant was that the mother never ever tried to use stories dishonestly again. In trying to simplify it I said something I didn't quite mean, because of course I don't mean that the mother never ever made up a story again.'

'A story is seldom published to universal applause,' Margaret told the Harvard audience. 'Over the years *A Lion in the Meadow* has been criticised for various imperfections . . . for using the word meadow (which is not part of average New Zealand terminology: a New Zealander would almost certainly say paddock), as being sexist because the mother is the one who is at home peeling the potatoes. But the criticisms I have had most occasion to think about concern the ending, which I have thought about every bit as much as I have ever thought about its beginning, though for different more external reasons.

'As it was originally written, it ends in a ruthless way. The mother, who did not take stories seriously, had patronisingly invented a story about a dragon in a matchbox — a story in which she certainly did not believe — to trick her child into less distracting behaviour. Stories suddenly roared into life around her. The lion, in which she had not believed, suddenly becomes actual, rushes into the kitchen crying, "Hide me! A dragon is after me!" and hides in the broom cupboard. The mother, horrified at the turn events have taken, protests, "But there wasn't a real dragon. It was just a story I made up." "It turned out to be true after all," her child explains to her. "You should have looked in the matchbox first." The child and the lion then go off together, and the tale ends by saying, "The mother never made up a story again." Or, once upon a time, the story ended like that. Once upon a time the mother learned that stories have power beyond parental condescension.

'"Do you think the mother really saw the lion?" my first editor asked me curiously. I replied that I did. "But that doesn't make sense," she said. "A lion doesn't suddenly materialise out of nothing. The artist will draw the pictures so that the reader can make up his or her own mind." I was perfectly happy about that. At that stage in my writing life if she had suggested that the lion be replaced by a pink elephant I might have agreed in the most servile fashion. I was so keen to be published I didn't have as much integrity back then as I can afford now. But I genuinely *liked* the ambiguity of the idea, and since I don't want to be a submissive reader, I can't afford to be a dictatorial writer, either. And yet I was puzzled. After all, the editor was right, and, even in these days of email and the Internet and three-dimensional imaging, lions don't materialise out of nothing. Anyone who praises rationality as often as I do has to acknowledge that. All the same, at some level I felt certain that the mother had seen the lion, and been overwhelmed by it . . . *seeing the lion?!* The mother never made up a story again, because she had *seen the lion*, and she kept on seeing it.

'As the story began its public life, I was sometimes reproached, usually quite gently, for telling a story with such a negative conclusion, and the people who expressed dismay were people whose opinions I respected . . . fellow librarians and editors, people on whose judgement the continuance of the story depended. "I love the story," a librarian acquaintance once said to me, "but I can't bear to read the ending." I began to feel rather guilty because of these judgements. Some 16 years after the story had been published, the publisher proposed a new edition with new illustrations by the original artist, and I was asked to come up with a kinder, more positive ending. I agreed to this with a certain relief, feeling I was being given a chance to correct something that I had not got right the first time. In due course the new edition appeared, and immediately I, along with those who expressed pleasure at the older ending, began to hear from people who were indignant at the change, who felt, in some way, betrayed because they had trusted the story the way it had been told the *first* time. I think they were right to feel like this, for I also found that, though I had so willingly altered the ending, I did not believe my own alteration. Now I consider *A Lion in the Meadow* very cautiously, feeling the ruthlessness of the first ending still lurking under the second kinder one, and believing it to be the true ending. Don't patronise the story, the outer sign of the pattern you are destined to fulfil . . . don't use it in the wrong way or it will have its revenge. It might pull itself out of your life and you will never make up a story again. Or it might rush into your kitchen and take over the broom cupboard. Every time you go to that cupboard, planning to sweep the floor, it will look out and roar at you. You will never make up a story again, because now you know you are living eye to eye with story every moment of your everyday life.'

As early as 1975 the lion had become much more than a favourite character for Margaret:

'In moments of exhilaration I still catch glimpses of it, bounding along golden and beneficent, usually silent. I recognise it in other people's lions — in C.S. Lewis's Aslan (though my lion has nothing of the moralist about it) or recently and more important in Russell Hoban's book *The Lion of Boaz-Jachin and Jachin-Boaz*. The lion has two uses — one is that it builds around itself a sort of area of acceptance and association which enriches reading among other day to day experiences. The other use is one of celebration — when the lion, as it were, takes over and roars or dances in those moments of happiness or vision which we all experience, sometimes most deeply in solitude.

'Everyone knows this feeling and all have their way of visualising what is going on in their heads. For me, as I have said, the lion has taken over and I am seeing the world through lion eyes, not the eyes of Elsa the lioness, or any of her African relations, but the eyes of the big black-maned Abyssinian Lion, a sort of personal archetype. The lion stories are usually slight, cheerful, fun stories where difficulties are resolved in unexpected ways. It puzzles me at times that something that I feel with great power in my imagination should produce amiable uninvolved poems and stories, but I think perhaps I haven't finished with the lion and some day he may really roar.'

The picture book of the first Mahy quintet that did least well in the English and American markets was, perhaps predictably, the 1966 *School Journal* horror story of *Pillycock's Shop*. Asked a few years later whether she was ever concerned about the question of taste, or suitability of subject matter for young children, Margaret replied: 'I wrote a story, *Pillycock's Shop*, which . . . has been criticised because it is a horror story. In fact it's a sort of Faust situation: in order to get something that he thought he wanted, a child gave up something — in this case it was a baby he was looking after — that was really more important, and then had to reclaim it before the sun went down. He went back and found the whole environment changed, like a nightmare. But because he was a child of resource, and also of some courage, he finally did find the baby. It's a play on words: the baby in the story is called Penny, and he sees a new penny on the table that wasn't there before. When the shop keeper, Pillycock, tries to divert him from it, he sticks to his request for it, and finally makes the statement which now, looking back, I can see as a statement of good, saying "If you don't give me back the penny now I've asked for it, the sun won't ever go down". In the context of this particular story he's making the statement that right must triumph or the laws of nature will be suspended — which is partly a religious statement, I suppose.

'I read a review of the book recently which said it revealed "real malignancy" and indeed it does, and indeed it was meant to. People seem puzzled by this book, and I think they're justified in that the picture book presentation seems to tie it in with a younger age group than that for which it was written. And the pictures (by Carol Barker) are rather horrific, although suitable to the story. There is, for example, a metamorphosis where in one picture everything is beautiful, a doll, an owl, and a variety of objects, which in the next are shown fallen into decay, with the doll's face broken, the owl reduced to a skeleton, and everything broken or destroyed. I'm not surprised, in a way, that the book has not been successful, but I'm always pleased when I meet people — and I do meet some — who really like it.'

Picture book authors, she also discovered, are not always delighted with an illustrator's realisation of their characters. The image of the clown in *The Princess and the Clown* was a disappointment, 'because they changed the quality of the clown to such an extent. In the original story he was very much a circus clown, a buffoon, the butt of humour. In the illustrations, and by cutting one or two phrases, they transformed him from the knockabout clown to a harlequin type, who is much more of a romantic figure. They had removed the ridiculous contract of a clown marrying a princess, they had somehow or another made the clown a figure of beauty — which he *was* — but they had entirely cut out the fact that he achieved this beauty by making other people laugh by making a fool of himself. It is an ambiguous figure, the figure of the clown.'

The impact of these five books, of finding herself almost

overnight a world author with American and British publishers (and soon, others, with editions in translation) cannot be underestimated, but the exhausting daily routine of family life, working and writing continued. There might now be a steady stream of books being beautifully published, energetically promoted and brilliantly reviewed overseas, but Margaret was by necessity a solo working mother first, and a writer and reader second, with a house to get built and a garden to develop.

Today a 33-year-old and impecunious solo mother hitting the literary big-time in New York and London — J.K. Rowling, of similar age and circumstances in the mid-1990s, comes to mind — might well be getting extensive media attention. There seems to have been little coverage of Margaret's achievement and the *New Zealand Woman's Weekly* piece was typical of women's magazines at the time: 'Mrs' Mahy was described as a 'tallish, strongly boned blonde in her early thirties, well-dressed in a tweedy "mod" style. One imagines she would be at home on a tennis court, on the back of a horse . . . but with a BA and Library Diploma, she has a responsible, full-time job with the Country Library Service in Christchurch.' The young mother, in a double-breasted trouser suit, was photographed with the 'two adorable little girls she is bringing up single-handed'.

In 1970, *A Lion in the Meadow* won Margaret her first literary award, the Esther Glen Medal given by the New Zealand Library Association for a novel or picture book deemed to be a 'distinguished contribution to children's literature'. It had been awarded only five times since its inception in 1945, mostly to books with Maori elements and most recently in 1964 to Lesley Powell for *Turi: the story of a little boy*. An unprecedented second Esther Glen Medal followed in 1973, with *The First Margaret Mahy Story Book*, published in London by J.M. Dent & Sons, who would be her principal publisher for more than two decades. By this time Margaret had formed a strong friendship with her editor at Dent's, Gwen Marsh. A few years later there would be an even more important friendship and professional relationship with Vanessa Hamilton, the forceful, astute Dent editor and, later, literary agent, who from *The Great Piratical Rumbustification* (1978) on, was to edit most of Margaret's picture books and, in due course, her major novels.

By 1973, Dent's was producing promotional fliers inviting English readers to 'step into the magical world of Margaret Mahy', detailing no fewer than thirteen books, and in New Zealand she was now being invariably described in journals like *Education* as 'New Zealand's best-known writer of children's books'.

It was inevitable that before long her overseas publishers would want to meet their rising young star in person, so in May 1973 Margaret flew to London at the invitation of Helen Hoke Watts, returning by way of Las Vegas to attend the American Library Association annual conference. Unusually for middle-class Kiwi women who, since the 1950s, had spent their early twenties travelling, it was her first adventure outside New Zealand, and a wonderfully rewarding experience. Her childhood reading had given her feelings 'of great familiarity and affection with a place I had never been in before — quite eerie, but far from unique'.

Typically she had agreed (as other more precious or more canny, established writers might not) to an exhausting programme: straight into a week of schools and libraries in Bristol and Birmingham, followed by a major speech to the Library Association in London and a visit to the huge Penguin Books complex at Harmondsworth.

Although Margaret had not yet done a great deal of public speaking, Constance Reed of the Bracknell Children's Book Group reported in a children's literature magazine that 'No summary of Mrs Mahy's talk can do credit to her gift of interweaving short tales and poems, and of gripping the attention of her audience'. As still primarily a working librarian, her own report on the trip to her Country Library Service managers in Christchurch comments soberly on professional matters such as book stock, remedial literacy advisers in schools and pointed comparisons between 'the very circumscribed nature' of New Zealand's school library service for pre-schoolers, and the English situation where young children were regarded as being 'of the first importance'. The occasional whimsical note breaks through: she describes the malfunctions of Camden Library's computer system cutting off the initial letters of author's surnames, resulting in 'Shakespeare and Chaucer, now both beginning with the letter "H" becoming unexpected neighbours'.

The visit had begun in fairy tale style with a Rolls-Royce at the airport, to take her to Mrs Watts's Belgravia apartment, and dining with her hostess at the Savoy Hotel Grill and the Hilton. She had some time for sightseeing and stood before Seurat's 'The Bathers' in the British Museum weeping for joy. Bedecked in borrowed coat, gloves and jewellery, she sat in a box with Mrs Watts at Covent Garden Opera House for a sold-out Rudolf Nureyev gala performance. And two valuable and enjoyable days were spent at the home of Margery Fisher, then Britain's leading critic and author on children's books, before she flew on to the Las Vegas conference. This was 'an incredible experience,' where she noted the 'earnest and rather conservative' approach of American librarians as opposed to the publishers' vast displays and their 'very hard and competitive commercial sell'. She also attended the banquet for the prestigious Newbery and Randolph Caldecott children's literature awards, with her hosts, the Parents Press. Though the meal was 'hardly lavish', the whole occasion, 'ritualised by repetitions over a number of years, was something a librarian would always recall with interest and even nostalgia'.

By 1975, as she moved into her eighth year of full-time work with the School Library Service, behind the occasional glamour of being an internationally published author in demand by schools and adult audiences, Margaret's professional life was becoming very complicated. There was a constant stream of mail from the United States and Britain (for every book, the publisher's contract to be signed and returned, the proofs at various stages to be checked and endless publicists' promotional requests to be met). For every appearance outside Christchurch, there were travel arrangements to attend to, titles to supply for as-yet-unwritten speeches, short biographies to write for organisers. By 1976 her books were being published in German, Japanese and Russian, which meant more contracts, and *The Wind Between the Stars* had been the only picture book in the English language to win an award at the recent international children's book fair, held annually in Bologna. She told a journalist 'I'm sure that Brian Froud's illustrations played a big part, but like to think that the story helped.' And then there were her readers' letters, from children, their parents, librarians, teachers, other writers. Like most children's authors, Margaret regards these personal notes, but above all those from children, as her most important and rewarding mail: every one is essentially a love letter that must be answered.

As she wrote in a short autobiographical piece for the prestigious American children's literature magazine *Cricket*, 'Every working day I get up and begin to arrange some sort of breakfast for a hungry family of two girls (Penny, 16, and Bridget, 10), two cats (Polly and Punch), one dog (Max), one horse (Blackberry), at least two guinea pigs, and one fish. I have to be careful with breakfast; for instance, it would not do if I gave Bridget the guinea pig grass and the fish an egg.

'When everyone is fed and some of us are dressed, Penny, Bridget, and I set off to school and to work. We travel up a zig-zag road that is very steep in parts with banks on one side and a cliff on the other. In winter when there is frost and sometimes snow on the road, we feel very adventurous as we wind carefully up to the top of the hill. We usually get to the city safely, though every now and then we are late for school and for work.'

This relentless routine was taking its toll, as she revealed to a *Listener* journalist:

'I used to think it didn't matter if I got tired, and in a way, it didn't. But over recent years the most terrible thing has happened — I not only get tired, I go to sleep . . . If I get to bed by midnight I am all right. If I'm up till one I'm quite likely to go to sleep at work, very compulsively and embarrassingly. I wouldn't mind being tired, that's something I can cope with, but going to sleep is a most terrible thing.'

Asked about future prospects, Margaret doubted that she could make a living from full-time writing. 'She likes to think that if she was on her own she would be adventurous enough to try, but with two daughters . . . such a venture would be "rather risky". So each weekend the dirty white Mini goes over the Hill to the Country Library Service where, as a "patchy librarian" Margaret Mahy has worked for the last eight years.' To add to her workload, 'she does correspondence courses in third-form maths and fifth-form biology — at present, in a rather disjointed fashion; the maths because she doesn't find it easy (she remembers that she never passed a maths exam in her life) and the biology because when the course says it is time to dissect a worm or a possum, worms don't seem very interesting and "possums prove difficult to catch".'

Significantly, in this *Listener* piece, Margaret signalled her desire to extend her range, perhaps even to novels. 'I suppose every writer has the dream that one day he will produce the story that will go beyond entertainment, that will involve people and maybe change them, even if only to an infinitesimal degree. That is what I ultimately hope to achieve. The trouble is, when you get involved in something like this, it is an emotional involvement and you have to be careful not to make what you are doing carry the full burden of your own hang ups . . .

'The stories about real life I wrote before were not satisfactory to me. They were rather wooden. I didn't feel the same involvement with them as I did with fantasy stories. Now, perhaps, I have come to the point of saying something I have realised for a long time — that real life is fantastic, too. Perhaps some of the stories I write from now on will be concerned with the sort of experience that could really happen. I would like to have a go at writing something other than short stories. It's not that I wish to give up writing the sort of story I have been writing — I enjoy that very much indeed — but I suppose there comes a time when you feel you have to move on. I suppose, too, with all the talk of confrontation and self-identification, that the process of writing is a way of growing up, which sounds odd coming from someone my age. Writing has been like going back over familiar ground, reinforcing the symbols and elements that were present in childhood, in a way like a sort of echo of growing up. The books are an outer symbol of an inward progression.'

Some idea of where she stood as the New Zealand feminist movement gathered force can be gleaned from a short and rather stern essay, 'Educating the Imagination — Women as Writers,' which she contributed, along with educator and editor Phoebe Meikle, poet Lauris Edmond and activist Phillida Bunkle, to a feminist magazine in 1975:

'If there is any area in the literary arena where women should feel encouraged to succeed, it is as writers for children. The training and moral direction of children has long been regarded as a proper interest for women, and success in children's literature can readily be seen as the development of a perfectly legitimate female interest.

'It is true that there are a large number of excellent children's authors who are also women, their number increasing as one approaches the 70s. Yet, for all the involvement that women have had with children over hundreds of years, the outstanding books for children, those which have changed accepted patterns and which now stand out as landmarks, are almost exclusively by men — Andersen, Carroll, Lear, Kipling, Twain and Stevenson write with a certainty and a freedom that Frances Hodgson Burnett, Mary Mapes Dodge, Edith Nesbit and even Louisa May Alcott cannot, for all their mastery and magic, quite achieve.

'The view is of course historical. It is not possible in an article of this length to build up a total picture of why men have proved so successful in a field that seems set up for female dominance. All one can do is to speculate on the social and literary factors involved.

'Perhaps the very closeness of women to children, for all that it offers unique opportunities of observation and involvement, has been a mixed blessing because of the weighty instructive responsibility women have had placed upon them. Women writers of the eighteenth and nineteenth centuries are the subject of some scorn today because of their constant moralising. Men, of course were not free of this fault . . . it can be seen very clearly in Kingsley, George Macdonald and even such rugged writers as Ballantyne and Marryat. However, men, rather than women, seem capable of breaking free from the instructive function of writing and producing books which, though originally written for a specific audience of children, are primarily personal celebrations.

'*Alice in Wonderland*, for example, was not only a remarkable innovation in children's stories when it was written. It was also a sudden manifestation of a new type of humour — one which is very much with us today.

'Girls do seem to show a higher initial responsiveness to language than boys do. However, in the past they could probably not enjoy the verbal latitude which men were allowed. Profanity was out, and even slang, that colourful and idiomatic field of invention and innovation, was generally forbidden to well-educated middle-class women — the very women who would want to write stories for children (and in some cases needed to write them in order to make a reasonable living. Edith Nesbit is a case in point). It is significant perhaps that Jo — the writer of the March family — was adventurous, not only physically but verbally too, and in the first few pages of the book is criticised by two of her sisters for using slang . . . I am not suggesting that women were brought up to be inarticulate — but they were certainly encouraged to be very careful in their choice of words, and the way that they said them.

'It seems as if women on the whole had to work twice as hard as men to achieve that spontaneity, that unselfconsciousness, which is so much a characteristic of writers like Kipling, Lear and Twain. Women have not felt free to experiment, and their natural joyousness is often tinged with caution. They do not seem to be able to make that curious act of unconscious surrender which is as much to the needs of the story and words as to the needs of an audience . . .

'My particular interest in education is perhaps the education of the imagination, for I believe a properly functioning imagination to be as much a part of a human being as a good clean liver. It need not function along the whimsical lines so often regarded as evidence of its excellence but it must bridge the gap between the rational intuitive aspects of human thought and feeling and help us avoid the disassociation that so often seems to threaten us today.

'It doesn't matter to me whether or not the books that inform the imagination are written by men or women provided that they are written. Certainly I believe that Twain and Stevenson are ultimately more liberating than any modern morality where the boy plays with dolls and his sister chops the wood. It is not beyond a female capacity to be Tom Sawyer or Jack Hawkins if ever she needs to be. Here is real adventure and style. I am equally glad to read *The Iron Man* by Ted Hughes or *Tales of Arabel's Raven* by Joan Aitken — as long as the combination of action and style is potent, then the sex of the writer is irrelevant.

'Nevertheless, I feel that only now — when it is increasingly recognised that children's literature is part of the literary spectrum and those who write it best out of their own necessity — are women writers able to be writers and not authoress-instructors. They are free to turn the universe upside down and kick the stars around like autumn leaves if they wish to, or to put a raven in the fridge with the milk bottles.

'Throughout this article I have been considering the strictly literary scene, of course, and overlooking the grannies and nannies and nurses and housemaids who in the past have told both sentimental and horrifying stories to the children in their care, touching them with that combination of delight and fear that is still necessary today. These people too were powerful educators of the imagination.

'That's another story.

'I have neglected too, the lady writer of our own times who produced literally hundreds of books, bristling with stereotypes, patronising in style, often lacking in compassion, who nevertheless appealed to the imagination of thousands of children. Two generations have responded to Enid Blyton with a wholeheartedness that few writers before and none since have equalled.

'VOTES FOR WOMEN INDEED.

'But that's another story too.'

In 1976, Margaret won a New Zealand Literary Fund Grant to enable her to take a welcome year's leave of absence from the School Library Service. Apart from the writer in residence fellowship at the University of Canterbury in 1984, it was to be her only acceptance of public money.

By this time she had published nineteen hardback picture books with artwork by some of the best illustrators in Europe, three story book collections illustrated by the acclaimed English artist Shirley Hughes, and two very short (and admittedly very light-weight) junior novels, *Clancy's Cabin* (1974) and *The Bus Under the Leaves* (1975). It might be expected that her regular contributions to the *School Journal* would diminish, but in fact some 20 stories and poems appeared in there between 1970 and 1975, including the four Tai Taylor books championed by Jack Lasenby. Some of these, like the first group of Mahy stories from 1969, would later appear as international picture books: *Sailor Jack and the 20 Orphans* (1970), *The Railway Engine and the Hairy Brigands*, *The Boy Who was Followed Home*, *The Boy with Two Shadows* and *The Princess and the Clown* (all in 1971), *The Man whose Mother was a Pirate* (1972) and *Leaf Magic* (1975).

Meantime Margaret herself was undergoing a gradual transformation from the rather plainly dressed librarian/working mother, often pale and drawn with tiredness, into the flamboyant Margaret Mahy, Storyteller persona now so embedded in the popular New Zealand imagination: the witty, beloved author of wacky picture books who, wearing an equally wacky green or multicoloured fright wig, regularly visits primary schools to captivate the children with readings from her books.

By the mid-1970s she had embarked on the first of her thousands of visits over nearly three decades to New Zealand school classrooms, mostly under the auspices of the New Zealand Book Council's highly effective Writers in Schools scheme begun in 1977 after several years' trialling by its then administrator, Dame Fiona Kidman. The scheme originally envisaged New Zealand authors of adult books visiting high school English classes but was increasingly extended into the primary and intermediate schools as Margaret and an upsurge of talented children's authors from the early 1980s became more widely known. Some see this initiative as a significant factor in creating the present keen audience for New Zealand books, both adult and children's.

In 1976 a *Woman's Weekly* journalist was one of the first to comment, rather breathlessly, on Margaret's celebrated wig. 'Her tousled, bright green wig swept spikily in all directions, green and purple patterned kaftan-like gown giving her a billowy, fluid shape, she drops her voice to a conspiratorial whisper. The children at her feet are entranced; here is fantasy come to life, a real person with just the right aura of magic and mystery to sweep young minds off on Technicolor flights of imagination. Margaret Mahy is in town. Doing the things she loves and is so good at: telling stories . . . all based on simple, everyday processes, magically coloured and soaring on the wings of imaginative anarchy.'

The wig helped in the early days of these school visits and library readings when she was unsure of her ability to hold an audience. 'Dressing up for me is partly a disguise. It's also an attempt to keep myself under some wraps. But it's also more than that — it's an attempt to be as entertaining as I can for the children. They are a captive audience, they don't necessarily ask for me to come and talk to them . . . I want them to be interested.' It originated as a bit of fun for the reading sessions, of her own and other authors' work, she arranged as part of her new job at the Public Library in Christchurch. But the hired wig was such a hit with children that she soon bought it for more frequent outings and indulged her growing taste for colourful (and now more affordable) offbeat outfits. From the moment she arrived in the school office, she was irresistibly fascinating and funny to children of all ages and soon became a skilled and mesmerising performer to audiences of any size — 'a bit of an exhibitionist, with nothing to exhibit', as she has more than once described herself.

By 1980 the wig and Margaret were thought so inseparable that the Christchurch children's book community was alarmed when hearing that she had unaccountably offered her unique headgear to a forthcoming telethon to be sold to the highest bidder. 'Margaret Mahy minus Wig . . . that repository full of ideas from which she plucks imaginative tales when needed?' Christchurch librarian Veda Pickles reported from the front line on this catastrophic prospect in the Children's Literature Association 1981 Yearbook. 'As well imagine Arthur without Excalibur, Morecombe without Wise, Buckingham Palace without corgis. My immediate reaction was one of horror. What would I, as a teacher, do next Book Week, without the Green Wig to talk to us? What would my pupils do without the Green Wig to encourage them to write and keep on writing?' The call went out, and 'within minutes members of the New Zealand Librarians' Association, the Children's Book Group and Children's Literature Association had swung into action, pooled their resources and saved the day.' On telethon night Margaret's supporters bid vigorously for the wig and returned it triumphantly to its rightful owner.

Margaret was always sensitive to the wig's powers and its impact on her audiences. 'Kids were very entertained. There comes a point though where kids will suddenly get embarrassed. You never quite know where that point is.' She describes with wry amusement the appalled embarrassment of 'big boys at country schools who are probably leading reasonably adult lives, doing useful things on farms, being addressed by somebody in a green wig. It must seem very denigrating.' When the green wig was lost, Margaret realised she'd 'got a bit sick of it' and thought she wouldn't be bothered wearing it again. But by then the wig had taken on a persona of its own. 'When I went to schools, almost the first question was, have you got the wig? — even at secondary schools. After a while I had to get another. It's rainbow coloured and I don't like it quite as much as the green one.'

In later years she would sometimes don a full penguin suit, given to her by the Gibson Group film company, confiding in a chuckling aside to the children (and sometimes adult audiences) that it was hot inside and that penguin flippers were not made for turning pages. Resulting from one of her many trips to Australia from the mid-1970s on, a possum suit became another addition to her wardrobe, though its bushy tail presented certain difficulties in sitting down and in getting through customs.

A story was later told of a Christchurch chief reporter's response to a breathless new reporter announcing to the newsroom that he had just seen a giant possum carrying an umbrella and riding a bicycle. 'Mahy,' said the underwhelmed chief. 'Surprised it wasn't the penguin.' The multicoloured wig arrived sometime in the early 1980s, a radiant confection of pastel pinks, yellows and lime greens, dramatic purple and electric blue, sometimes decorated with twigs and leaves for a 'forest sprite' effect. Later again, any ethnic or more classic outfit would be regularly transformed by a jaunty hat (sometimes decorated with a feather of alarming reach), and/or a hand-knitted scarf of impressive length, made weighty and clanking by several hundreds of badges collected from a huge variety of sources — schools, associations, booksellers, publishers, probably hotels, airlines and so on — all over the world.

The year's leave of absence presented Margaret with the appealing picture of what it might be like to be a full-time writer rather than a full-time librarian. 'Working does cut time a lot, and it also cuts leisure time in which you think and turn over ideas almost unconsciously . . . letting different things come in, turning them over, turning them into images, metaphors, into jokes, and I do think I suffer from this now, where work is concerned.

'Once on a television programme they commented on the fact that some of my stories had been described as *stories of genius*, and asked if I thought this was true. And I think it's very true to say that I'm not single-minded enough for this. I certainly love the writing, but I'm just as interested in a different way, a more public way, in the library, in reading, and in what other people write. And I'm interested in pursuing private studies of things, and in doing things with my children. I wouldn't wish to give any of it up.'

In early 1977, about to turn 41, Margaret was not quite ready for the uncertainties of full-time writing. After her year's leave, she accepted the position of children's librarian at the Canterbury Public Library. This would be a significantly more 'public' position than the School Library Service, involving greater interaction with many more adults other than teachers, and with children of all ages from toddlers through to high school students.

Looking through comments on Margaret's development as a writer in the 1970s, one is struck by certain preoccupations and perceptions. First, why does she write for children, and second, why does she not write New Zealand stories for New Zealand children like other well-known New Zealand children's writers of this period, Jack Lasenby, Anne de Roo, Elsie Locke, Ruth Dallas, Ron Bacon and Eve Sutton?

'She has often been criticised because her books lack any distinctive New Zealand flavour,' noted a 1976 newspaper profile. 'Even the word "meadow" in her best-known story is seldom if ever heard in the mouth of a New Zealand child. (Paddock is the vernacular New Zealand word here.)' Baffled interviewers wanted her to explain why she should want to focus so obsessively on 'little stories' for children. Although 'little' was not always articulated, it was often implied by adults who, though possibly parents themselves, may never have actually considered that, in all the best picture books, a highly sophisticated, adult layer of meaning lies behind the simple words and folk tale manner of telling. This is certainly the case in all Margaret's short fiction, especially the miniature masterpieces like *A Lion in the Meadow*, *Pillycock's Shop*, 'Small Porks', *The Girl with Two Shadows* or *The Wind Between the Stars*.

One of her earliest written opinions on these issues was a long interview entitled 'One Great Frolic with Words', which appeared in *Education* in 1973. Her polite, slightly tentative answers (almost as if she were still searching for convincing intellectual justification for the literary activity she had now been compulsively engaged in for nearly 20 years), foreshadowed major speeches she would make in several countries. The unnamed interviewer asked, circumspectly, whether the places she had lived in affected her work.

'Not a great deal, because the things I have written are basically from the inner landscape of a personality. They are concerned with things that I have found funny or amusing — eccentricities on the whole — but sometimes I will use a story in a single image that I have observed in the outside landscape. The other day when I was at a school the teacher asked me where I got my ideas from. I tried to explain to the children how ideas can come from anywhere at all. You just are, you know, *open* to them. I said, "Suppose a witch was to get on a bus." A bus, you see, is a very self-contained (if temporary) community. (I wrote it as a story later on.) The witch starts to make trouble and it ends with a bus load of people fighting and throwing eggs and hitting one another. The witch is laughing to herself and then she slides out, leaving the bus in this chaotic condition; but on the way out she catches her foot and she falls in a puddle. Everyone looks at her and some of them remember that she had started the trouble and others are ashamed because she found it so easy to cause trouble and then they all start to laugh and with the laughter the chaos is cleared up. They clean up the eggs and the oranges and everything. The bus goes on its way, filled once again with a happy warm self-contained community. When people give up stamping and start laughing, there is no way to tell where it will all end. This is a story that obviously comes from ideas rather than environment but it is still affected by environment.

'I do believe quite strongly in the therapeutic value of the happy ending. I think that not only is it very pleasant for children to read a happy ending, but I think it can make you go out and want to *make* a similar happy ending, make you want to be brave, strong and true. People nowadays are very suspicious of happy endings and think they have to be contrived . . . I think that the prince and princess in the fairy tale take on a symbolic quality, and that the happy ending is a much more dynamic thing than people nowadays tend to give it credit for.'

Was her kitchen sink fantasy deliberate?

'Well, yes, I don't wish to sound at all precious about this but I believed that any commonplace object has a capacity to become a thing of wonder. I don't think this is a coy fantasy. I have been reading a lot over the last few years — on a very popular and simple level, admittedly — about the structure of matter, and the quantum theory and things like this and it gives me the feeling that any object has a capacity for being wonderful, that at any moment any part of the landscape, a tree, say, can turn into a burning bush with the voice of God speaking out of it. A table can be all sorts of things to me, depending on which way you look at it. A box of matches on the kitchen sink is as intricate as the Bach partitas. I couldn't write about atomic theory for children, though I find this sort of thing extremely moving, but I try to suggest the ordinary/miraculous double nature of things.

'I think that a lot of writers are like this, each of them is a receiver and a transmitter; one receives signals from outside and transmits them in one's own particular way. This is why I think that perhaps any object in a story that I write could become a vehicle for a miracle or a remarkable happening.'

So who did she write for, children or herself?

'I write for myself entirely, but nevertheless it would be unrealistic to say that I don't have children in mind. I write about the things that entertain me — that entertained me when I was a child and haven't stopped entertaining me. I suppose I have a certain faith in my judgement where this is concerned but I feel that I was ordinary enough as a child for there to be a lot of other people whose children would be entertained by the same things. It is really a way of sharing a joke.' And on responses from children: 'It is very hard to distinguish my own stories from other people's stories in that I take just as much delight in other people's stories too, and looking backwards I find that reading and writing tend to merge into one great frolic with words.'

Did she consider that childhood was the best time in one's life?

'Oh no. The most exciting and interesting times I have had really have been as an adult. I don't wish to go back even two or three years. I don't wish to go back to being 21 again for that matter. So far, to me at any rate, it has been more interesting to go forward. I don't exactly know why it is that I write for children and not for grownups, perhaps there is an element of nostalgia too.

'My adult life is very full and I am reading a lot of other things that people have written and I find it good, by writing for childhood, to maintain a sort of feeling of time past and time future being here all at the same time. Childhood is not a separate part of a person's life, it is just part of the way in which we become a particular person. I think that this is why I have a lot of old people in the stories I write — people do tend to treat children and old people as if they were much more separate. They put them here, and they put them there and make plans for what to do with them. Old people seem to be deprived of their autonomy to a certain extent, and actually they are just different points in the growth of individuals.'

Did she consider herself a religious person?

'Oh yes, I think that I am probably very religious in a way. If I am asked to write down my religion I usually put "agnostic" because it seems easier, but it depends, I suppose, on what you mean by religious. I have trouble where basic acts of faith about a personal God and creation and questions like this are concerned. It is very difficult to me to line up with a particular form of dogma, but sometimes when I am talking to people who are Christians I think that our views are probably very similar.

'I believe that I have a reverence for life, for stars and cells, for structures. I said before that I find it extremely moving to read about the structure of matter; it ties up with a lot of other things as well. I have very little education in these areas, so I have to be very careful what I read because it is important to me to know what is true about these things.

'I remember once many years ago — it must be about six, I was expecting Bridget at the time — I was levelling a piece on the section, pushing a wheelbarrow of clay. I was doing this for about three weeks and I remember this as a remarkable experience — rather like what people describe when they have been taking some sort of drug — every object burning with a deeper significance. Everything that happened was significant; the way the sun and the moon arranged themselves across the sky. As I walked along, one was on one hand, and one on the other, so that I was balanced in the middle of them like a sort of Blake personage. The way the birds sat on the bare branches of the trees looked like some isolated thing from Haiku poetry. It was late in the year and next door a liquidambar tree burned like a flame. I saw it simultaneously as a tree and as a fire burning against the sky and the sea and, without necessarily at the end of this time understanding more what a tree was, I felt that I had moved deeper into its meaning. This is a religious experience. I can't remember anything as sustained since that, but, even once in six years, it's something to look back on with a feeling of gratitude.'

The formal speeches from this period, which grew in confidence and never underestimated her audience's intelligence, considered why she wrote as she did:

'[After 1969 I] was soon called on to make some statement of why I wrote for children, and more particularly why I wrote for children rather than adults.

'To digress for a moment there are some assumptions about writing for children which crop up continuously either directly or implicitly in the questions people ask. These assumptions are not irrelevant but they are surprising to me because they suggest that the motives for writing children's stories are very circumscribed in people's minds. One such assumption is that you write children's stories because you love children although no one assumes you write adult stories because you love adults. In fact I do like children — babies and all — because I like people and the degree of liking or disliking depends on the individuals concerned. There is nothing very esoteric about it. Another belief is that one begins writing stories because one has children of one's own to tell stories to. This was not so in my case. I chose to write stories for children well before I had children . . . But it is certainly true of many outstanding writers for children, including Carroll, Milne, Grahame and Kipling. Even so I would like to suggest that in many cases the presence of children in the author's life has been a starting point only and the story has become, consciously or unconsciously, a vehicle for the author's own self-expression. It certainly seems to be hard for people to accept that, in writing children's stories, one writes, as William Mayne says somewhere, for oneself in childhood, that there is some area of one's childhood unappeased to which one must return and give sustenance, or that the symbols and images of childhood reading have laid so strong a hold on the writer's imagination that he must come back to them again and again for strength and refreshment. And when one takes such a familiar journey over again, one often finds it is not, after all, familiar. The old signposts and landmarks may still be there, but they signify new directions on this second journey. The waves still scribble their message on the sea, but they tell you something different from what they did when you were a child. Meaning is always an interaction between word and reader and even though words may remain constant the adult has different experiences to bring to bear in his part of the negotiation, than those he had when he was a child.

'In 1969 when I was asked why I wrote for children I said it was simply to entertain them. I now think that the fear of appearing pompous caused me to over simplify. The old explanation no longer satisfies me for its very openness is a distortion and delusion. "Simply to entertain" is an odd statement in itself, for the sources of entertainment, to paraphrase Oscar Wilde's comment on truth, are rarely pure and never simple.

'Like any writer — any communicator — I am not indifferent to my audience. I am certainly not indifferent to my audience out there or the fact of their childhood. Certainly I select and modify my aboriginal fancies to meet them half way. But I am also concerned that my story should do something for them, complete some circuit or exorcise some demon. I have come to see these stories as shadows cast in the conscious world by unconscious actions and journeys, the crests of icebergs shining in the sun while their greater part remains drowned in green water. If it is the hidden part I am talking about today, I hope to justify it by showing that the shining crest, the story the child reads and understands, is made possible by the depth and weight of the hidden experience that produces it. And some children at least are able by a mysterious process or faculty that we roughly call "imagination" to apprehend that part of the story that is hidden and use it to illuminate their own hidden experiences . . .

'To get a true picture of ourselves we are increasingly required to understand ourselves as points of tension in a field of opposites, to acknowledge and cope emotionally with paradox. I think imagination is the mechanism by which we achieve a position of balance, not a cloudy decoration hanging on the outside of life but a vital part of our structure. Part of its function I think of as a sort of coding which gives you, in moments of need or crisis, rapid access to images and energies which will enable you to interpret and to act. The definition of imagination which I prefer therefore is not simply the power to create in the mind, images of things not present, but that it is the ability to deal creatively with reality, one of the definitions given by a dictionary.

'How can we study this intangible but important faculty? It is so very intangible. I suppose in the same way that we are forced to study so many of the basic constituents of matter by looking, not at the thing itself, but at its shadow or its footprints. Sub atomic particles reveal their nature by the tracks they leave in cloud chambers. Provided we don't allow ourselves to become dogmatic, to understand that we are dealing with possibilities and probabilities for the most part rather than fact, I believe we can find out a lot by tracking the paths imaginative processes leave in the mind, by looking at shadows, dreams, analogies, symbols, images and actions based on these things.'

Some characters and images are particularly potent for her. 'Perhaps we are all born with witches, lions, magicians and heroes in us, who recognise their counterparts in the outside world and invite them in to sleep or dance in the various spare rooms that open off the main corridors of the human mind.'

Occasionally, a good-humoured defensiveness is evident as she reminds audiences why her stories are so determinedly universal.

'I am a New Zealander by birth and by a sense of tradition, so when people say to me "Why don't you write New Zealand stories?" my answer is that I do, but I am aware at the same time, that this is almost an evasion, a deliberate twisting of the terms. For what people mean when they ask this, is, why don't I write in terms of a particular locality, in terms of people, surroundings and experiences that couldn't be anything else but New Zealand?

'I have wondered at times about this myself and have come to the conclusion that it is in part because the external landscapes with which I identify so closely and which impose themselves in such immense images in my inner landscape (the landscapes of personality and identity), do not do so in terms of their locality . . .

'At present I am living on an extinct volcano on Banks Peninsula which has been broken into by the sea and has become a harbour. In the heart of this harbour you can still see the little hard core which has become an island. Every morning when I get up and go out to test the day and to guess what sort of a day it's going to be, I see hills and sky and trees and sun. Far off I see

Lyttelton perched in accidental fashion on the flank of the hill. It's only a few miles away as the crow flies but already it looks like a mirage — it looks as if it is there in a very temporary way, as if at any time these big hills might shrug it off into the sea. As I look out I see this, and I see hills which have been robbed of their bush, except in streaks where the folds of the land run down to the sea. There is a sort of arrested stillness as if the hills have a great deal more mobility than the sea itself, a great deal more fluidity. I have this feeling that if I'd looked out a moment earlier I would have seen these hills moving in some sort of way, moving in a motion as tidal and instinctive as the sea . . .

'I very often . . . while looking out the window and catching a glimpse of this landscape, have the feeling that it is growing and evolving around me. In actual fact, perhaps I am seeing my own shadow cast upon the hills, seeing in fact, my own growth, my own evolution, recognised at some partly conscious level and reflected in the exterior landscape. Being small in a big landscape produces the feeling it is mobile and you, the observer, are standing still . . .

'. . . Finally we get off and we go along the road . . . And we climb up till we get to the top where the rocks come through. Here perhaps, one is aware of the rock coming through the soil and one feels the very bones of one's body move in sympathy with this breaking through, and one feels one's substance of flesh identified with the rich soil. Then we reach the top of the hill, and there's the Sign of the Takahe as we follow down the other side towards Christchurch.

'Here something different happens, because although there are trees and rocks, and corners with which we identify, and though we see these trees through the years as slow clocks ticking away the season, and although they are still a continuation of the same scene, I feel we are imposed upon this landscape, not sifted through it.

'On the other side of the hills we are incorporated in our own landscape.

'Many of you will know exactly the sort of experience I am

talking about. When you've chosen a landscape to live in and you've lived in it for a number of years, watching the seasons pass over it, you become part of it in a very special way. Like any other form of love it is a double-edged emotion — it can hurt you as well as reward you. Any violation of this familiar landscape feels like some sort of personal injury, because you identify with this landscape to such an extent. Inevitably it is a distinctively New Zealand landscape with which I have formed this sort of relationship.

'In talking about this outside landscape, this exterior landscape, I've probably already given intimations about an inner landscape too, because it's hard to separate them. On the whole the outside landscape is much more predictable than the inner one because although there are places you can go to, and perhaps infallibly recognised, in your inner landscape there are also places you can go to where the landscape changes, where the milestones don't stay the same for two days running. You go there along the road that you thought was well sealed and laid, and you find it's already a mosaic of doubt. This is the inner landscape where you find yourself coming face to face with changes; you find yourself coming towards a puritan, or a nymphomaniac, or some shadowy stranger and as you come up to them you recognise that they all wear your own face. This is the place where your surrogates, your other selves, act out your own particular dramas, dreams and devices. The inner landscape is a much more dangerous place and a much more personal place, too.

'I'm still talking about this inner landscape in terms of scenery, because you have to limit it in some way or otherwise you have chaos . . . And look [sighting an autumn poplar beside the road] there's the tree burning up from the ground like a flame in all its autumn colouring. It comes into my eye and into my mind through a complex system of nervous reactions which I can't attempt to describe, and I see, simultaneously almost, an autumn tree, a flame, a shower of bright arrows, somebody standing in a golden robe, a magician, an enchanter and an ancient spirit whirling in a spindle of gold. In a moment the boundaries between outer and inner landscapes are down, and they flood into one another and combine. Then I, myself, dissolve into a swarm of golden whirling cells and am knitted up again between one world and the next, so that, even the most malignant and observant traffic-officer probably couldn't fault my driving. Yet in a second, I feel I've been infinitely enriched and my direction has, in some way, perhaps infinitesimally, been altered.

'This really can happen. Some days may go by and it doesn't happen; sometimes it can happen several times during the day. One such spell of it extended over a period of about three weeks — I seemed to live with this thing almost continually. Once I went almost without it for three years and looked at the landscape, the outer landscapes around me, and knew they had this ability to transform me, but I knew too, that I was shut off from this magical experience. In the inner landscape the identity of things changes — the tree becomes a spirit, the spirit a flame, the flame a clown and the clown can become the very axis of the world with all the planets dancing around it. There is nothing whimsical in this. In fact it can be frightening, and beautiful, and merciless. Time too, changes in the inner landscape . . .

'Were I able in the same way to stand outside of time in the outer landscape, I would see my volcano creating itself, seething, building its walls up, falling into silence, and wearing down and down into the hills and the road and the sea that at present exist. At this point several things become obvious, I think. Just any landscape, anywhere in the world, is capable of this sort of interpretation, and this sort of feeling; it's not a particularly New Zealand thing to do. Although the inner landscape is enriched and developed by the outer landscape it is ultimately defined in terms of language and images and things that are heard, things that are read and things that are said. If a person's inner landscape has been as closely defined as mine has by reading and listening, then when the moment of union comes . . . when the inner landscape widens and coalesces with, and interprets the outer landscape, then it does so in words which are the closest approximations to the state it perceives. This isn't some particularly New Zealand thing. It's a universal phenomenon.

'The words and images that are at our disposal to use, in order to interpret our landscape, tend to be — at least in my case and I suspect in the case of many people — those that turn back to a European background . . . But when we have a totara tree, we don't have any of the build-up of language, we don't have any of the background, if you like, that gives this word the same quality of meaning on the inner landscape. Many of our local words are still only half real. They're real on the outer landscape, but haven't yet attained the associations that we need to make them completely real on the inner landscape . . .

'So I suppose what a New Zealand writer should hope to do is to build up the associations for the inner landscape with the things that are particularly New Zealand. He should try and strengthen this sort of association so that it becomes part of the inner landscape of our children and when they read for example "totara tree" or rimu (or something like that) instead of feeling this self-conscious, slightly unnatural feeling that we appear to have about it, we come to feel as natural and strongly about it as we do about willow or poplar.

'In actual fact this has been happening in New Zealand . . . I think it began with the poets and goes on with poets . . . I think that the process begins here and works its way down ultimately to people who never even read the poems. At present we have novelists, historians and children's writers, who, again, are doing this sort of thing. So perhaps it's partly a feeling of guilt because I don't seem to be doing much in this area myself, that makes me want to stand up and say that, while the development of local associations is one of the good functions a children's story, or any other sort of writing, can perform in New Zealand at the present, I'd like to speak up also perhaps for some of the things I'm doing when I write. I feel they're just as "New Zealand" as anything else. I feel that perhaps our tradition of writing is dictated partly by the idea that we must express ourselves as New Zealanders. I'm now over simplifying it perhaps to an unforgivable degree. But I do think there's more to New Zealand's outer landscape than the football match or the good keen man. I do think that this rather mystical interpretation of New Zealand landscape has relevance and enriches it. I think that perhaps our whole tradition has been touched upon partly by the fact that we use words, almost entirely to convey information. Very few of us really use words as a celebration — and I personally am very fond of a celebration. Then we have a paternalistic rather than a pantheistic form of religion, so that we don't expect a religious experience to come to us out of the trees — we still think of it in terms of something "way out there". . .

'I think that science with its emphasis on relationships and structures and things like this can add to our feelings, not only about our outer landscapes, but about our inner landscape . . . How exactly does this lead to the writing of children's stories? I don't rightly know, because personally I don't regard myself as any sort of child — I think I'm a mature adult. I don't think I write children's stories out of any sort of whimsicality, only out of necessity. I find that the stories I write can use all the feelings, all the command of language and all the passion I have at my disposal. If I had more they could use it all . . . I don't want to be the tree, just one of the voices singing within its branches. The sort of story I write, would, I hope, tend to leave the children who read it, with their options open to choose in a whole lot of different ways. I like to think that they will be able to see the tree as the tree, as the clown, or as a king. I like to feel that they too will be overwhelmed by what I called earlier the shower of golden arrows. I think to think too, that if they're confronted with something like the structure of the DNA spiral, they will be changed by it, as by a good poem. I like to think also that the children who read these stories are left with a tremendous number of voices and able to use this fantasy as an instrument of accuracy. I hope ultimately for children who come in contact with this sort of story that the poet and the scientist may dance together like lovers each wearing the child's own face in the child's own inner landscape.'

For many admirers, it is the language that sets any Mahy writing apart. Whatever the genre, she uses English as few other writers can do, across a wide range of comic, ironic, poetic and lyrical styles.

In 1987 University of Auckland MA student Jenni Keestra analysed some of the more straightforward characteristics of Margaret's language: the repetition, the extravagant use of alliteration, and less frequently assonance, by which playful rhythmic patterns are established and played upon much as a composer might do. Keestra quotes from *The Midnight Story on Griffon Hill*: 'His stories were so funny that doctors gave them to people suffering from dejections, doldrums, despondency or even those who were merely down in the dumps. As the patients read his stories they would begin to simper and smile; they would grin and giggle and guffaw, and at last they would laugh loud and long until they were light-hearted again.' As Mark Williams has commented, Mahy's patter song *Bubble Trouble* (included in Bill Manhire's *100 New Zealand Poems*) is amazing 'if only by showing how many permutations of the letters b and l are possible'. Many audiences have been delighted with a perfect, rapid fire rendition, starting:

> Little Mabel blew a bubble and it caused a lot of trouble . . .
> Such a lot of bubble trouble in a bibble-bobble way,
> For it broke away from Mabel as it bobbed across the table,
> Where it bobbled over Baby, and it wafted him away.
>
> The baby didn't quibble. He began to smile and dribble,
> For he liked the wibble-wobble of the bubble in the air.
> But Mabel ran for cover as the bubble bobbed above her,
> And she shouted out for Mother who was putting up her hair.

At the sudden cry of trouble, Mother took off at the double,
For the squealing left her reeling . . . made her terrified and
tense,
Saw the bubble for a minute, with the baby bobbing in it,
As it bibbled by the letter box and bobbed across the fence.

Her alliterative bent comes out most outrageously in *The Birthday
Burglar*, in which a boy called Bassington has a predilection for
things beginning with the letter 'b'. She says she was slightly
disconcerted at how easily alliteration came to her in this story: 'I
increasingly became addicted to using the letter b . . . when read
aloud *The Birthday Burglar* should have the quality of an extended
tongue twister. Part of the fun of the story is working out the
ending from the clues that the words beginning with b provide.'
Then there are the words heaped on top of one another — 'Oh,
she was a scold, a shrew, a vixen and a virago — and a proper
tyrant and tartar to her poor husband' (*Mrs Discombobulous*) —
and the escalating lists in descriptive passages, as when the little
man sees the sea for the first time in *The Man Whose Mother was a
Pirate*. The sea, notes Keestra, is acknowledged as having more
than one image, one character:

> He hadn't dreamed of the BIGNESS of it. He hadn't dreamed
> of the blueness of it. He hadn't thought it would roll like
> kettledrums, and swish itself onto the beach. He opened his
> mouth, and the drift and the dream of it, the weave and the
> wave of it, the fume and the foam of it never left him again. At
> his feet the sea stroked the sand with soft little paws. Farther
> out, the great, graceful breakers moved like kings into court,
> trailing the peacock-patterned sea behind them.

Or, later, the long, surrealistic dream sequence in *The Changeover*,
in which powerful details are added to lists:

> . . . she saw dwarfs, lost princes, beautiful girls who had

committed themselves to silence in order to save brothers turned into swans or ravens, young men who thrived on sunshine and dwindled with darkness, mutilated maidens who wept over their own silver arms, and then the simple people, three bears, the girl in the red hood, the lost children who found their way home, the lost children who didn't and were covered with leaves by the robins.

In raising language to an 'exciting art-form', warns Keestra, Margaret Mahy does not allow readers to take it for granted: fullest pleasure and enjoyment depends on careful reading, lest any delights be missed. She cites the invented adjectives and especially, expletives, worthy of Edward Lear; the jokey transfer of meanings recalling Lewis Carroll, such as a meal of shenanigans, peccadilloes and paragon soup (in *Raging Robots and Unruly Uncles*). Then there are the names, always as inventive, sly, ironic, fanciful, funny or classically allusive as necessary for the characters and the story. Others have had similar fun in picture books — Jill Murphy, Babette Cole, Joy Cowley — or gone for similar allusive seriousness in novels — J.K. Rowling, Jan Mark, Roald Dahl, Terry Pratchett, Philip Pullman or Sonya Hartnett — but not both at the same time.

Consider pirates called Peregrine (*The Horrendous Hullabaloo*), Orpheus Clinker, Terrible Crabmeat, Roving Tom, Wild Jack Clegg (*The Great Piratical Rumbustification*), Lionel Wafer (*The Pirates' Mixed-up Voyage*) and Grudge-Gallows (*Tingleberries, Tuckertubs and Telephones*); teachers called Ms Marigold, Mr Sogbucket (*The Horribly Haunted School*) and Mrs Desiree Thoroughgood (*The Blood-and-Thunder Adventure on Hurricane Peak*); a beautiful librarian named Serena Laburnum (*The Librarian and the Robbers*).

There are the families — the Terrapins (*The Great Piratical Rumbustification*) and the Scholars (*The Haunting*); Wicked Uncle Jasper and his seven sons, Caligula, Nero, Genghis, Tarquin, Belshazzar, Adolph and Julian (*Raging Robots and Unruly Uncles*);

sisters Alpha, Cathabelle, Elodie, Icasia, Zamira (*The Five Sisters*); the Likely family, brothers Hardly and Scarcely, mother Pretty and clown Uncle Flipping (*The Great Millionaire Kidnap*).

Then there are the villains and magicians — Rancid Swarthy, Whizzy Tambo and Crambo Tambo (*The Riddle of the Frozen Phantom*); Carmody Braque (*The Haunting*), Sir Quincey Judd-Sprockett, Amadeus Shoddy and Voltaire Shoddy (*The Blood-and-Thunder Adventure on Hurricane Peak*); Squidgy Moot (*A Villain's Night Out*); the robbers Salvation Loveday (*The Librarian and the Robbers*) and Buckbounder (*Beaten by a Balloon*); the magicians Quando (*Alchemy*) and Heathcliff Warlock (*The Blood-and-Thunder Adventure on Hurricane Peak*); sinister brothers Felix, Ovid and Hadfield (*The Tricksters*), wacky sisters Ursa, Leona and Fox Hammond (*24 Hours*), difficult, demanding older sisters Ginevra (*The Other Side of Silence*) and Christobel (*The Tricksters*), difficult stepsister Jake (*Aliens in the Family*), feckless young male Jackie Cattle and the damaged bully Christo (*24 Hours*).

From the novels come heroines Laura Chant (*The Changeover*), the besieged Troy and talkative Tabitha (*The Haunting*), beautiful Angela and her betrayed mother Dido (*The Catalogue of the Universe*), secretive Ariadne (*The Tricksters*), Bonny Benedicta (*Memory*), Winola (*Underrunners*) and mute Hero (*The Other Side of Silence*); the heroes and interesting young men Tycho (*The Catalogue of the Universe*), Sorenson Carlisle (*The Changeover*), Jonny Dart (*Memory*), Ellis (*24 Hours*), Roland (*Alchemy*) and Norvin (*The Great White Man-Eating Shark*).

Witches, grandmothers and assorted crones? The Carlisle witches, mother Miriam and grandmother Winter (*The Changeover*); bustling granny Mrs Oberon (*Busy Day for a Good Grandmother*), poor senile Sophie (*Memory*), creepy Miss Credence (*The Other Side of Silence*) and cold, pale Miss Gibb (*The Wind Between the Stars*).

For explorers and scientists she comes up with Tycho Potter (*The Catalogue of the Universe*), Jess Ferrett (*Alchemy*), Boniface Sapwood and Corona Wottley (*The Riddle of the Frozen Phantom*),

Belladonna Doppler (*The Blood-and-Thunder Adventure on Hurricane Peak*); for babysitters, Daffodil (*The Riddle of the Frozen Phantom*) and the unforgettable Mrs Fangboner (*The Catalogue of the Universe*). Mr Prospero is a dutiful but vulnerable father (*Down the Dragon's Tongue*); Mr and Mrs Flip are ballroom dancers (*The Queen's Goat*). Then there is *Mrs Discombobulous*, and *Pillycock's Shop* and Small Porks and dogs named Nightshade, Oberon and Titania, a sculptor named Uncle Pygmalion, a home decorator called Jacques Spratt and a boss called Mr Fat and an alien spy from outer space called Bond and a ghost named Lulu . . . As she explained in a 1975 speech, Margaret is fully aware of the symbolic, philosophical, visual and aural possibilities of language.

'Language seems at times to have a separate existence from the people who use it. We talk about respecting it, about the damage that can be done through misuse of it. At times it seems as if language is man's creator as much as a thing created by him. Without language we remain potential rather than actual.

'After all, what is language? A way of symbolising! Some words stand for ideas with very well-defined boundaries. We can use the word "four", meaning the idea of "fourness", understanding precisely what is meant. No flexibility is possible here. Other words stand for ideas with which we are less apt at dealing. "Ultra-violet catastrophe", for example, is a phrase with a highly technical meaning which only a physicist can fully appreciate. And yet we feel a response to the words, to their richness, their unexpectedness, to the explosion in their heart. Our response gives us pleasure and moves us on into other areas of verbal speculation. Sound alone has an impact beyond the necessities of sense.'

Then there is the word that has a boundary, but the boundary is constantly changing. The poor abused word 'love' is an example.

'I once had an aunt who had very definite ideas about love. It had to be "unselfish" or it was not "true love". Love between the sexes had to lead to marriage. Not to intend marriage was to exhibit "selfishness" and therefore the feeling involved was not "true love".

'I remember arguing against these views, saying that she was making the criteria too narrow — that there were many cases outside the boundaries she had laid down that deserved to be described as cases of "love". We could not agree. We obviously understood different things by the word and yet we continued to use it meaningfully to one another, stretching this way to cover point A, and back again to cover point B. You cannot stretch the "four" to cover "fiveness" or "threeness" but sometimes the definition of "love" can be stretched until it meets itself coming around the other way. We speak of love-hate, a term which is meaningful to us, though it encompasses two ideas that we understand as opposites.

'Being aware of the definition of a word capable of such treatment is to understand it. Being open to the nuances possible within the boundaries of that meaning, nuances which at times extend the boundaries like frontiers in strange territory, is to be open to the intuitive field that such words build up around them . . . some of the more obvious ones are emphasis and expression (in conversation), irony and understatement.'

Intuitive listening, she believes, is a matter of practice. 'The ability to use words so that they simultaneously satisfy the need for rational discourse between two people, and at the same time extend into a variety of private satisfactions to the individual, is one which is often initiated in childhood and develops the very thing it relies on — the tuned ear listening to associations, to meanings underlying the pattern of words.

'The person listening in to the field spread out around each word becomes an explorer of language, a taster of words, whose every encounter with reading or conversation has a potential, both in terms of momentary beguilement and more permanently, in that it may be one of the experiences by which future encounters are interpreted and defined. For such a person the world is full of messages flashed urgently, exhibited briefly and gone. Who is the sender? Sometimes it seems the universe is constantly revealing itself in a curious shorthand inscribed everywhere. Sometimes the inscriptions are moving and expected. Sunshine, storm and seasonal change write themselves across the city and we make guesses at what we are being told . . .

'In writing for children I often find, on looking back, that a story written purely for entertainment at a particular time is nevertheless full of clues suggesting to child, adult, author, and reader alike that words are capable of many uses which are purely individual, even though they relate to the needs of social communication. The mother says there is a dragon in the matchbox and behold — there is a dragon in the matchbox. Her word has taken a green and purple body to itself, breathes smoke and fire and terrifies the lion. Her words, working through her son, achieved a validity she would never have imagined. She must never tell a story again unless she dignifies it with belief, even if it is a belief in the symbol that underlies her story.

'In another story, recently written, an old man uses the phrase "ultra-violet catastrophe" as a magical phrase, a spell which will recall him always to a realisation of himself, of his own identity. He shares the phrase with a small girl and it becomes, not just a magic formula, but a password between them. "Ultra-violet catastrophe" she says instead of "Goodbye", and it means "Goodbye" and "We will meet again" and "We are good friends" and "We had a wonderful, adventurous time together". The listening mother and aunt cannot hear any of this. The message is given but the secret is kept.

'I hope there is enough in this to amuse and satisfy a reader without it being necessary to understand the phrase. It actually means, and my understanding of it is very imperfect, a catastrophe that would occur if energy were not contained in little parcels, in quanta. If energy were not restricted in this fashion, it would escape away through the ultra-violet end of the radiation spectrum — ultra-violet catastrophe, with apologies to any physicist. So there is a literal meaning hidden in the story, a funny surprise for any child who reads the story and then encounters the phrase in its literal form later in life. On the occasions that I have had such encounters I have certainly been amused and have felt, moreover, the literal situation enriched by the fantastic, and vice versa. I suppose one of the author's satisfactions lies in establishing circumstances for this to happen for a like-minded person, in thinking of a child grown up and involved in physics suddenly encountering the phrase and saying "My God! Ultra-violet catastrophe" and feeling the spaces between thought and feeling, childhood and adulthood, symbol and reality, close up and everything become one, for the space of a second. In the present is the password for the future and part of the pleasure for the author is that it is speculative. It might never happen. It is a message sent out blindly like the broken plaque in the Mariner space probe that carries the image of our humanity outward to the stars.

'Just as, for me, and at least some other people, too, all journeys are basically symbolic and just an outer manifestation of an inner exploration, so I think all statements are statements of self and one's place in the universe. As we plan and commit ourselves to certain ideas and actions we watch ourselves carefully, see ourselves using words to give ourselves form, like ghosts using ectoplasm to materialise.'

Margaret spent three years as the Christchurch children's librarian, adding to her by now encyclopaedic professional knowledge of children's books. Some older writers can remember her from this period, a jolly and welcoming presence clad in the unflattering smock that librarians of the time wore. Other librarians, such as her long-time friend Cathy Thompson, saw her as their 'scribe', composing poems for people leaving, organising book days, quoting Chaucer. 'But the abiding memory everyone has is of an exhausted Mahy falling asleep at her desk.'

Some fascinating scraps survive, in the library's Margaret Mahy Archives, of the scribe's contributions to in-house newsletters, such as the 'Library Advisor's Song', accompanied by an Edward Lear-style cartoon of a giant cat, with bearded librarian astride as driver, and behind him, back-to-back, a woman with a machine gun trained on a fierce pursuing dog:

> We always know just where we're at
> Travelling by trusty cat
> Petrol troubles are all gone
> Milk is what we travel on.
> On we speed, though once or twice
> We have to stop to take on mice.
> Goodbye to every mileage sorrow,
> Cats! The transport of tomorrow.

'A Library Christmas Carol or The Consolations of Literature' is also written and illustrated (lizard on trumpet, mouse on violin, hedgehog on drums) by Margaret Mahy. The librarians are discussing what to do with their library on the 24th of December.

> 'We should close the library down,' said one. 'No one ever comes in on the 24th of December. Everyone is busy buying balloons or posting a last minute Christmas card to Aunt Minnie or trying to get a card of Christmas string. No one comes into the library.'
> 'But somebody did come in once,' said a high minded librarian. 'Once some people from a lighthouse came in looking for books. Suppose we had been closed! Those people would have been denied the consolation of literature over Christmas.' All the librarians were silent. None of them wanted to deny members of the public the consolations of literature over Christmas.

No members of the public come, of course, but a man in a red coat and white whiskers does, and borrows

> . . . a book on woodwork, three detective stories and a thick book called 'An analysis of the work pressure systems revealed

by the dream of reindeer'. This book had only been issued once before.

'That was me,' said Mr S. Claus pointing to the date. 'I had this book out in 1947 and I've never forgotten the whole new field in reindeer-employer relationships it opened up for me. I don't know how to thank you for staying open on the 24th of December and letting me get this fine book out once more.'

'Yes I do!' he suddenly cried. 'You may keep that Christmas tree. It is loaded with rich gifts and seasonable viands and was intended for the Town Hall, but I'll give it to you instead . . .'

Virtue was rewarded. Librarians enjoyed the rich gifts, and when '5 past 5 came and they were legally allowed to go out and buy their last minute Christmas string, theirs were the most cheerful Government faces to be seen on the city streets . . .'

Librarians crop up in many of her stories as figures of fun. 'What has she got against the poor librarian?' asked one commentator. 'Apart from having been one for many years herself and therefore understanding what it is like to be a librarian, she sees in the image a dichotomy between form and disorder.' In *Cuckooland*, the television series that she was to write around 1985, Margaret hugely enjoyed the 'inappropriateness' of pairing up a librarian who heads a group called the Library Task Force who go out to reclaim books that have been kept overdue. 'They simultaneously have the persona of the librarian and also of the SAS. They arrive in a balloon and speak through a loud-speaker saying, "Mr Branchee, come out with the book above your head and you will not be harmed."' In other speeches she has noted that 'Jorge Luis Borges was national librarian of Argentina though he was blind, and the fact that he had 800,000 books in his library was apparently one of the few facts he ever bothered to remember. The post was a sinecure, and one he felt ironic about. Casanova was not only a writer but a librarian too, a fact not commonly noted. Still such illuminaries [*sic*] do not really define the profession, except to suggest how wide the abilities of librarians need to be.'

But she could also be deadly serious about libraries' roles in communities.

'Human beings are driven, within their cloud of limitation, to struggle towards some sort of understanding of what is going on around them. There isn't any escape. They live lives in which they observe, record, theorise, detect significant patterns, invent fairy tales that elucidate the human situation, and over and over again they need to record. Babies are given puzzles that challenge them to fit flat painted wooden horses into the empty horse-shaped spaces, and in a way we never outgrow such confrontations, though the shapes and the spaces grow stranger and the correspondences more tenuous. The library exists to maintain human records, but over and above that it also exists to impose form on the chaos of human perception and, through giving it form, to make it universally available. The library struggles with ambiguity, puts books on the shelves in an order that theoretically makes knowledge readily obtainable to all rate payers, and trains people to help other people when it comes to solving the increasingly complicated electronic maze which is also the respository of human information.'

Occasionally, for the local press, she would write encouraging, wise — and very funny — columns aimed at parents:

'Do you have anything on disasters?' asks an anxious mother. 'He needs something on disasters for a school project.'

The librarian answers her question by asking another.

'How long has he got to do the project?' and the parent looks both deprecating and anxious as she replies, 'He's got to have it in by tomorrow. He only mentioned it this morning at breakfast. You know what kids are.'

The librarian, quite possibly a parent as well as a librarian, knows what kids are and slides an apprehensive glance at the section of the non-fiction shelving that houses books on the world's great disasters. A suitable book may actually be there. What relief, what vindication of the library service if it is. And contrariwise, what feelings of inadequacy all round if the various books on disasters are all issued to other children for similar projects and the parent has to depart with a mere token earthquake or worse still, totally disasterless…

Many children, with or without their parents, never make it over the library threshold. The aura of intellectual privilege is too alarming, though the librarian tries to conceal this by cheerful displays and by cultivating an easy informality but many children and parents see through this and refuse to lower their defences. I recently encountered one mother, brought to the library by her daughter, who seemed about as comfortable there as a criminal in an electric chair. She apologised for being there at all, said she did not want to cause any trouble, mildly scolded the child for bothering the librarian (by asking for books on erosion) and then finally and rather wistfully admired a book with a pink and particularly pretty ballet dancer on the cover.

'Take it out!' I suggested. 'Take it home and look at it. You can have it on your daughter's card.' But she began retreating in little short scuttles, dismayed by this confrontation, saying as she left the library . . . 'No, no, I won't take it. I'll leave it for some other kind of people.'

I recall this mother very exactly because I feel I should have made her understand that the library belonged to her just as much as it did to me. Should I have been silent? More insistent? Whatever I should have done I failed to do and she left me there, monarch of all I surveyed, 'another kind of people'.

Between the person who knows exactly what the library is there to do, and the person who is unsure of anything about it except that it is full of hard books, there are many people who are well informed but want to be better informed.

A considerate parent gives children time to choose books — time to browse around and see what is to be seen. Sometimes of course one has to dash in and out, but children choosing books need a little bit of space. I recall one parent, very impatient with a book-loving child, saying over and over again, 'Take the first one on the shelf . . . it doesn't make any difference.' In fact, it makes a lot of difference and children should be given the chance to choose whenever possible.

Her own unique humour — ironic, self-mocking, subversive, sometimes sharp but always generous and never cruel — was now at her command. By the mid-1970s she was giving the serious, but occasionally comic and always entertaining speeches that, with new successes as a novelist, would take her all over the world in the 1980s.

A talk, she told an Australian audience in 1977, is not so dissimilar to a story: characters need to be established boldly, so she proceeded to describe herself:

'I am a solo mother aged forty-two, a really entertaining age. My oldest daughter is seventeen and the youngest is twelve. I am a full-time librarian — children's librarian at the Canterbury Public Library, Christchurch, New Zealand, and just over a week ago at two in the morning I had, for the first time, the experience of washing a young cat in warm soapy water (because it had fallen in a drain, not purely for personal diversion). I once drove a traction engine and I can go to sleep standing up or, very occasionally, walking. I have written twenty-seven or eight books and have been writing for thirty-five years, but I am still capable of making misjudgements in my own favour. I am capable of behaving in a terrible fashion — for instance once recently at an innocent library party I got drunk and ate the flower in somebody's buttonhole, not pretty behaviour in a children's librarian of forty-two. I live merely twenty-five to thirty minutes from the centre of Christchurch . . . but I am divorced from some of the amenities of civilisation having an outside chemical lavatory and being dependent on rainwater for a water supply. I am the custodian of four cats, four hens, a fat despicable dog, a rooster called Tarquin and a guinea pig. Once I had ten pheasants. I think reality is largely an act of the imagination but I am not very clear about who is doing the imagining. I live in a place which was once a volcano and is now a harbour. Someday it will be something else and so shall I. In fact, I am the usual mixture of fairly conforming public elements and singular personal elements. And yet the most important element of all is missing from that description. If I had to describe myself as one thing above all other I would describe myself as being a reader, meaning not just a person who reads, but a person who has, to some extent at least, been made by reading . . .

'. . . It may be worth recording that [my father's] catholic diet of stories, many of them read to me when I was about seven or eight, meant that I could identify with any mortal of any age or sex whose role in life interested me. I could identify with boys, girls, animals, with great white elephant hunters, pirates, cowboys and space men. It is true that when I was ten I was greatly interested in women like Belle Starr, Calamity Jane, Mary Read and Anne Bonney but for many years it seemed that the people with whom I identified most closely were middle-aged men travelling through underground caves, the pockets of their shooting jackets filled with diamonds. It resulted in a great build-up of energy that had to be used up somehow, and opportunities for travelling through underground caves with or without diamonds were very limited in Whakatane when I was a girl.

'Perhaps therefore the desire to belong in this compelling world of discomfort and adventure became too much for me. At any rate from the age of seven onwards I began writing stories.

'The effect of reading on the choices that people make is the subject of much speculation. There are probably degrees of resistance, some cultural, others, possibly innate . . . I have never found any account of the possibilities of influence or indifference that satisfied me . . . I know that many decisions I have made in the past have been made in an effort to match up with the challenges and excitements depicted in books. Some of these decisions, decisions about what to do next, have affected me for years. Others are more ephemeral. We live at one end of a road . . . a wild road in many ways, always on the look out for blood, throwing down rocks on travellers, or dissolving itself, crumpling its edges in slips. People do go over the side and fall sometimes hundreds of feet. I have a friend who escaped such a fall unscathed but every now and then someone is killed. In the winter when there is a heavy frost and the corners of this road are glassy with ice there is always the question of whether or not to take this treacherous road or to go by the easier, longer, less dramatic, less beautiful road through the tunnel. It sometimes seems we submit all such decisions to Allan Quartermain. High winds, frosts, trees down over the road or mysterious fog that makes strangers of familiar corners — all these journeys touched by these elements are journeys through an internal landscape as well as an outer one.

'As I stagger up the library steps on a frosty morning I say, aloud if need be "Well, another triumph for Allan Quartermain. Keep up the good work, Allan!" and similar encouragements. Rider Haggard's resourceful hero has become an emblem, a heraldic device, and I am not so much addressing him as some part of my imagination which he has come to symbolise — a sort of imaginative energy which can be released and used by locating and invoking the emblem that is its representative . . .

'Rather than thinking of imagination as the ability to summon into being the vision of things that have no real existence I think of it as the ability to work creatively with reality. It may sometimes choose to entertain itself, sometimes very meaningfully, by invention by producing the sort of sub creation that Tolkien names and describes (he goes on to say that such fantasy produces in us recovery, escape and consolation) but part of its work is to provide us with symbols and analogies that give us some sort of control over an incredibly complex world. (Incidentally Tolkien, for no doubt very sound scholastic reasons, would disagree with my view, thinking imagination simply the power of summoning creative images.) At any rate I want to express an opinion that imagination is not simply a pretty decoration hung around the neck of humanity but a working part of the intellect. Part of our intellectual process in an essential way, promoting survival rather than hindering it. And I would like to speculate that children's stories, the myths and legends, tales of adventure and love and laughter with which their society presents them (and today this mostly means children's books) operate with great power, not only establishing a present relationship but actually determining what the adult imagination is going to find acceptable.'

In the second half of the 1970s the picture books kept coming: four in 1975, two, including one of her best, *The Wind Between the Stars*, in 1976, three in 1977, one each in 1978 and 1979, and Horrakapotchin! — none in 1980. This was the only year between 1969 and 2004 when there has not been at least one new Mahy book (and sometimes four or more) on the market. By the eve of the new decade, royalties were coming in from some 21 picture books, in English and a number of translations, also from six collections of stories and three junior novels. *School Journal* stories and poems (more than 60 had been published in over 20 years) would continue to bring in money, though these always involved only one-off payments, no royalties. In addition, income could be generated from school visits, from speeches and very likely from other areas of writing, such as the burgeoning educational market and children's television, developing strongly at the time. Full-time writing at last seemed possible.

In another major Australian speech, given in Melbourne in 1978, Margaret talked about the unresolved problem of being a New Zealand writer in a global market, and of that fault line that still 'divided my interior landscape from my outside one, from my town, from my home . . . Some component, some correspondence was missing. "Every writer," says V.S. Naipaul, himself in an ambivalent position, "is, in the long run on his own, but it helps in the most practical way to have a tradition. The English language was mine but the English tradition was not." I was not altogether in Naipaul's situation. The English language was mine, and disconcertingly, so was the powerful and beautiful English tradition. But I was not English, and nor were others like me.

'This then is a circular problem. We cannot exist as total New Zealanders until our imaginative focus, our imaginative reality is established and the fault line that separates inner and outer landscapes is bridged, or until the power of our collective vision applies pressure and makes both landscapes move together. We cannot become New Zealanders in our imagination until someone has already become a New Zealander in his or her imagination and said, "Look. This is what there is to see. Listen. This is what there is to hear. That light between rose and lavender colour that falls on the thin soil and rocky outcrops of the hills around Lyttelton harbour once fell on those hills when they were the walls of a volcano, not of a harbour. Come over these hills in the evening and there are places where there are no houses to be seen and such trees as there are have been absorbed back into the shadows. The lush landscape you so often see promoting New Zealand in tourist brochures is never present here, and now in your imagination the world has become ever starker and leaner and you are back in Gondwanaland, the old continent, with the ancient ocean Tethys sighing at the edge of the land. This is something that perhaps you can see. And listen: even the sounds are ranked, each marking its place in time — the bleating sheep and the distant barking dog, the older sound of the bellbird; wind, oldest of all, and the silence that underlies all sounds underlying these. On these hills our eyes and our ears make time travellers of us, particularly if there is a writer to give us the passwords."

'Fortunately this circle is not a closed circle. Little by little people make breakthroughs, catch accents, see details and pass on their discoveries about them. No need to copy — once someone has succeeded, successors have a place to stand, and with language for a lever, they can be Archimedes moving the world in some private direction.'

In this speech Margaret also gave a shrewd and frank assessment, as librarian and writer, of the problems still facing children's publishers in New Zealand, where mostly older writers, still capable of submitting manuscripts of children playing in snow in Nelson at Christmas, were caught in the same trap as artists who attempted, unconvincingly, to draw Maori or early builders who built their houses facing south, because, 'in their building imagination, south-facing houses were strongly established and that was what they built, because the reality inside mattered more than the reality outside'.

She was unusually blunt about the standard of those books that were published 'by New Zealanders, featuring New Zealand, many of them dreadful enough to justify the common suspicion among New Zealanders of the recent past that a thing produced within the country was bound to be of poor quality'. Though sympathising with local publishers' difficulties in a small market, she declared that, in her opinion, 'our local publishers frequently lack precision and inspiration in their judgement, and books are slow selling because they are books of only moderate quality . . . and their promotion in the book shops is often very casual'. New Zealand–British co-publication was a possible answer; more professional book production was another, as was more government support, especially in the form of equal recognition for picture books in Authors' Fund payouts. (This fund compensates authors for the borrowing of their books from public libraries; in 2004, picture book writers and illustrators are still disadvantaged.) More awards and grants would also help; it was, she concluded, an altogether uneasy and anxious scene. She ended this talk on a personal and significant note, signalling the coming change in her focus and, possibly, her own career:

'I find myself in an odd but by no means unique situation where my own writing and publishing life is concerned. The stories that I write are published overseas, they are illustrated overseas. I sometimes don't see the illustrations until the books turn up in my letterbox, so that in a way I am an expatriate writer, even while I live within New Zealand and don't ever contemplate living anywhere else. Everything that happens with the production of my stories takes place at some point of removal and I think that this is a very strange state of affairs. I have a friend in Christchurch [Gavin Bishop] who has illustrated and written a story which is in due course, I understand, to be produced by Oxford University Press. He is looking forward to joining in the production of this book throughout the whole process. Now I might not want to do that, but I think that one of the things I would love to do is to work with an illustrator on a book. There is no real reason I suppose why I shouldn't do this, except the usual lack of time, and the commitments that already exist to people overseas.

'Nevertheless, I do feel that I have come to a point where I would write a story which had a New Zealand setting, but that setting of New Zealand would be inside the character, they wouldn't be "living in New Zealand", New Zealand would be inside them. Like myself, the characters would have to incorporate the fault lines, the uneven movement of volcanoes becoming harbours that are part of the landscape . . . It is an enviable position perhaps to be in, having to make a tradition. If I have any ambitions for myself as a writer for children and for other writers in New Zealand, my ambitions would be that we would make it possible for our children to build houses that don't have to face south.'

She would not regret leaving full-time library work, much as she had enjoyed it.

'Back then when I really was a librarian at the front desk,' she wrote in 2003, 'there were times when someone would come in and ask, say, for a red-covered book about wild horses remembered from a first reading back in 1946. Not always, but on a significant number of occasions, I was able to recognise from such intangible clues the very book they were searching for. Such successes filled me with an enormous pleasure, as if I had truly become, at last, the witch I had once claimed to be. I had found something I was good at. But the prospect of more money moves librarians away from the confrontations of the front desk to other less rewarding puzzles like staff organisation, writing reports and so on — all excellent and necessary work in the contact between order and chaos, but not front-desk work any more. I had left my particular area of excellence behind me. As an administrator I was never as good a librarian as I had been at the front desk, knowing how and where to find that longed-for book. In due course I left the library and became, at last, a full-time writer.'

Part Four

The Full-time Novelist —
1980 to 1993

The transition, in 1980, from five-day-a-week librarian and part-time writer to full-time writer working from the solitude of home, required faith and courage. With this new, hard-earned 'gift of time', Margaret sat down to daily (and often nocturnal) hours at the typewriter, 'delighted with the new space in my head'.

No longer would her modest and unreliable cars have to negotiate the steep road up and over the Port Hills to the Christchurch library and back twice a day, its driver frequently doing battle (after only a few hours' sleep) with rain, gusty winds, cloud, smog, ice and, occasionally, snow. Her house was still tiny, and would have an outside loo for some years yet, but it was homely with toys, cover artwork, small statues, china cats, masks, paintings and photographs gathered up in ten years of increasingly public life, as well as family clutter and ever more books. Progress was being made in the garden, too. Penny, now 20, had been away from home since she was seventeen; Bridget agreed to spend a year at boarding school so her mother could spend more time writing. Realising that Governors Bay was not a great place for teenagers, Margaret allowed both her daughters to get their driving licences at fifteen, which she described as 'a very scary thing for a parent. If they were late home — and they often were — I'd worry.'

The decision to leave the library was a huge turning point. 'I was 44 when I finally went full time and I had reached a stage in my life where I felt I would stop writing if I didn't. I was starting to fall asleep over my stories at night. I'd had one or two things rejected and I'd started things and hadn't finished them or rushed through stories too quickly because of time pressure. I had a lot of ideas but I didn't seem to be able to do anything with them, so I decided to have a go at being a full time writer. I'd always wanted to, but I had all the anxieties of making a living and financing the mortgage and I wasn't sure how I would manage. When I finally took the plunge . . . I swore I'd do anything that was compatible with self-respect, to make money.' Though she had written three short children's novels, *Clancy's Cabin* (1974), *The Bus Under the*

Leaves (1975) and *The Pirate Uncle* (1977), she had no conscious intention of immediately embarking upon further long fiction. But two unfinished stories that had 'grown too long and somehow too complex to think about' suddenly presented themselves as possible novels.

Compared with the earlier novellas, the story that became *The Haunting* was a 'rather different kettle of fish' and she found herself 'rather thrilled with what I was writing. Both this and *The Changeover* came quite easily, because I'd been thinking unconsciously about them for some time, carrying them around, you know, while doing ordinary things. After I'd finished the first one, it seemed that Tabitha was quite a self-portrait: the talkative girl who wants to write, quite bossy and commanding, managing to work mention of my stories into conversations in an effort to show other people how interesting I was.' The key role played by the silent, powerful, mysterious older sister Troy in the dramatic dénouement takes most readers by surprise, but Margaret mildly rebuffs any suggestion of deliberate 1970s feminism. 'I didn't then and in many ways still don't have very strong politically feminist intentions. However, being a female I suppose that means a certain set of experiences at my command, and there are times when I quite like making a strong female character.'

The Haunting did, though, establish an often mentioned characteristic of the novels: that, in almost all her stories, the women appear to be stronger than men. They are either bringing up a family on their own and trying to juggle careers and looking after a home, like Margaret herself; or they have suffered and been made stronger by the experience; or they exchange roles with men. The girls, too, generally show more initiative than the boys. This is not because Mahy thinks men are weak but because she has been surrounded by strong women: 'I've lived in a family where there have been a lot of women, most of them fairly resilient and fairly tough. They've had their troubles, but they've come through without becoming alcoholic or having nervous breakdowns, or becoming nasty about the world, or bitter.'

She knew she was 'almost possessed' while writing *The Haunting*. 'Suddenly everything that happened to me, everything that anyone said, seemed to connect up with the story. Other writers have had this experience too: you have an idea for a novel and suddenly there are all these strange signs of it in the outside world: "Look, there it is again." . . . I'd finished writing the novel and suddenly realised that I'd written all about myself in it without ever once realising it. Now that's scary.'

Even more disconcerting was the realisation that the young girl, Tabitha, in whom she recognised herself, was, in the words of *Listener* writer Pamela Stirling, 'not the sort of person whom the book necessarily suggests that one should feel very sympathetic towards. Tabitha, in fact, is a real pain. The problem is that Tabitha, whom Mahy describes in *The Haunting* as "having the important, excited look of a person swollen out with secrets", is such an extremely *talkative* child. Tabitha talks. And talks. Despite being with "stuck with ordinariness", Tabitha is determined to be a world-famous writer, and she never stops reminding people of it. Much of her prattling is quite entertaining . . . It's just that Tabitha never shuts up.' As Stirling reported, 'Mahy was quite honest about the problem of "unbridled ego" in a child. Like Tabitha, she would often, as a child, find a way of "showing off" the fact that she was writing a story. "I can remember carrying my notebooks around in an effort to introduce them into the conversation." When she was five, her idea of striking up a mature conversation with an adult was to say something like, "And would you happen to know if there are any woodpeckers in this district?" When one of her uncles once threatened to cut out her tongue, she wept bitterly: "Not because I thought he'd do it, but because he obviously wasn't enjoying my conversation."'

In what seems at first deceptively like a short family fantasy novel, *The Haunting* demonstrates the key aspects of Margaret's long fiction: the family setting supercharged with fantastical or supernatural elements, and the genius for twisting and twisting and again twisting a story until something extraordinary emerges.

Barney is thought to be the one grappling with inheriting the absent uncle's powers, but no, it is his older sister, the brooding Troy; furthermore, in the penultimate chapter, the most malevolent power in the family is discovered to reside in the austere old great-grandmother, one of the most memorable of Margaret's many old crones.

The Haunting was launched by Dent's in Britain in 1982, and published in the States by Atheneum in New York. Critical acclaim on both sides of the Atlantic, and in Australia and New Zealand, was immediate, consistent — and surprised. In Britain, the influential *Junior Bookshelf* critic wrote: 'We know Miss Mahy best as a distinguished writer of texts for picture books. It has always been clear that this is one of the most taxing of all literary exercises. It comes nevertheless as a surprise to discover what a commanding writer of the full-length novel she is. *The Haunting* is masterly in its conception and above all in the way it uses words to overcome scepticism and to give a vivid actuality to a fantastic theme.

'The theme, and the mechanics of its magic, are handled with the mastery of a virtuoso performer. But the strength of the book lies in the way Miss Mahy relates the fantasy to the relationships of ordinary life. The Scholars and the Palmers may be unusual but they are real people, and it matters greatly to the reader that the harmony of their lives should not be destroyed. Even Great-Granny Scholar, "a terrible old lady, a small, thin witch, frail but furious", is not only convincing but sympathetic. These positive factors would in themselves make this a most memorable book. What lifts it into an altogether higher class is the way Miss Mahy tells her story, using words as if they came fresh from the mint. Here's Tabitha, on the subject of Great-Granny Scholar: "I don't mind her being wrinkled. It's just that all her wrinkles are so angry. She's like a wall with furious swear words scribbled all over it."'

For the American *School Library Journal*, Michael Cart, from the Beverly Hills Public Library, commented: 'Here is an

absolutely first-rate contemporary novel of the supernatural
. . . The principal characters — Barney and the members of his
family — are beautifully drawn, and perhaps because they care
so much for each other, readers care for them too. Their growth
and development as individuals and as members of a family unit
are as important to the story as its supernatural chills, thrills and
puzzlements, a fact that lends this genre book unusual richness.'

In New Zealand, children's book authority Tom Fitzgibbon
described *The Haunting* as 'a plea for the liberating power of the
imagination with all its richness and poetry against those like the
Great Granny who repress life into a series of rigid lines', while
the Australian commentator Agnes Nieuwenhuizen thought it 'a
dazzling piece of writing . . . crammed with extraordinary images
and similes which infuse ordinary events and small domestic
details in the lives of children with fresh and deep significances.
Mahy's characterisations and portrayals of the nuances, fears and
strength of family life are superb.'

Consistent with Margaret's previous work and the story's
folk tale associations, *The Haunting* is set in some unspecified
Western country. She told one audience:

'Many people comment on the lack of setting for *The Haunting*.
Readers in Australia began thinking it was set in the USA. Some
people have thought that it was set in England. There is a family
living a reasonably realistic day to day life. They garden, wash
dishes, go to school, feel concerned for one another and all in a
sort of void. There is reference to a city and to hills, but there is
no statement of place . . . [It is] the landscape of the imagination,
with little idiom or local reference . . . The fairy tale, however, is
universal. The family story, even when it calls on folk tale sources,
is somehow unique.'

A later assessment, by Stephanie Nettell in the new edition of
The Haunting as a Puffin Classic, told a new generation of young
readers that a 'straight ghost story was not nearly enough for
Margaret Mahy. She also wanted to give you a glittering fantasy
about enchanters, and a family saga, about the misery inflicted on

one generation by an angrily unhappy mother and reawakening of another by a loving young stepmother. And then she gives us still one more story, about the secret anxieties of a small boy . . . her glimpses of magic are thrilling, full of mystery and beauty . . . By the end of the book you realise there are, in truth, no evil villains, only confused, despairing people. The construction of *The Haunting* is flawless . . . its action takes place within a few days in the life of one family, and encapsulates her philosophy as neatly as any of her more complex books for older readers.'

The Haunting also marked a new and important phase in Margaret's relationship with her British editor, Vanessa Hamilton. South-African born, slight in stature but of energetic personality, Vanessa combined editorial skill with a boundless enthusiasm for Margaret's writing, sustained over three decades, and continuing after Vanessa left Dent around 1988 to become a literary agent and freelance editor right up to her death in January 2002.

Few authors enjoy such long-standing consistency and commitment, leading to confidence, trust and deep friendship. For every book, as in-house and later freelance editor, Vanessa edited the text, chose and guided illustrators and designers; Margaret often did not see the illustrations until the last proof stage or even until the completed book, but trusted Vanessa's judgement. As her agent, Vanessa attended to contracts for new books, for translations (any one book might have as many as fifteen translations) and for reprints, when the rights reverted, as they normally did after a period of time, to the author. Managing the fast-growing Mahy backlist was in itself a huge, never-ending task. There were frequent long-distance phone calls between London and Governors Bay, and lengthy faxes, then emails.

Vanessa was usually the first person to see any Mahy manuscript, although Margaret would often have read it first to her daughters, especially Bridget, and valued their comments. Margaret never viewed editors as potential adversaries determined to prevail in any dispute and put their stamp on the manuscript, though in 1992, as her output became ever more international, she was to write of the difficulties of working with three different editors: her agent, the publisher's editor and then the American editors who could be 'diabolical', wanting to change vocabulary unfamiliar to American children. '[A] bit prudish, unexpectedly moral', they did not like references to sex, alcohol and violence — although, with typical pragmatism, she conceded that book sales were the crucial factor and editors were not 'quite as wishy-washy as I make them sound'.

Margaret has been generous, respectful and professional towards the many editors she has worked with. 'Good editors can take the place of passing time, can read with fresh judgement and be of great help, particularly towards the end of the process, which is usually when they come in. I hope for an editor who has better mechanical skills than I have, more business contacts and acumen. And whose judgement, while it may more or less parallel my own, will be more incisive and constructive at the final stage of the story. Much editorial comment on my stories is concerned with the fact that I tend to make things too long. The editor also picks out incoherencies of various kinds, both verbal and in terms of the action of the plot. I suppose one is always upset at some level by criticism, but it is essential, and at times, can even be welcome because the editor has seen a way to improve things which you, as author, have been unable to see.'

There was no respite in Governors Bay when reviews for *The Haunting* started to arrive. The second short-story-turned-novel, becoming a longer and more complex narrative than anticipated, was well under way; there were always smaller stories being worked at simultaneously as ideas struck; and even more invitations to conferences which required the researching and writing of major speeches. Margaret never took these appearances lightly, or trundled out earlier talks. Some, such as the long, scholarly, lengthy assessment of 'attitudes to children in early Australian and New Zealand children's books', delivered to a librarians' conference in 1981, drew on her library experience. Others, such as the challenging discussion of the relative 'truths' of fiction and non-fiction and the dichotomy between art and science, presented to a gathering of teachers in 1982, offered the opportunity for an intellectual workout.

The overwhelmingly positive reaction to her first serious novel must have been gratifying, but no one was prepared for what happened next: a phone call from London, early in 1983, advising that *The Haunting* had been shortlisted for the Carnegie Medal, given annually by the British Library Association for the best children's book published in Britain in 1982. Then Margaret heard that she had won the Carnegie: would she please arrange a flight to London.

In the history of New Zealand literature, there are few comparable achievements, most notably Keri Hulme winning the 1985 Booker Prize for *the bone people*. The Carnegie is the Olympic medal for children's writing, the ultimate seal of approval from the English-speaking world's strongest literary tradition.

Bursting with delight but sworn to absolute secrecy, even from her family, Margaret hit upon a practicable solution only she would have come up with. Aunt Francie, now housed in a small cottage next door bought by her niece, was suffering from Alzheimer's and remembered nothing she was told. 'Aunty, I've won the *Carnegie Medal*!' 'How splendid,' her 84-year-old aunt answered, blissfully unaware that Margaret was about to join a pantheon of children's writers that began with Arthur Ransome in 1936 and included Noel Streatfeild, Eric Linklater, Walter de la Mare, Elizabeth Goudge, Eleanor Farjeon, Rosemary Sutcliff, Philippa Pearce, Penelope Lively, C.S. Lewis, Alan Garner, K.M. Peyton, Anne Fine, Berlie Doherty, Jan Mark, Gillian Cross, Robert Swindells, David Almond, Aidan Chambers, Terry Pratchett and Philip Pullman — and the only other writer from outside Britain or America, the Australian novelist Ivan Southall, who won the Carnegie for *Josh* in 1971.

Margaret's new award-winning stature cranked up the demand for appearances, both around New Zealand and internationally. Shortly after travelling to Britain to receive her

Carnegie Medal, she paid her first visit to Auckland schools, to entertain more than 1500 children in West Auckland classrooms over a period of three days, with adult gatherings at night. To the organisers of that author tour (and to many since), her immediate appeal to children and performing skills surpassed expectations, and there was 'apparently no limit to her affability and stamina'. The Carnegie Medal was celebrated with 'extreme delight and excitement', particularly by her elderly mother who had made the long trip up from Whakatane specially to hear her famous eldest daughter speak for the first time.

Only two years later, Margaret won a second Carnegie Medal for her second novel, *The Changeover: a supernatural romance*, still regarded by many as her finest piece of fiction. Only four other authors, Jan Mark, Peter Dickinson, Berlie Doherty and Anne Fine, have ever won the award twice, and Margaret Mahy is the only one of the four from outside Britain.

The Changeover was her first work for the slightly older age group known as young adults (YA). Vanessa Hamilton had been jubilant when she received the manuscript, writing to say that there was almost nothing she wanted changed. As Margaret has noted, the young adult genre entails special considerations: 'It is to do with the difference between writing books for adults and writing even for young adults. Elements of melodrama (though I must admit I quite like them in adult books) are quite desirable in books for young adults. Partly it's because it's often a more florid and melodramatic and less ironic time of life. People are looking very anxiously for something that's going to make them marvellous. Whereas, as you get older, you make more use of irony.'

Told of the news of her second Carnegie win, Margaret was 'absolutely swept away. *The Haunting* had come right out of the blue. With *The Changeover* I knew it was a possibility, but when I heard that it had won, it was with a different sort of astonishment. I didn't think it would win, not twice to the same person quite like that.'

She was unable to attend the second Carnegie ceremony so her acceptance speech, vintage Mahy, was read by Vanessa Hamilton.

'The pleasures of being awarded the Carnegie Medal are unlimited. My delight in winning it in 1983 was so great, and I spoke about it with such fervour when given the opportunity, that, though I was equally overwhelmed by winning it a second time, I find I have already said all the easiest things. It does not seem enough to reiterate that I was surprised and delighted (both true reactions) particularly as it was a different surprise and a different delight, the first occasion reaching out of the past to alter the second . . .

'Accepting the medal for *The Haunting*, I told a story about my aunt who lives with me. Having lost her memory to a great extent her comments, now detached from the world of reality, have the enigmatic quality of oracular utterance. When the news that *The Changeover* had won the medal was announced in New Zealand it was featured on the national evening news. A reporter came with a cameraman and interviewed me in my house. More material than is going to be used is always recorded, and, since I felt I had answered some of the questions well and others not so well, I was actively interested in finding out just which answers it had been decided to make public. Not only that, I was uneasy about how I was going to *look*. Sometimes when I appear on television in New Zealand, a make-up woman at the studio improves me enormously, making me look smoother and more or less the same colour all over. But on my home ground I felt the truth would show, and, exposed on television, who could possibly want that? After all, television ought to leave the truth alone and concentrate on illusion which it does very well.

'In the evening, reinforced by my daughter and my aunt, I sat poised in front of the television, listening impatiently to trivial accounts of famine, terrorism and economic recession, waiting for the *real* news to be announced. "Margaret Mahy does it again," said the announcer. I was about to find out just what it was I had said earlier in the day. However, at the sound of my name my aunt sat up quite sharply and an expression of great pleasure crossed her face. "Margaret Mahy!" she cried, "I used to know her. Well, I'm interested to have heard that, and the next time I'm in Whakatane I'll tell her mother I saw this. *My* father used to write you know, and he was a great help to us with our school work . . ." And so on and so on through a fine, old family anecdote. I never ever heard what I actually said on television. I wasn't meant to know. The oracle had spoken, and all I could do was listen to my aunt and watch my own face, every bit as faulty as I had suspected it would be. How old I look! I thought, so you see the moment turned out to be far richer and more mysterious than I could have imagined.

'This in an oblique way of coming to the point which is this: that excellence, an area of great confusion to start with, is composed of many parts, and no matter what excellence a book achieves in the author's head, and later, unrolling through the typewriter, there is an important aspect of excellence that only comes into existence when people read the book. That is the point where the book begins to work. Obviously I want to write books that work for people. This particular aspect of excellence is composed, in part, of elements that the readers bring with them, in interrogations which I cannot guess at, except in the most general terms. I want with a great deal of anxiety to know what my editors think, what librarians think and what readers think of anything I have written. For these people are my professional family . . . I think most writers know they have a limited bag of tricks, and there is no such thing as a story that is ever good enough. Somewhere, there is a wonderful story, a platonic *form* of story, promising infinite amazement and wonder, never worn out by repetition. Readers and writers reach out for it continually, tracing it through other stories that come their way. To receive the Carnegie Medal is a way of being reassured that some people have traced something of that marvellous still unwritten story in one's own writing.

'Virginia Woolf wrote: "What is the use of saying one is

indifferent to reviews when positive praise, though mingled with some blame, give one such a start-on, that instead of feeling dried up one feels flooded with ideas."

'I think that is what I really wanted to tell you — that this award fills me with elation, not just because it is good to feel one has done well, but because it also makes one feel released to new possibilities, infinite and undefined, but somehow *there*. One may hope to do even better. I know I am, that we *all* are, part of a pattern of shared excitement and response as old as human kind, and possibly, since we can't be certain of the exact nature of creation, as old as time itself.'

The genesis of *The Changeover* is now part of the Mahy mythology, and probably known to many a children's librarian, or teacher, who has stamped an inky image on a young child's soft, trusting hand.

'One day when I was working at the front desk in the library a woman and a little boy were taking books out and the child smiling with pleasure put out his hand to have a Mickey Mouse stamp on it. I often put stamps on children's hands in those days, taking pleasure in making them clear and straight. On this occasion however I suddenly felt very sinister, as if I were a goblin king branding a stolen child of a slave. I felt myself acting out something of this ominous thought, looming over the child and putting the stamp on his hand. Then, filled with dismay at myself I glanced rapidly and placatingly at the child's mother, who stood by smiling and having no idea, I hope, of what was passing through the kindly librarian's mind. This incident was the beginning of the book *The Changeover* which I originally saw as a short story about the impossibility of retreating to a state of innocent once innocence has been exchanged for knowledge. You can't forget what you know — or if you do you are subjecting yourself to a sort of violence. You don't become innocent again. Like the idea for *The Haunting* before it, this idea attracted action and characters too varied to make a satisfactory short story . . . there is no doubt that, once I had that initiating moment, which sprang from every day experience in my power, it immediately made connections with a lot of other things I was unaware of, but it is also true that the experience I described took the form it did because I was monitoring the world as the possessor of a literary imagination. Though later I was to have little goes at being both Laura and Sorenson Carlisle, the first person I acted out was Carmody Braque, the evil and pathetic spirit of the story stuck in a perpetual immaturity. There might be a lesson to learn from this but on the whole I try not to think about it much. In my head at least fantasy and real life are Siamese twins, joined at the heart. *The Changeover* springing from a real event expressed itself from the beginning as fantasy but immediately attracted all the reinforcement of real experience to such an extent that some people object to it, and others, often teenage girls, assume that I have had supernatural experiences myself, which I have never had. I am a determined rationalist.'

With the starting point of the stamp, and drawing on themes that had been in her head for some years, Margaret began writing the manuscript 'on the same level as *The Haunting*, with Laura having an encounter with a girl at school who turned out to have supernatural powers. I wrote a certain way into the story, but something was a bit flat, not satisfying. Then I suddenly thought to make the girl into a male character and immediately I found the possibilities of the book changing. It stretched up a level and it became a YA novel, and the sexual relationship between Sorry and Laura became quite different. The underlying idea was of one of the Grimm fairy tales, though there are all sorts of folk tale connections, but it's also the story of a romance, of a girl growing into a new maturity and power for herself, so that a changeover variety of relatively realistic elements are involved along with folk tale. It came quite quickly.'

The Changeover is dedicated 'to Bridget and other midnight visitors'.

'At this time, Bridget and I lived in Governors Bay and she, along with her friends, were about 14 — too young to legitimately drive over the hill and restructured, when it came to social life, to what was next door or just down the road. I worked late at that stage — well into the early hours of the morning and restless adolescents were likely to turn up, regularly, at our house as late as 11 o'clock at night and sit around talking into the early hours of the morning. There are many stories I could tell about this time in my life, many of them disreputable by a sort of displacement. However the point I am making is that I did hear, from out in the kitchen, as I made yet another cup of coffee, the authentic voices of New Zealand teenagers. They were in the air around me.'

The last stages of the novel were written in 1984 while Margaret was writer in residence at the university where she had graduated more than 20 years earlier. The choice of the first children's writer to win a New Zealand university fellowship against 'adult' contenders raised a few eyebrows. 'I was told, as one so often is, that there was opposition to the appointment on the grounds that I was not an academic writer.' One interviewing staff member, journalism teacher Brian Priestley, was apparently bemused enough by the prospect to explode, 'Goodness, for the life of me I can't imagine what a children's writer is doing at a university!' Margaret reportedly replied, 'So I told him — I need the money. He nodded well yes, there is that, there is that.' As the *University Chronicle* reported in March 1984, this was an author who insisted that writing for children was not something totally detached from the rest of literature, but simply a genre with a very special character; like many authors she still wrote her first drafts in longhand, in old but large diaries, then typing second and third drafts often late at night, using music and coffee to keep awake.

The university year was inevitably one of concentrated work but also distractions: students, schools, journalists and, increasingly, readers' letters all deflecting her from the final stages of *The Changeover*, intensive work on two further novels, the beginning of a film adaptation of *The Haunting*, and the new venture of plays and adaptations for Christchurch's Court Theatre and Canterbury Children's Theatre. It also, however, offered her the chance to become a student again: she enrolled for the philosophy of science and the philosophy of art at 200 level.

The reviews for *The Changeover* were as good as any author would ever hope to get, and translations into ten or more languages were soon under way.

Once again, some critics expressed their surprise. 'Who would've expected such a triumph from her first attempt at a full-length novel for older children?' wrote one British columnist. 'Well, any admirer of Margaret Mahy's possibly. In a couple of dozen books she'd already testified to her conviction that "a fairy tale is often the truest way of talking about real life . . . that humour has a more spiritual function that people are prepared to admit".' Margery Fisher, who had hosted Margaret on her first visit to Britain eleven years earlier, wrote in *Growing Point* that here was a book 'about the whole human condition encapsulated in one small part. This is no thin blueprint for growing up. It is a metaphor for living rising out of a recognised, sharply drawn picture of reality . . . this new story triumphantly fulfils the promise which has for so long tantalised the admirers of Margaret Mahy's picture book texts and short stories.' Another English reviewer said that *The Changeover* went 'well beyond a simple story of witchcraft to achieve a moral and psychological subtlety similar to that in the stories of the great British fantasists C.S. Lewis and J.R.R. Tolkien'.

American reviews were equally enthusiastic. At the 1985 American Library Association (ALA) annual conference, the editor of the Centre for Children's Books at the University of Chicago, Betsy Hearne, spoke of *The Changeover* as a book that fulfils both popular and literary criteria, explaining that it had been 'selected as an ALA Notable Children's Book, a YASD [Young Adult Services Division] Best Book for young adults, a School Library Journal Best Book, and an ALA Booklist Editor's Choice. In at least two of those selection panels, the vote was unanimous . . . Its critical success is unquestionable.' The influential *Kirkus Review* stated: 'Again, as in *The Haunting*, New Zealand writer

Margaret Mahy proves that all-out supernatural stories can still be written with intelligence, humour, and a fearful intensity that never descends into pretentious murk or lurid sensationalism . . . Mahy thus invests the occult evils here with a metaphorical, psychological undertow; at the same time, however, while filling out all the characters (including the witches) with textured charm, she never stints on thoroughgoing creeps and scares. In sum, the best supernatural YA fiction around, with Stephen King power and Mahy's own class and polish.'

And Sarah Hayes in the *Times Literary Supplement*: 'The double aspect of things — man and beast, good and evil, young and old — intrigues Margaret Mahy. In the manner of all good supernaturalists, her stories always have a perfectly possible rational explanation. This one could be about the products of a young girl's fevered imagination during a period of physical and emotional turmoil; or about the influence of a boy traumatised by a cruel foster father and years of psychotherapy; or about a miracle cure, a single parent, and a dirty old man. These explanations are never offered, merely there for the reader to think about if he chooses.

'It is rare to find a novel which captures so well the changeover from child to adult, and from what is real in the mind to what is real outside. Readers who have grown up with Margaret Mahy will recognise here that land of infinite possibilities, discovered out there so many years ago by the lion who might or might not have been in the meadow.'

For a writer so firmly linked to picture books, *The Changeover* required a new appreciation of Margaret's work. This was indisputably a young adult novel, and as one British interviewer wrote, the story contained 'some heady stuff then, and Margaret Mahy was keen for readers to be warned. There was the sub title, the blurb and the fairly disturbing cover picture on the hardback. "I did the best I could. But I still find people who haven't picked up the clues and who give the book to a nine-year-old 'because she's such a good reader'. People must have to take some responsibility.

You can't say that such books shouldn't be published, any more than you can say we shouldn't have the sea, just because a few people will go in too deep."'

Some praise was, inevitably, qualified. In his 1990 book of essays on contemporary writers of fiction for children and young adults, *What Do Draculas Do*, British novelist and commentator David Rees wrote of a 'considerable difference in quality' between Margaret's two Carnegie winners. '*The Changeover* is a rich, powerful many-layered novel that thoroughly deserved its award, but *The Haunting*, well done though it is, seems rather a slight work to be given such a prestigious accolade as the Carnegie . . . *The Changeover* is on an altogether different plane. It is another tale of the supernatural . . . but "changeover" is a double metaphor: this is also a realistic book about an adolescent girl experiencing another kind of shift, that of becoming adult and adjusting to new relationships, particularly with her mother . . . on a third level it is a romantic women's magazine type novel about Laura's relationship with her boyfriend, Sorry Carlisle . . . The mixing of such different genres could have been a recipe for disaster, but the triumph of *The Changeover* is that the author manages to fuse all three with total success . . .'

Rees was, however, critical of what he regarded as the lost opportunity 'to reveal a unique place and culture' to the outside world: 'if readers expect New Zealand to be a central issue, as Australia is in the work of Patricia Wrightson and Ivan Southall, they will be disappointed'. He cited Wrightson and Southall, and English writers like Jane Gardam, Lucy Boston and William Mayne, and Americans like Virginia Hamilton, who 'make their own particular patch a major theme for their books . . . but Margaret Mahy does not find this important'. Place is there in her work, he conceded, but 'with the exception of the differences between the seasons (Christmas in *The Tricksters*) we could be almost anywhere in either the northern or southern hemisphere'. He also speculated, incorrectly, that Margaret's career seemed to be following the not uncommon phenomenon of 'growing up' with her own children, like, say, Penelope Farmer, who moved from picture books to teenage and then to novels for adults. 'But with Margaret Mahy, the approach to a novel has been remarkably gradual. Thirteen years is a long time to spend being a prolific creator of fiction and *not* write a novel.' A New Zealand commentator, even unaware of Margaret's story but familiar with the bleak local publishing environment and the attitudes of overseas editors, would not have made such observations. ('I think it was *The Changeover*,' Margaret has said, 'where the editor said it's wonderful to have a New Zealand story and then proceeded to cut out a lot of New Zealand references.')

Few reviewers anywhere remarked on the consciously New Zealand setting of *The Changeover*, a first in Margaret's writing. And that setting was not a farm, bush or beach, but, much less common in contemporary New Zealand children's literature, a city. As Margaret wrote in the postscript to the 2003 Collins Modern Classic edition, 'this was the first story that adequately repaired an imaginative displacement within me,' even a 're-entry,' but she had not been able to resist an ironic little in-joke in the opening paragraphs of the novel:

Although the label on the hair shampoo said Paris and had a picture of a beautiful girl with the Eiffel Tower behind her bare shoulder, it was forced to tell the truth in tiny print under the picture. *Made in New Zealand*, it said, *Wisdom Laboratories, Paraparaumu.*

Just for a moment Laura had had a dream of washing her hair and coming out from under the shower to find she was not only marvellously beautiful but also transported to Paris. However, there was no point in washing her hair if she were only going to be moved as far as Paraparaumu. Beside, she knew her hair would not dry in time for school, and she would spend half the morning with chilly ears. These were facts of everyday life, and being made in New Zealand was another. You couldn't really think your way into being another person with a different morning ahead of you, or shampoo yourself into a beautiful city full of artists drinking wine and eating pancakes cooked in brandy.

Exotic by name it might sound, but New Zealanders know Paraparaumu (pronounced as Para-para-umu, the first 'u' accented) as a rather featureless little settlement on the flat coastal strip north of Wellington, near to a long, grey, very tidal beach of no great appeal. Earlier generations of Pakeha corrupted it to 'Para-pa-*ram*', the last syllable nasally emphasised. Wellingtonians have holiday cottages there, travellers hurry through northwards on State Highway 1, a small shampoo-making factory could fit into its light industry. In England, an equivalent might be Wigan. Not much of a move, indeed.

By the end of the first chapter, it is clear to New Zealand, or at least Christchurch, readers that this is indeed a 'New Zealand' novel, but Margaret was apparently delving deeper than that.

'And yet, as I wrote the story, I found myself for the first time naturally drawing on the place around me by way of a setting. The story took on not the traditional New Zealand setting of bush and sea, but the character of the city around me. As I drove through Christchurch I found myself confronted with statements and signs, as the story melted into the city and the city transformed around me. Shopping malls and video parlours (relatively new features of the time) suddenly seemed to take on a curious surreal dimension. Street names and road signs took on the character of magical announcement. I had never imagined I would find my way into my own ostentatiously rural land by invoking a city.

'I now think that all cities have both universal and particular characters, and I was able to use the universal form to begin nudging my way imaginatively back into the city I actually lived in, and then into a place from which I had been along with many other New Zealanders, unconsciously expelled. Having found my way in I have never left it but continued to move deeper in with increasing pleasure and confidence. The hills and sea and summer holidays of a later book (*The Tricksters*), the waterfront and jetty of the picture book *A Summery Saturday Morning*, would not have come to me as easily and naturally without the re-entry made possible by *The Changeover*. Though I hope its folk tale references make it generally recognisable and accessible, I still remember with pleasure the exhilaration of what was a sort of homecoming.'

After two Carnegie Medals and a university fellowship, Margaret's increased standing in the literary community was reflected by a New Zealand Literary Fund Lifetime Achievement Award in 1985, although at close to fifty she was not even (as it turned out) anywhere near full flower. Interviewers were no longer asking her why she wrote for children, or why her stories were not 'New Zealand'. The many lengthy interviews and profiles that appeared from this period often shone small, revealing beams of light on her earlier years or on the challenges of the professional writer's life she was now energetically carving out. One unnamed British reviewer compared her habit of walking, muttering to herself for inspiration, around the edge of Lyttelton Harbour, to Wordsworth stomping around the Lake District, and saw similarities between their homes, with their large gardens, many cats and thousands of books. Margaret, though, with daughters as her sharpest critics, took herself 'much less seriously'. Indeed, some suggested, passages like this, from her 1983 comic novella, *The Pirates' Mixed-up Voyage*, placed her firmly in the tradition of the *Goon Show*, *Monty Python* and *The Hitchhiker's Guide to the Galaxy* (all Mahy favourites).

> The pirate captain charged forward and slashed at Mrs Hatchett but she, with tremendous skill and a sword of razor sharpness, parried his lunge, and cut through his thick leather belt so that his trousers fell down. He dropped his sword and seized at them desperately, then stepped on to one half of the banana and shot across the room winding up in a dusty corner with the classroom wastepaper basket.

She was not always pleased by her previous work. 'Many of my books I don't like at all now . . . I am becoming less and less capable of giving a simple answer to anything, and try to justify this by maintaining that there are no simple answers, and there may not even be any real answers, only points where people agree not to argue . . . I am . . . untidy with things (not people) and entertained all the time. I am slowly disintegrating but I don't mind, and would quite like to turn into a tree some day, but not immediately.'

The Changeover was always going to be a hard act to follow. In terms of order of writing, the third novel should have been *The Tricksters*, Margaret's most complex book so far, but the shrewd Vanessa Hamilton suggested that, coming so soon on the heels of two Carnegie Medal winners, both with supernatural themes, the next title should not be a fantasy but something quite different.

The Catalogue of the Universe appeared in 1985, the year in which she also spent a month in Perth as the writer in residence at the Western Australian College of Advanced Education. When asked to name her favourite novel, Margaret has sometimes expressed a particular fondness for this book, and admitted that, of all her characters, the shy, brainy but ungainly young astronomer and philosopher Tycho Potter is more of a self-portrait than any other, even Tabitha in *The Haunting*. He is named after the 16th-century Danish astronomer Tycho Brahe — partly because of that telescope she once put together, with her father's and uncle's help. 'It was a very transforming moment when I looked through and saw the craters on the moon and knew that it really was a small planet. It's part of my own past experience that I've passed onto Tycho. But I also think that his interests, his judgements about the contradictory nature of the world, contain some of my own fascinations in a very direct form.'

The Catalogue of the Universe is 'social realism' or, perhaps better, 'a realistic fairy tale' set firmly in Christchurch and the Port Hills and described by Tom Fitzgibbon as 'a love story of Angela and Tycho [which] revolves around the nature of truth'. As in

The Changeover, the heroine is a teenage girl living with her mother — the struggling solo-parent family once again. The storyline deals with Angela's compulsion to meet the father about whom her mother Dido has invented, as much as for herself as for her daughter, a romantic fairy tale of hopeless love for a handsome married man whose child she bore while knowing also she could never expect marriage. Angela, though deeply disillusioned by the cold, unloving businessman she finally confronts, maturely settles for a greater understanding of her relationships with her mother, and the plain but clever Tycho.

In lesser hands, wrote British reviewer Audrey Laski in the *Times Educational Supplement*, such elements could 'have piled cliché upon cliché', but in fact Mahy spins something 'entirely new and golden . . . the happy ending imposes a sense of complete rightness because the reader so much desires it'. And although the 'substantial paragraphs in which Tycho meditates on the philosophy of astronomy could be off-putting', there is the final delight for young readers, of 'the moment when Angela puts *The Catalogue of the Universe*, the book within the book, to an entirely different purpose from that for which it was intended — the moment when the Frog Prince gets the spell-breaking kiss. Such pleasures should be widely shared.'

One of the best of many further fine reviews came from the Australian world authority Walter McVitty, who speculated that *The Catalogue of the Universe* could quite conceivably win Margaret a third Carnegie.

'Margaret Mahy is now one of the most popular and prolific of children's authors. She is also one of the best. With the exception of English writer Jan Mark, I would say that she is probably without peer today . . . her books, however simple, are affirmations of life: set your mind free of its shackles and reach out, grab it and embrace it, make it yours. And the wonderful things can be as wonderful as you hope they'll be, as I discovered in reading *The Catalogue of the Universe*, Angela describing her mother: "It's not as if she's a real eccentric. I mean she's not what I'd call colourful. It is more as if she was on loan from another planet, almost like ours but not quite — a sort of near miss." That's exactly the way I would describe the author herself. Eccentric is certainly not the word for Margaret Mahy. She does, however, have such an extraordinary intellect, combined with rare insight into human nature and such a breathtaking control of words that one could easily believe her gifts to be supernatural. She expresses ideas in the most carefully crafted, felicitous prose — which never takes itself too seriously, being enlivened by a constant undercurrent of humour.'

If children's book watchers in the English-speaking world were beginning to wonder what the writer from New Zealand would come up with next, they could hardly have anticipated the four books that appeared in 1986: two story collections, the short novel (also with a New Zealand setting) *Aliens in the Family* and the major, complex novel that had been written hard on the heels of *The Changeover*.

It had taken her a year to write *The Tricksters*, the only one set entirely away from Christchurch and probably the most audacious of her novels. She said later, 'I couldn't work out what was making me so slow. At last I realised that I had never previously written a book with so many characters. It had twelve people in it, and I was used to writing a story with only four or five at the most.'

The genesis of the book's bold and colourful Antipodean summer Christmas setting was the subject of a major lecture she gave in Auckland some years later.

'One day some years ago I was in Great Britain in New Zealand House, listening to some flattering things being said about my work. I was consumed with gratification and at the same time by dismay, since not only my upbringing but my rationality prevents me from believing the flattery in the conditional way I would like to . . . in the way that instinct seemed to be prompting me to accept it. You know what it is like. Just as at one level part of you is listening and thinking "How true! How true!" other more sensible strands are telling you "They have to say that". Or "What about all the things that you know are wrong with your story", looking furtively sideways at the shiny wall. Some sort of marble I seem to remember, I saw a whole company of dark reflections standing apparently on the other side of the reflecting surface, listening intently, reproducing almost exactly our own attentiveness. I say almost exactly, because there was something menacing about the reflected featureless crowd which was certainly not present in the actual one. I was reminded that in Jorge Luis Borges' book *A Dictionary of Imaginary Beings*, he tells in a section called *The fauna of mirrors* that a creature called the Fish could be occasionally glimpsed in the depths of mirrors. (One must bear in mind that his account may be apocryphal because Borges is not only an astonishing scholar, but makes a literary point of inventing scholarship which has all the appearance of being genuine.) Once he says, apparently quoting a Cantonese myth, there was a time when the images in mirrors did not imitate us, and men and women could come and go even more freely than Alice through the looking glass surface. However, a battle developed between the world of men and the world of the mirror people. In the end the reflections were shut in behind glass and obliged to repeat, "as in the actions of a dream", the actions of me. One day we will see an essence called the fish in the glass . . . a very faint line of no describable colour. From that point on our reflections will start to rebel, little by little they will begin to move in their own ways. They will break out through the water and battle will be joined again. Staring at the reflecting surface there in New Zealand House I wondered if I was possibly about to see the fish there among the dark listeners. It was at that point that I began to think of the story subsequently published as *The Tricksters*. I am sure my ego, replete with the energy of praise, began darting around, searching for a way out . . . and ran off on its own through the familiar escape route of a story. I was aware of the story because of the stories I had already read, and out of the stuff of these stories and out of what I was seeing I began to construct another story and hide in it.

'At first I had the idea of people coming out of a picture . . .

but not because they were painted in the picture which I imagined as an oil painting of a countryside, and painted with a dark shiny surface. Reflections of people in real life of the story would pass over the surface of the painting. They would live briefly in the painted landscape, and give possible forms to life coming out of it ... the residual energy of the painter maybe. It was not an original idea, of course I had read stories that touched on possibilities like these for years. Once as a child I began writing a book about a reflection that came alive, though I never finished that story. Once the reflection had come alive, once that fearsome moment of transformation was past, interest faded. Our reflections and shadows are often candidates for an extended or haunting life that is part of our own lives, yet separate too. *The Picture of Dorian Grey* [*sic*] is a notorious tale of a man living in a particularly exploitive relationship with his painted image. Vampires do not have reflections. In a way they are already reflections among us, yet belonging to the other side. In this first speculative version of *The Tricksters* characters came off the surface of the picture once shapes were provided for them. They came, because they were desired. They were desired by the most powerful of all desirers . . . a reader, a reading girl.

'As I wrote the book changed, the picture vanished, though the reflecting surface remained. It became the surface of the sea, big reflecting skin of the world. I see the sea every day I am at home. The water of Lyttelton harbour is still water, and is a particularly vivid reflecting surface. I have often commented on the fact that it has been hard for me to write a story set in New Zealand and that when I began to do so in *The Changeover* the story was set in a city, an environment which has many universal qualities rather than local ones. *The Tricksters* was the first book I had attempted in years which came directly from my immediate surroundings, and was possible because those surroundings, though real enough, suddenly took on a fantastic dimension. I was able to mediate with my environment through fantasy, the zone into which I had been projected in childhood. I re-entered Lyttelton harbour, the same but different, via London, via reflecting mirrors. Via remembered stories, in the end I wound up at home again . . .

'*The Tricksters* always seems to me a moral story because compassion and forgiveness triumph over betrayal. In the end it is the older sister Christobel who manages the heroic act . . . by vanity she is genuinely determined to force happy endings out of disaster and brave enough to begin to do so . . . Her friend Emma has after all betrayed [her] by usurping Christobel's own father, and indeed (as father of Emma's illegitimate baby) assuming knowledge of him that is forbidden to Christobel herself. Christobel however persists. She rings Emma and invites her to join the family for New Year, only to find that something from the other side of another imperfectly reflecting surface, from the other side of morality if you like, advances to meet her. It is something connected to ego perhaps, but greater than ego. She is surprised to find she is more sincere than she realises. And sometimes this can be done . . . take my word for it. It is part of the perceived reality of children's books to end with hope, but that doesn't mean such endings are impossible. Self-sacrifice or, if you like, the suppression of one's own ego is not particularly fashionable at present, partly because it was so damagingly insisted on in the past, particularly in the lives of women and the poor. Now it sometimes seems like a false myth or sometimes like a myth insisted on by one part of society in order to command another. Nevertheless it is part of my direct experience and therefore I suggest on its possibility . . . It is adult reality, built on guilt as well as experience that suggests such endings are necessarily cop outs . . .

'It now seems to me that *The Tricksters* and *A Lion in the Meadow* have the same plot and spring from the same experiences. The little boy in the picture book and Harry in *The Tricksters* both imagine or desire so strongly in their respective stories that their belief or desire makes a connection and alters reality.'

A 1986 interview picked up an aspect of *The Tricksters* that some have found a step too far, just too bizarre, even for Mahy. Harry becomes 'romantically involved with a ghost, one of a trio of charismatic reincarnations who range from violent to sensitive . . . but Margaret Mahy doesn't believe in ghosts. She confirms that her phantoms are teenage desires come to life.

"'They aren't meant to suggest that I have any belief in the supernatural. The ghosts are imaginative projections or metaphors, or psychological devices. They work for me by producing mysterious moments which though fictional still manage to enlighten mysterious moments in real life." Margaret Mahy sharply recalls her own adolescent confusion at the sexuality of adults, and with it the fear, when she was on the brink of womanhood, that next year wasn't going to be as nice as last year. It's an aspect of adolescence she thinks should be dealt with. "Adolescents can't opt out of their physical changes, and these developments are very important. Sexuality is one of the central preoccupations of the novel from *Pamela* onwards. I think most people, including adolescents, want to lead passionate lives, so I allow my characters a certain amount of liberty where this is involved . . . I think happy endings are therapeutic, but even in my adult life I find some acknowledgement of my troubles in literature helpful. I think I am writing about something that is very real. The books have a fairy tale structure, even though I'm writing for older children, but they're disguised fairy tales. They have a lot of realistic reinforcement. In many ways I think I still write for adults.'"

At least one American reviewer agreed, describing the book as strong, heady stuff and suggesting that 'it would take very little to market the book as an adult novel . . . her writing is sensuous and lush; the story is magical and compelling', while Diane Hebley, in the *Listener*, felt that *The Tricksters*, being 'both credible and incredible', moved beyond 'children's' literature as exemplified by Mahy's earlier Carnegie winners. Other critics drew attention to the affectionate and vivid description of the spectacular Lyttelton Harbour landscape. In a long and particularly astute piece in the *New York Times Book Review*, Robin McKinley stated that, as in her two earlier novels, 'Ms Mahy has proved she can handle, as no other writer has, the first terrifying awakening of teenage sexuality. She seems to know the delicate balances of the highly indelicate things that hormones start doing to you at around age 14, and she describes them in a funny, real, significant and haunting way that no one old enough to write as elegantly as she does should be old enough to remember . . . there is more going on in them than just the mechanics of a clever plot; on different levels *The Tricksters* is a parable of the responsibility of the artist, or a simple ghost story, or a tale of the girl's first understanding that adulthood will mean a more complex vision of situations and people that through childhood have been taken for granted. I am in danger of doing Margaret Mahy a disservice by recommending her too enthusiastically, but she deserves the recommendation, and she is a strong enough writer to stand up under it . . . [though her material is universal], it's that in her hands the matter of living in the world we must share with other people becomes cleaner, kinder, more involving and more exciting.'

The publication of *The Tricksters* completed a kind of fantasy hat trick, one that had demonstrated Margaret's increasing willingness to take risks, both emotional and literary. Margaret told one interviewer, '*The Haunting, The Changeover* and *The Tricksters* aren't a trilogy — they are about different characters — but they do form a triptych. Each one is more disturbing than the one before and the three supernatural brothers in the latest one are more obviously sinister. They are figures summoned up by the girl Harry's own writing.' When asked if she was disturbed by what she was conjuring up, Margaret immediately agreed. 'We like to test ourselves against something that's dangerous and thrilling. The idea of being overtaken by something that's overwhelming and too strong to resist appeals to both men and women. I did feel disturbed when I wrote *The Tricksters* and I wanted my readers to feel uneasy because I enjoy reading that sort of book.' She did concede, however, that she had gone as far as she wanted along that path, 'and there won't be any more books of that kind' — unless she gets an idea she can't resist.

Now, as the writer of four acclaimed novels, Margaret was increasingly being called on to share some of her writing methods and her secrets.

'Reading [a manuscript] all through again one sometimes finds ideas one doesn't like! How have they got in in the first place? I don't always recognise the first time round just what is going into the story. Frequently I make things too wordy, or too dramatic. I always have to simplify. Sometimes something I meant to sound touching sounds sickly and sentimental. At second draft stage I start looking very seriously for things like that, as well as for places where the plot stops working, where people might stop believing in the story. At this stage too, however, just to make things more complicated, I also add many things as the network of association comes into play — with parallels, analogies, metaphors, other literary references, ideas and echoes from other areas of knowledge.

'For a longer book I usually have a third and even a fourth draft. I find it good to get all the different versions together and to cut them up and put them together in an even better order with sellotape. Then I get them typed (or type them myself) for the last time and send them to the publisher.'

As well as the requests for writing tips, there were the children's letters and the long queues for autographs now standard at every public appearance. From the early 1970s, conference or school visit organisers knew that no matter how long the queue or how tired the author or how pressing the next engagement, every child waiting for an autograph would probably get, along with the distinctive signature, a little drawing of a crocodile, a dragon or a dog as well as a cheerful, interested comment.

There might be at least one letter a day: 'I mean to answer the letters I get, but I feel I should do them properly, so I wait. Look at this one. Fifty-seven closely typed pages by a 10-year-old girl. Very sophisticated . . .' She has admitted to often being late with her responses. 'Even with a word processor, it takes a long time, and sometimes, where a school project is concerned, there are many questions. In all the years I have been answering letters one boy has replied, not only saying thank you, but enclosing a petrol voucher. I was very touched.'

And what, she asked one interviewer, 'do you make of this one I got from a little girl the other day?' The letter begins in a hearty, complimentary fashion. She enjoyed a particular Margaret Mahy story very much in fact, "I enjoyed it so much I nearly went to sleep." Margaret Mahy looks perturbed. 'Is she finding a secret away of telling me the truth, do you think?'

By the middle of the 1980s, Margaret's output had reached new levels made possible only by regular ten- to eighteen-hour days.

'I almost never turned down work,' she told Murray Edmond in one of the first 'literary' interviews published in *Landfall* in 1987, 'until recently when I've had a bit much. I am a professional in the sense I chase after opportunities. I've almost never turned down any invitation to talk to a group or to visit a school. It's not just for reasons of making a career, but it's also for supporting what you're dealing with — the idea of reading, of books, of story, to exemplify it as a way of making a living. If children ask me how much I make I answer pretty honestly. And they're often very impressed. I don't know if land agents would say how much money they make — people are often very shy about money. I do work long hours . . . Sleep? I have more in the last couple of years. But I'm almost never in bed before midnight. In my case the best work is often done in the early morning — I tend to push the cutting edge of the story along at night when what matters is movement forward rather than precision of judgement. To charge forward and then retrace my steps the next morning and look at where I've been has developed into a fairly natural pattern for me. I also show children the number of rewritings of things that I do, partly because process writing in schools involves them in doing some of the same things.'

Although her range had now expanded into novels for both children and young adults, and into film, television and theatre, her overflowing, inexhaustible storehouse of ideas and sheer enjoyment in writing very short stories found another outlet in the books for children learning to read, published first by the Department of Education (*Ready to Read* series), followed by Shortland Publications (*Storybox* and *Jellybeans*) and Wendy Pye Ltd (Sunshine Books), among others.

From the early 1980s these reading programmes, comprising small child-sized books and larger, teachers' versions for classroom use, began to earn New Zealand a formidable reputation overseas, challenging the huge corporate publishers producing expensive hardback textbooks based on phonics. Even today these 'readers' account for the majority of New Zealand's book exports.

Key authors for the larger educational publishers were Joy Cowley and Margaret Mahy who, according to Sunshine's Brian Cutting, kept faint-hearted British editors on their toes by introducing words such as 'sinuous', as in 'While a sinuous shark of the good-hearted sort/Shared egg-and-cress sandwiches auntie had brought'.

As with her picture books, some of Margaret's school readers had appeared originally in the *School Journals*, but in the new format they (and new stories) could be presented over and over to children learning to read. Typically, 'despite a terrible temptation to save one's best ideas for the more prestigious trade book area', Margaret has kept some of her finest stories for these programmes. The 1984 Sunshine book, *The Girl Who Washed in Moonlight*, an exquisite, haunting tale of good and evil, light and darkness, is a good example.

'There are books I have written for educational publication which I like as well as anything I have published in the trade book area, though in a curious way books in a reading scheme are still books that are widely used but publicly hidden. But a true whole book practitioner will have not only various reading series in the classroom, but many trade books too . . . the Whole Book method of teaching reading has resulted in a large number of short books being published within New Zealand, an increased possibility for authors and illustrators to make a living . . . as a greatly increased chance for children generally, not just children in homes with a bookish tradition, to make contact with stories that reflect and confirm their own environment.'

She was not initially attracted to the idea of writing for these programmes.

'When I was first approached I thought it just possible that educational publishing might not be compatible with self-respect, largely because I was remembering the books that were used in the schools of my childhood and the childhoods of my brothers and sisters. I learned to read from the Whitcombe and Tombs Progressive Primers . . . I remember these with a great deal of affection, for they did tell real stories, though these stories were universally selected from British anthologies and, being made up of folk and fairy tales, had an attractive otherworldly feel to them. Still, people of my generation do remember these stories quite vividly and will recite the good lines they remember to one another. For example, the repeated cry of a character called Teenchy Duck — *Quack! Quack! Quack! When will I get my money back!* It is a curiously modern entrepreneurial cry, and one I mutter of myself from time to time as I go up to the mail box . . . [yet] in all my conversations with people on the subject of reading series over the years, I have only encountered one person who recalled [the later Janet and John books] with affection and pleasure . . .

'It was the memory of such stories, stilted by their didactic intentions, which made me hesitate when asked to write for the *Ready to Read* series. Along with the passion to make a living went the wish to be passionate about what I wrote, and I had the feeling that I would not be interested in writing the sort of story that children could learn to read from. I was not a teacher. I had no idea about how one introduced new words, or how many or how often and no idea about the sort of basic vocabulary appropriate to each level, and I wanted to have a good time as a writer.

'However, when I expressed my doubts I was told that I should not worry about details such as these. That was the job of the editors and the reading advisers who would assess the stories I came up with. I should write stories as they came to me and make them simple — yes — but as good as possible in literary terms, without restricting myself by anything other than common sense. Occasionally, a good long word, or a lively phrase, I was told, constituted such drama that its strangeness would be compensated for by the interest of the reader. Although, as I have confessed, I enjoyed many of the stories that I learned to read from, my enjoyment of the stories had not, as far as I know, been part of official intention. It seemed to me that the underlying expectations where reading acquisition was concerned had changed in some very basic ways since I was as child. I proceeded rather doubtfully to submit stories that seemed to meet the criteria suggested to me, and to my surprise and pleasure they were accepted for use and I was paid for them. It was a powerful incentive. Writing for the *Storybox* series I found I could send stories off one week and be paid the next. It set off a sort of pavlovian conditioned reflex which has never left me.'

'We need to remember,' she said on another occasion, 'that for some children . . . these were the only books with which they made any extended contact, and this is true for some children into the present day. Moreover, they had traditionally never been counted as part of literature in New Zealand, even though from early in the 20th century they sold in hundreds of thousands.'

'So I begin my stories usually starting from a gleam, some fleeting moment, an unexpected juxtaposition, a typing mistake ("They went out into the sinlight" or "He was like a shop-wrecked sailor"). I tell the story to myself and then begin the process of externalisation, and the consideration of for whom (after myself) the story is intended. Editors are obliged to protect children from taking ill-regulated lives as models, particularly the authors of educational material. Spending public money, they are publicly accountable, and they have to cater for and to gratify a wide proportion of tastes and philosophies. In addition to that they are trying to produce literature by committee, for it is a deep-seated part of the philosophy of teaching reading in New Zealand that children will learn best from a genuine, though very simple, literature rather than graded readers. This underlies all the schemes I work for . . .'

To see what can be done with just sixteen words and a good illustrator, imagine a five- or six-year-old encountering this little gem, from the author who 'never ever doubted that she was adored':

There was once a wonderful baby. The cat thought she was wonderful. The fish thought she was wonderful. The bird thought she was wonderful and her mother and father thought she was wonderful. And the baby knew she was wonderful.

Or, for the emerging reader, *The Cake*, a Shortland's *Jellybean* reader that elevated cake-making into an existential discussion on identity crisis.

The Cake

Mary's mother put some sugar into a bowl.

'What's happening?' thought the sugar. 'A moment ago I was sitting around with the rest of the sugar in the sugar-pot. Now I have been chosen for something. I must be special and this must be a special day.'

Then Mary's mother put some butter in with the sugar.

'Hello!' cried the sugar. 'I can tell we're going to be friends.'

'How sweet of you,' the butter said admiringly.

Mary's mother turned on the electric mixer.

Whirrrrr! went the mixer.

'Listen!' cried the butter, 'they're playing our tune.'

'Shall we dance?' asked the sugar.

The butter and the sugar danced together until they

were so mixed up you couldn't tell where the butter left off and the sugar began.

Mary's mother beat up some eggs and put them into the bowl.

'The more the merrier!' cried the butter and the sugar. 'Another friend to dance with. Let's crack a few yolks.'

The butter and the eggs and the sugar danced together.

Down came a soft rain.

'Hello everyone! Here I am!' said the flour.

'I'm here too!' cried a funny little voice. It was the baking powder.

The mixer sang its whirring song and everyone danced together.

'Why are we here?' the butter asked the flour.

'Who invited us?' asked the baking powder.

'Something very exciting is going to happen and we have been specially chosen,' said the flour.

Down came the currants, the raisins and the cherries.

'Don't forget us,' they cried.

'What are we doing here?' asked a cheery cherry.

'There must be a reason,' declared a raisin.

Whiizzz! went the electric mixer. Then they were all turned upside down.

'Let me help you out?' offered the kindly wooden spoon.

'Let me take you in,' cried the round baking tin.

'I'll give you a warm welcome,' said the oven.

They were all put into the oven together.

'It's dark in here,' said the eggs.

'Warm too!' yawned the melting butter.

'Which of us is which?' asked the flour.

'I think I'll puff myself up,' said the baking powder. 'This is such a cosy oven.'

They were all quiet then, enjoying the cosy oven. No-one spoke for a long time.

Then, all of a sudden, a new voice spoke.

It was an eggish, buttery, floury voice — sweet as sugar, and as cheery as a cherry.

'I know what I am!' it said. 'I am . . . I am . . .'

But it couldn't quite think of the right word.

Someone opened the oven.

'Oh Mum!' cried Mary. 'What a lovely cake!'

'So that's what I am now,' said the voice. 'I'm a cake.'

Mary's mother iced the cake.

'Now I'm wearing my best coat,' said the cake.

Mary sprinkled the cake with hundreds and thousands.

'Now I am wearing my jewels,' said the cake.

Mary's mother put four candles in the cake.

'Now I'm wearing my crown!' the cake cried.

Mary's mother wrote on the cake. She wrote, 'Happy birthday, Mary.'

'I knew I was special,' cried the cake. 'I am a birthday cake.

Hooray hooray for the birthday cake.'

And that's just what Mary said too.

Margaret has confessed to her delight in the part where the butter says to the sugar, 'Listen, they're playing our tune' and the sugar replies 'Shall we dance?'. 'I'm very fond of that line. It seems to me it works well enough to describe the creaming of the cake, and for an adult it has all sort of ironic associations with romance.'

She has always found the story 'very satisfying . . . though it is, in many ways, a concealed story . . . in strange ways *The Cake* discharges some of the functions commonly associated with literature in the academic — what I jokingly called the *noble* — sense. Underlying the simplicity of the language is a set of ideas that add up to a joke about the world and the way we fit ourselves in it' — suggesting pleasure, women's lives ('in my mother's generation they were often judged according to the quality of cake they produced'), and a moment of glory for a particular child; while 'a teacher might think, privately, that it is concern with identity crisis and emerging self-definition . . . the butter, sugar, eggs, flour and dried fruit, their initial bewilderment, their existential speculation and their final melting together to form the one inclusive character, the cake . . . even a text in a school reading series can contain ideas that fulfil the imaginative speculation of the writers and which are also ideas for the reader to grow into.'

By the end of the 1980s, Margaret's 'school readers' had dramatically increased her output to something over a hundred and fifty books, 'most of which are very short, because, if ever I count my published works (and I don't think I have ever done so for my own gratification) I always include the books I have written for three reading series all originating in New Zealand, but available internationally.

'This is not simply to inflate my total. I regard some of these educational stories with as much affection as anything I have ever written . . . [but] I have become rather more hesitant — a little dismayed by various series which display the same writer's name over and over again — even when it happens to be my own. I think such a series looks claustrophobic and my own experience suggests that though writing many stories can be a powerful financial inducement, on the whole one is better to be rather more circumspect. A series, intended to support a whole language approach to reading acquisition in the most truthful way, should offer a large number of books in a classroom, but it should also ideally display the freshest possible ideas from a wide variety of authors and illustrators . . . [although] simple, very simple, as emergent texts, have to be, one can still sometimes hear a particular voice, a particular perception coming through, and it seems to me that, ideally, these voices should be as diverse as possible.'

Margaret's best 'school reader' years were for the Department of Education from 1982 to 1985, for Shortland between 1984 and 1992 and for Wendy Pye Ltd from 1986. It would be a formidable task to track them all down (and impossible to calculate how many millions of children would have read them in English or many translations around the world) and they comprise a body of work greater, with the notable exception of Joy Cowley, than most authors of this very specialised and difficult literary genre would hope to achieve in a lifetime. The best are miniature poetic masterpieces.

In the mid-1980s Margaret was able to tell an interviewer: 'I think I have made a lot of money over the past three years, relative to a lot of other writers anyhow, but I have been writing since I was seven and have only recently felt financially comfortable.' Now, at last, she was able to contemplate a major addition to her house. Around the original modest 1965 structure was wrapped a handsome, three-tiered addition, giving her a spacious high-ceilinged living area with a huge stone fireplace capped with a burnished copper hood. Picture windows framed the view up Lyttelton Harbour to the Pacific Ocean, and one wall was lined with bookshelves so high a librarian's ladder was needed to reach the volumes at the top. At last, too, she had a room of her own.

'The room where I write is my bedroom but it is my workroom too. I sit with my back to a view of trees and, in winter, of the hills behind the trees. It is always there, when I turn around. My room is lined with bookcases full of books and there are many books on the floor. The pictures over my bed are from books of my own, but there are pictures done by my daughters Penny and Bridget. I have several filing cabinets and a chair and a bed which is covered with papers during the day. On a bench along one wall is my word processor, a fax machine, a photocopier and a tape recorder. On the wall behind this bench are pictures, notes about work I must do and so on. There are several clocks and usually a few cats, particularly in the winter when it is cold outside. One cat likes to sleep behind the printer of the word processor.'

The word processor, and later the more upmarket of big-screen computers, entered her life around 1986. It was a long way from her apprentice's notebooks and pencils, or even her large clunky typewriters, and not entirely the blessing it might seem. 'Lately,' she mused to Greg O'Brien, 'I've taken to thinking about the word-processor as being associated with some form of immorality or hellishness — a new form of industrialism.'

Those, like O'Brien and Betty Gilderdale, who visited the Mahy house from this period commented on the thousands of books, spread around every room: the encyclopaedias, dictionaries, atlases, philosophical and scientific texts, adult fiction from around the world and an enormous historical collection of children's books. On the bedroom shelves sat hundreds of her own books, not only in English editions, both hardback and paperback, but multiple copies of the American editions and many translations: Italian, German, French, Finnish, Norwegian, Danish, Swedish, Dutch, Spanish (Catalan and Mexican), Greek, Thai, Chinese and Japanese.

Then there was the stuffed snake descending a staircase, a rocking-horse and a fine Elizabethan toy house, many dolls and toys; on the walls, blank-eyed masks, children's paintings, book cover artwork and brooding New Zealand paintings; later visitors might notice a small upstairs room given over entirely to an amusingly eclectic collection of perhaps 500 videos — action and horror movies and old classics alongside Shakespeare and Shaw. Around the bricked patio outside are two-metre storks, wooden garden seats straight from Kate Greenaway, a goldfish/waterlily pond and, not far away, a spa pool; in the garden, many varieties of fruit trees, raspberries and roses climbing over archways. Margaret has always found solace and pleasure in being a gardener, almost single-handedly creating an enchanting physical world while creating her many imaginative worlds.

This was the routine behind the incessant, some might say obsessive creativity, as explained to interviewers a few years later: 'She writes for long hours (at least 12 a day) and sometimes, in the past, has ended up working through half of the night. Now that she is getting old, she has had to change her routine. Her working day comprises getting up every morning at 4.45 am, having a cup of coffee and working for an hour or two.

'She then walks her dog, (she also has cats and rabbits) returns home and then writes again. Margaret used to type her manuscripts but now uses a word processor. This change has altered the way she writes and edits. Novels like *The Tricksters* she would end up typing out four times completely, but with a word-processor she says, "I write on screen, print it out, read it — I try to operate between word-processing and reading the page. I used to have a word-processor, a photocopier, a fax machine and laser printer in my bedroom and then I used to have to go outside the house to the loo. It certainly stopped you from getting too conceited about your technology."'

Not surprisingly, as Margaret moved closer to her 50s, many observed how tired she looked, quite thin and even 'gaunt'. They marvelled at her workload, and sympathised with the days that inevitably got interrupted, but not many knew that, as well as her writing commitments, international travel, house renovations and garden improvements, for nearly four years another domestic responsibility was being attended to daily. And typically, the experience was to provide Margaret with the knowledge and compassion for a later major work of fiction.

'If any story I have told has the mark of social realism on it, it is certainly *Memory*, and in it I have told young readers a lot of the truth I know about the metamorphosis of a rational human being replete with knowledge, memory and the power to make a cup of tea several times a day, into a demented old woman losing command of all the things in which self-respect is traditionally established, and driven to wear a tea cosy instead of a hat.'

Aunt Francie Street, her mother's sister, who once mailed a wartime birthday cake to the five-year-old living in a caravan in Northland, came into Margaret's domestic orbit around 1982, as sole resident of the little next-door cottage her niece had been able to buy. For nearly four years, through Francie's increasing dementia, Margaret cooked her aunt's meals, dressed and toileted her, did her laundry and rescued her when, increasingly, she went wandering.

In the later stages, some help was available: 'The support services were good, partly because I was sufficiently well-educated to know where to go and what sort of things to say, and also because I was prepared to cope with quite a lot before I asked for some support. A district nurse and a housekeeper appeared once a week and things were tidied up quite quickly. In between times things went downhill, but neither my aunt nor I bothered too much about a certain amount of squalor.'

From the early days of this arrangement, the writer in Margaret had recognised the potential, one day, for a story. Sophie in *Memory* is the only character she acknowledges as being based on a real person.

'There's very little written for children about adult senility, and I think they could identify with a character who is like a child. My aunt, for instance, hides biscuits and I would like to develop that into a story. When she does bring out the biscuits, she brings out Biscats. You can see how her mind is working, though. A cup of tea for her is now made with a milk token and hot water. It's sad, because she used to make such a good cup of tea.'

The incidents involving Francie were always poignant, sometimes very funny. 'When Bridget was working up at the shop, Aunt Francie showed up one day dressed only in her petticoat and Bridget said, "Francie, do you know you're only in your petticoat?" Francie stiffened and said "Child, I never tell you what to wear".'

She would laugh uproariously, while slightly shocked, at Benny Hill on television, and mistake her nieces in jeans for young men being familiar with her, or put on three dresses, or retell certain anecdotes endlessly, or constantly wash clothes and check the mailbox and walk right past the lavatory she needed to visit. Once, sent off at bedtime with a torch to negotiate the short bricked connecting pathway to her cottage, she returned with the torch in her mouth, asking 'what was she supposed to do with this trumpet?' As she got older, she became fixated on her handbag as the symbol of identity. 'As long as she had that she had her bankbook, the symbol of having some money and position; she felt in charge of herself . . . her search became very simple, so every time she looked for her handbag which she used to hide because she was afraid it would be stolen, she was searching for herself too, and she would feel diminished, lessened, if she didn't have that handbag.'

Francie provided Margaret with one of the most chilling moments of her life (one she was to use to full effect at the climax of *Memory*), when she 'turned around and her mouth was "bursting with teeth". She had tried to wear two sets of false teeth at once. "It was like those scenes in horror films, where someone goes to touch something familiar, and suddenly it becomes a ghastly face."'

Nev was coming towards Jonny, not fast, but very deliberately indeed . . . Yet, in the very moment when he might have destroyed Jonny, Nev stepped back, dropped his left hand and revealed a face twisted not only by pain, but by such horror, that Jonny turned involuntarily to see what had horrified him.

The green door was open and coming out of the darkness was Sophie, armed with the hearth brush, and resplendent in her petticoat, suspender belt, crimson hat and one shoe. Over one arm she carried her handbag. She looked like an old, old spirit, her thin silver hair turned into a phosphorescent nest by the street light, her eyes nothing but two black holes under her high forehead, her mouth bursting with more teeth than any natural mouth could hold. Her lips were stretched thin trying to accommodate the impossible number of teeth which extruded over her lower lip, making it seem as if she were beginning to devour herself.

Involuntarily, Jonny flung up his own good arm as if to defend himself. Before he could remind himself it was only Sophie, every nerve in his body told him to put himself out of mortal danger . . .

Margaret has often acknowledged that some of the happenings and conversations in *Memory* are directly transposed, but 'if the story lacks the nastiness, the sheer fatigue of response involved in looking after a demented person, it is partly because, though those elements were present, they were not a commanding part of my life with my aunt. Because I had a background of story to draw on she never lost her imaginative function in my life . . . ' Occasionally the strain told. 'I don't wish to suggest that she didn't drive me crazy from time to time . . . the collapse of rationality is wearing to live with. Nevertheless the alteration in the frame of reference which a lifetime of stories enable me to make, made this a rewarding and mysterious relationship as well as an infuriating one. My aunt took on some of the aspects of an oracle. "How beautifully blue the sky is today," she said, peering at the sky as we drove up the hill. "It doesn't seem to mind us getting any closer to it."'

Memory provides a fascinating glimpse into Margaret's frequently quoted belief that it is the fiction writer's job to create imaginative originality by finding new and interesting connections, to detect (on getting an idea) 'the compressed ending, to tease it out, to coax it into public view . . . or perhaps to goad the beginning out of the end, for sometimes one gets the idea for the ending first'.

She has denied that *Memory* is a novel '*tackling* the subject of Alzheimer's disease'; rather, it *recognises* Alzheimer's in a story, with its origins firmly in fairy tale, about a troubled young man and a strange, helpless old woman. In essence it is a 'magical encounter between two unlikely people, both of whom are possessed, in different ways by a dissolving rationality'. She has also acknowledged the novel as yet anther example of her subconscious haunting her stories, this time in the fatal fall of the hero Jonny's sister. 'I had an imaginary picture in my mind of the place where she fell and when I was back home in Whakatane recently I *saw* the place. I couldn't believe it. I told my sister Patricia and she said somebody *had* once fallen off those rocks, a girl at her class at school, and you know, even then I still could consciously remember it.'

Yet the actual trigger for *Memory* was none of these, but an image that stayed with her until she found a place for it. This was a strange and haunting vision, 'seen when I was driving home through the city in the early hours of the morning. Passing a supermarket car park, empty and strange with its daytime function gone, I saw a very old man coming out of the car park pushing an empty supermarket trolley . . . when I finished *Memory*, when I was reading it through afterwards it occurred to me that what I had written was still at heart a fairy story about a young men setting out to search for a girl whom he remembers as very mysterious, beautiful and clever. He encounters, in the empty car park of a supermarket, an old woman who asks him a question, "Are you the one?" — a question my aunt once asked me, having in the course of going to a public lavatory, forgotten just who she was supposed to be with. In the beginning of my story the young man does not know if he is the one or not, but by the end of the story he feels that he does.'

Memory won a third major British award for Margaret: the Observer Teenage Fiction Prize for 1987 from a shortlist of six that included Anne Fine's *Madame Doubtfire* (later to become a Hollywood film starring Robin Williams). The book, said judge Elaine Moss, was 'so close-grained and all-embracing that it defies categorisation . . . a compassionate and intelligent novel, brilliantly crafted, simultaneously involved with social concerns and with universal themes'. Another eminent judge, Claire Tomalin, wrote that Margaret Mahy 'strikes me as one of those few writers who has actually retained the strengths of a child's imagination in her work; she deserves to be read by teenagers — and by more adults than the statutory librarians and schoolteachers'. In the *Times Literary Supplement* Doug Anderson commented on the novel's overtly New Zealand (Maori) political allusions. Double Carnegie winner Jan Mark in the *Times Educational Supplement* admired the elegant writing and good-humoured wit: 'only a churl, surely, would wonder if [the book] might perhaps, given its subject, have been a little less charming'.

Nineteen eighty-seven was a particularly triumphant year, with Margaret's literary and television achievements lifting her public standing and recognition internationally to a new level. The five, internationally acclaimed novels she had produced in as many years were earning this sort of comment from British authority Julia Eccleshare:

'More recently, especially in her long novels for older readers, Mahy's spectacular originality has injected a force or energy into her writing which has the unusual and outstanding quality of charging up the reader. She plays with fantasy, twisting the strands of fantasy and reality together into a continuous thread with no visible joins. She doesn't divide the world into "real" or "imaginary". To her, the unseen forces which surround us are every bit as real and powerful as the table top on which she writes . . . in each of these full-length novels she has shown the full extent of her invention, humour and control, giving to her readers books of exceptional intensity and intelligence.'

Eccleshare felt there was 'nothing intrinsically New Zealand about any of her books. [Margaret] was brought up on a diet of British literature and her books are, therefore, part of that literary tradition. As she says, it takes a long time for an indigenous literature to develop.' But 'landscape and locations can occupy more important, and more precise, places in Mahy's books than is always recognised . . . [she uses] indirect and playful ways of locating her story without excluding the non-local reader, as more local allusions are bound to do'.

Her exotic non-British voice could even, for some key people, work in her favour. 'As a writer, and as a person,' wrote one commentator in an influential British magazine, reprinted in a major American reference book, 'Margaret Mahy isn't easy to categorise. She both loves and resists her New Zealandiness [*sic*]; she wards off all attempts to turn her into a moralist yet fiercely defends the significance of the craft she practises; she's a fantasist who claims "I always write about real life"; she has a zest and flair that can bring her a bullseye where many other authors don't recognise there's a target . . . and at the same time she can't offer any guarantees that a new book of hers won't misfire completely. In short, she's a writer who takes risks, who's always changing, already capable of growth.'

Back in her own country, Margaret was beginning to find extra support from some loyal and well-informed quarters — notably, reviewer and historian Betty Gilderdale's breezy and useful hardback for young readers, *Introducing Margaret Mahy*. In 1987 two University of Auckland academics, backed by the esteemed literary journal *Landfall*, were among the first to mark Margaret's work out for academic attention: Murray Edmond with a lengthy, entertaining taped interview which he began by announcing that Margaret was an 'indefatigable and supremely entertaining talker, a genuine intellectual' and Claudia Marquis with the first New Zealand study of *The Haunting*, in a paper called 'Feminism, Freud and the Fairy Tale: Reading Margaret Mahy's *The Haunting*'. (Later she produced a 1991 paper on fantasy, notably Mahy's.) Marquis seems to have been a lone academic voice until work by Kathryn Walls, Rose Lovell-Smith and Diane Hebley began appearing in the mid-1990s.

Today Mahy is taught at Auckland (Marquis and Lovell-Smith), Wellington (Walls) and Christchurch (Anna Smith), and in the Canterbury College of Education's national children's literature diploma run by John McKenzie and Doreen Darnell. There is still, however, according to one leading Auckland academic, a strong notion in New Zealand university English departments that children's literature will never be a proper or worthy area of study and, since it cannot really be classed as 'literature', it is better taught and researched in colleges of education — this despite compelling evidence to the contrary in overseas universities and growing interest by students, such as Jenni Keestra's 1987 MA thesis, and Joan Gibbons' paper on Mahy's families and especially when seen in the light of the parallel rise of interest in the academic study of 'popular' culture.

By contrast, from about the time of *The Changeover*, papers on

Margaret Mahy have consistently appeared in overseas literary and educational journals and books by British, American and Canadian academics. For example, Elliott Gose, professor of English at the University of British Colombia and author of a book on Irish fairy tales, has written a detailed analysis of Mahy's connections with myth and folk tale. Massachusetts teacher Adam Berkin's long 1990 paper draws parallels between *The Changeover* and the Sleeping Beauty, concluding that novel performs a double service: 'it appeals to the whims of the adolescent reader by providing humor, suspense, and romance, and it subtly educates. The book ends with optimism. Sorry and Laura do not get married; that would be too traditional and unrealistic, but the book hints that they might get together in the future when Laura has grown up a bit more. This romantic and young adult rewriting stands between Sweet Dreams Novels and rewritten traditional fairy tales. *The Changeover* is a stepping stone to a feminist literary awareness.'

In 1988 one non-academic New Zealand publication did recognise Margaret as having a place among the country's 21 leading writers. On his earlier visit to Governors Bay poet and editor Greg O'Brien had clearly enjoyed Margaret's 'exceptional intelligence, which underpins her hilarity'. He noted, too, her ready agreement with 'Nabokov's notion that writing is a process involving the loss of energy. Starting with the original idea, energy is lost through writing it down, and then another loss occurs as it is revised. "The challenge of writing is to somehow recapture the originality of the idea," she says.'

This uncharacteristically bleak, ironic scrap appeared in the same book:

Sensible Questions

'Suppose the land turned into the sea?'
'Don't be stupid! It couldn't be!'

'Suppose the sea turned into the land?'
'It wouldn't happen. You don't understand!'

'Suppose I waved this grassy stalk,
And Max the dog began to talk?'

'Your fancy's foolish. Your ways are wild!
I often think you're a silly child!'

But Marigold waves her stalk of grass
And all she had asked about came to pass.

The land rolled up and the sea rolled over
The waves were covered with grass and clover,

While Marigold and her reproving aunt
Who'd kept on saying 'Don't!' and 'Can't!'

Were up to their necks in a wild green sea —
And Max the dog said 'Fiddle dee dee!'

By the late 1980s Margaret was describing herself as 'one of the oldest writers for children in New Zealand . . . something that takes me by surprise because I often feel that I am only just beginning to understand what is going on . . . and I am probably the most internationally known. I certainly have the biggest output, which is not boasting, for it might not necessarily be a good thing. Anyhow it doesn't have anything to do with my inner view, my own platonic form of what it is to be a writer, who I see as someone purer than I feel myself to be. I write trade books. I write extensively for instructional reading programmes and for film and TV. I have been a full-time writer since 1980 and over the last three years I have made what I think of as a very good living at it, partly because I work very long hours, and I never take a holiday and partly because I've been around so long

I am increasingly well known. I am fortunate enough to be able to make my living in a way that means there is little separation between work and real life. I enjoyed being a librarian, but when the time came for me to leave the library at the end of the day, I always felt that now my real life was beginning. This does not happen with writing, although parts of it are tedious, and parts of it are desperate in a way that I don't enjoy, so it isn't simply to do with having a nice time. I suppose I feel that, when writing, every part of me is usefully engaged, subjective and objective skills, judgement and memory, and that at the same time, just as the outer space probe Giotto transmitted (in the short time before it broke down) information about Halley's comet in a concentrated burst which it will take a long time to decode and understand, so I am decoding intricate information which I have been receiving in concentrated bursts and storing for years, incapable of doing anything with it when it first came in. One of the things I do when I write is to decode that information, sometimes, I hope, accurately, sometimes speculatively. It doesn't much matter that much of it is understanding personal experience, because, as I pointed out earlier, one thing that decoding reveals is that one's most individual experiences are part of another pattern, and the great originality that one is capable of. Depends upon that network, even when it is extending the network into new areas of perception and response in the writer or reader. I am usually working on several things at the same time . . . while it takes me over a year to write a novel, and during that period the novel is the story to which I surrender my own life, I am always working on other things as well, for I am never sure that the next long book is going to be as acceptable as the last one, and by now I have come to recognise various stages with attendant moods in the evolution of any book through my life and out the other side.'

The three books published in 1988 included another surprise for her loyal readers around the world. *The Door in the Air and other stories*, her first, and so far only book of short stories for teenage readers, was written in response to a request by her publisher.

Some reviewers, this time, were not quite so beguiled. The *Guardian* reviewer Mary Sullivan dismissed the collection as fairy tales of 'an embarrassing daftness . . . Or like a fiver's worth in the sly folds of Pseud's Corner', and an American reviewer, while praising the wit and lyricism, inexplicably bemoaned the general lack of plot. But these were handsomely outgunned by the *Times Educational Supplement* reviewer who compared Margaret to the great Scottish fantasy writer George Macdonald; others praised the language as spirited, incandescent, the collection as invigorating, crackling with high-voltage imaginative energy and altogether a book that should further enhance her reputation. 'A Work of Art', in which Mrs Baskin's cake finds itself being enthusiastically admired in an art gallery, was praised as a wicked, robust satire, while 'The Two Sisters,' with powerful Jungian imagery, leaves readers with the notion that 'all people should be dappled, shadows and light both, and not wholly one thing or the other'.

And there are two stories in this book which many single out as among her finest fantasy: 'The Magician in the Tower,' a surreal, lyrical dream-like narrative of Matilda's loss of innocence and transformation into (maybe) an artist, and especially, 'The Bridge Builder', with the dazzling succession of fantastical bridges that only Margaret, the bridge builder's daughter, could have dreamed up.

Her inspired, obsessive bridge builder constructs his masterpieces out of increasingly fanciful materials: cobwebs for spiders, flowers and beautiful climbing plants, horsehair and vines for little animals to cross, golden wires for singing birds, glass balustrades for fish, silver thread and mother of pearl, bamboo and peacock feathers and violin strings; he builds bridges with harps for handrails, going over volcanoes to the sounds of music, or going nowhere, bridging air and then time itself, crossing over hours and days. At first people, becoming part of a work of art, go out of their way to cross his bridges: 'Mystery became a part of crossing over by my father's bridges'. His power becomes dangerous and threatening; he must be stopped. Wrote one reviewer: 'The bridge-builder's son can transmute him magically into one of his own creations — a theme of death at the hands of the next generation . . . which turns up in several of the stories.' The father turns out to be 'a very ordinary-looking bridge himself — a single-span bridge built of stone over an arch of stone . . . he looked as if he had always been there, as if he would be there for ever, silver moss on his handrails, on his abutments, even on his deck . . . still, perhaps the job of some rare bridges is to cross over only briefly, and then bring us back to the place we started from.'

No writer is spared occasional bad reviews by thoughtful, competent reviewers, or silly or destructive comments by incompetent ones, though some authors claim never to read reviews, good or bad. Margaret candidly admits that she reads her reviews with a 'great deal of anxiety, because I believe them, even though I know how relative all such opinions are . . . I am sufficiently snobbish enough in a literary way to get pleasure from good reviews in "literary" journals. In some ways this is all a little bit of a literary game which, since I often get good reviews, I quite enjoy playing. However, I know that there are many good books that are well reviewed and impeccable from a literary point of view which have left me unmoved, and other, much more imperfect books which I have loved.'

Truly bad reviews leave her anxious for a day or so, but she adds with customary generosity, 'Some people have said that they hated my books, usually because of the supernatural elements in them. What can one say? I am sorry and feel a bit guilty because I want people to enjoy reading what I write, but I also want the freedom as a reader to dislike certain books written with every bit as much sincerity as mine. People like different books and so they should.' But bad reviews still hurt, and tend to be remembered verbatim: '[The Australian critic] Walter McVitty once reviewed *The Railway Engine and the Hairy Brigands*. The review began "It is terrible when paper is in such short supply that it should be wasted on a book like this.'" She finds it interesting that she remembers this so precisely yet cannot remember any line of any good review, no matter how pleased to receive them, 'but I must add I admired Walter McVitty: he was never sentimental about children's books'.

She was now enough of a New Zealand celebrity for her image to be of interest to the women's magazines. Her clothing choices? At home, she liked to be comfortable in tracksuit trousers, a drab jumper, an old Moroccan robe 'which makes me look like some sort of medieval monk, but if I was in Morocco people probably wouldn't notice'. For going out, slightly dressier trouser suits, two favourite Homburg-style hats to help keep her thin and fly-away hair in control, 'the sort of thing you'd imagine Bogart wearing . . . I don't spend a great deal of time thinking about clothes. But I do like the feeling of dressing up when I go out. I like patchwork — it's colourful and varied, and no two pieces are alike. It seems to relate to a certain sort of clownishness.' The cover photograph on Gilderdale's book certainly helped to bring squarely into the public domain the fanciful image that had hitherto been seen mostly in schools and newspaper pictures: Margaret appeared in frothy, pop-art wig and gold-trimmed jade costume, the benign word-witch of popular imagination.

The Door in the Air collection proved to be Margaret's last serious work for young adults for six years. Perhaps, as she neared the end of a decade of intense creativity, it might be considered time for a slight let-up of the pressure, heeding the rather dispiriting advice coming from Vanessa Hamilton in England and her American publisher Margaret McElderry in New York that overall the young adult genre was currently selling less well than expected, and that she should now concentrate on books for younger readers.

But now, as well as the constant stream of smaller stories for picture books and reading programmes, the constant New Zealand and overseas travel, as well as the new delights of grandmotherhood (the first of Penny's five children was born in 1986), much of her creative energy was going into television

— three series and a TV movie for children, and a major six-part drama series for adults, which screened in New Zealand and elsewhere between 1986 and 1994.

Back in the early 1980s Margaret had cheerfully decided that she would do any form of writing 'compatible with self-respect' to earn money. Selling the rights, writing storylines and sometimes actual scripts for television brings rewards undreamed of by most writers of books, except when, as gradually happened for Margaret, international sales and translations of multiple award-winning books start to accumulate in huge markets like the United States, Britain, Europe and Asia.

She has always been fascinated with film, building up that huge library of video housed in both her Governors Bay home and the Cranmer Square apartment. Her favourite film is *2001 — a Space Odyssey*, which she watched over and over again when first approached to write for television, to see how effects were achieved. 'I don't think I'm a born scriptwriter,' she said, 'but I've learned a lot over the years, and I'd be really sorry if I never wrote another script.' Working with television 'had meant an end to being an innocent consumer, even if it means being a much more knowledgeable one: I'll never again see films in the same way — it's even changed my way of listening to them.'

Her first scriptwriting was for Kim Gabara and a programme called *Seagull*. She quickly discovered that writing for film and TV is very different from writing a book, involving teamwork, a pragmatic acceptance of compromises and, compared with a book, a certain detachment. Nevertheless, although, from the very beginning, 'the story's never your own', she found working as part of a team very entertaining; 'you don't feel as alone with it in the very intense and exciting way you sometimes do with a book. I think this feeling is modified in the case of a TV script, but I like working with people, and I like the surprises they give me.' She found that her dialogue was often far too wordy, 'more than the medium can bear', and was often spoken by actors in ways quite different from what she heard in her head. And there were often surprises, usually pleasant but occasionally disappointing, in how her script was visualised by prop makers and set and costume designers.

And if she was pushed too hard? 'Yes, I probably have been at times and probably have backed off, but what's happened is a certain disinterest has crept in; I try to do as well as I could, but I'm no longer interested in it or connected with it in quite the same way. The script becomes a professional commitment with its own interest and enthusiasm but it's no longer my story in quite the same way.'

Her principal collaboration was with producer Dave Gibson and director Yvonne Mackay, of the Gibson Group, with, first, *Cuckooland*, a zany six-part television series that screened in New Zealand in 1986 and collected a gold medal in the New York Film and Television Festival in the same year. As Mackay has explained, *Cuckooland* was the result of Gibson's decision, around 1975, to move into children's programmes, following a successful adaptation of a Frank Sargeson short story, and first-hand experience at Cannes of the interest in children's TV. They were led to Margaret via the *School Journal* (and, coincidentally, to Joy Cowley, for an acclaimed adaptation by Ian Mune of her novel *The Silent One*).

With Margaret's patter songs set to music by the eminent Wellington composer Jenny McLeod, *Cuckooland* was, says Mackay, a 'way over the top' musical show, about a mother and her two children dwelling in a 'living' house. Margaret was given a free rein and no one who knew her comic books would have been unduly surprised by the family whizzing along a highway in a land yacht, a crocodile handbag with snapping jaws alarming passers-by, a letter-box with quivering red lips, a bath in a tree constructed of power pylons, or the layer, for adult amusement, of a used car salesman who becomes a pirate, mafia-like tax inspectors and a stern SAS-style librarians' taskforce in search of overdue books. One reviewer described it as 'weird, wacky, loud and almost incompletely incomprehensible in parts'.

Cuckooland was followed by *The Haunting of Barney Palmer*, a one-hour TV movie adaptation by Margaret of *The Haunting*, which Mackay had read and immediately wanted to film. The movie, filmed in and around Wellington, was shown in the United States nearly a year before New Zealand viewers got to see it (admittedly in prime time) in October 1987. The film, said producer Dave Gibson, was as close to the chiller genre as a family movie could get at that time.

Largely on the strength of Margaret's reputation and her screenplay, the 52-minute film was pre-sold to the Public Service Broadcasting Network and TVNZ. In return for what Gibson described as a 'substantial sum' of money, the contractual agreement stipulated an American actor, who turned out to be Ned Beatty (*Deliverance*, *All the President's Men*, *Superman* and *Wise Blood*) who played Great-Uncle Cole. This, says Yvonne Mackay, required some rewriting, to make the character an uncle who had lived overseas for many years. 'I remember Ned Beatty arriving here, as many stars do, needing to be placated, not a happy chappy, wanting to discuss the script. That really means changing his lines, to make them acceptable to him and a US audience. It was extraordinary: he met Margaret and sort of fell in love with her, and she with him — I remember them at the wrap party, dancing round, and by this time Beatty had decided that we were a real bunch of troupers, just like a New York repertory company. She won this extraordinary respect from him, and everyone — especially for that quite thoughtful way of speaking, with her eyes going off to one side, a giant pause while she thinks, finding the precise word, making connections with maybe something from a newspaper item which she's wondered or puzzled about, and which she'll work back into her response — which is *always* worth waiting for. Everyone on the set was fascinated, and very respectful.'

The Haunting of Barney Palmer was the Gibson's Group first experience with a production for overseas television; a stunning review in the influential *Variety* magazine was the best of gratifyingly good reviews both overseas and, when it was finally screened, in New Zealand. While 'not a merry prank, by a long shot . . . Margaret Mahy's script, taken from her own novel, doesn't spell everything out, and the results are neatly alarming — with the suggestion that it might all be too true,' said *Variety*. Overall, the child actors, Yvonne Lawley as the crabby Great-Grandmother Scholar, music again by Jenny McLeod and the special effects all earned high praise from reviewers. And for the *Evening Post* a children's panel, aged between twelve and fourteen, gave the film its seal of approval: '*The Haunting of Barney Palmer* wasn't weird — it was scary. We don't think it could have been any scarier — like the time that gloved hand came down on Barney's shoulder, or when the mirror cracked and water flowed out of it — really creepy. The music and their facial expressions helped too. The storyline was excellent and the special effects were brilliant . . . to enjoy the storyline we think you'd have to be a bit older but the special effects would attract younger kinds — about six — they might also scare them. When you're a kid you don't really seem to worry about what the story is about. We think the whole family will like it.'

Gibson's also seriously considered making *The Changeover* into a feature film. 'After *The Haunting*, we had a possible French buyer who struggled with *The Changeover* for a long time, but they were worried with the sexual aspect and it came to nothing,' says Mackay. 'I've carried a candle for it also for a long time and we have struggled with the young adult genre problem, but in the end, in film terms it is neither one thing or the other.' In addition, she notes, films for younger audiences present producers with special problems: they are harder to finance and promote than an adult film; audiences of half-price children's seats means returns are lower; and children's movies are screened on TV at times when your colleagues are not watching. 'But currently the *Shrek*s are changing that line of demarcation, in that adults will go to a "children's" film without accompanying a child, so maybe the time has come for a second look at Margaret's young adult books.'

Within a year of *The Haunting of Barney Palmer*, another Margaret Mahy script was being enjoyed by young television viewers in several countries. This was *Strangers*, a six-part story about four children who belong to a secret society and who witness a robbery of antiques. It was Margaret's first drama written specially for the medium. Described this time as a 'mystery thriller', involving a typical Mahy mix of 'spying, chases, kidnapping, the police, great danger and fire-eating', *Strangers* was commissioned in 1987 by TVNZ head of drama Brian Bell and producer Chris Bailey and the eleven-week shoot in Auckland was directed by Peter Sharp. This trio was largely responsible for TVNZ's strong 'kidult' genre reputation built up during the 1970s and maturing with fine series by writers such as Margaret and Ken Catran during the 1980s.

'Margaret's got a beaut feel for character and New Zealand dialogue,' Bailey told the *Listener*. 'When the children start piecing things together, they find a somewhat intricate arrangement of personalities who are not quite what they seem to be.' The enthusiastic reviews and a further major prize in New York make it even more lamentable that the political changes of the late 1980s (which resulted in cynical, ratings-driven television and a disastrous effect on locally made children's programmes) have in effect kept writers like Margaret and Ken Catran and quality New Zealand children's drama away from the small screen for over a decade.

Reviews for *Strangers* were warm, typified by the *Dominion Sunday Times*'s Colleen Reilly commenting on the writer's 'wonderful story,' taking stock-in-trade elements of children's books and adding to them 'elements of magic, social comment, sexual satire and humour and easy analyses of physical and psychological disabilities'. Editing, photography, pacing and cutting — all earned high praise, along with the puzzlement of just 'why TVNZ does "kidult" series so superbly and adult drama series so poorly'.

Hard on the heels of *Strangers* came another Mahy book

adapted for the small screen, this time a six-part BBC series of her 1986 book, *Aliens in the Family*. The story, not scripted by Margaret, was relocated to Britain and shot there with English actors. It went to air in New Zealand in September 1988. For some time after 1987 her scripting energies were employed in response to a suggestion, somewhat ahead of its time, by Yvonne Mackay that they should work together on an adult thriller on genetic engineering in the tradition of the BBC series, *Edge of Darkness*.

Mackay had earlier read of an American scientist being allowed to do field tests in genetic engineering at the Wallaceville Research Station in New Zealand that he was not permitted to do in the United States; that set her thinking 'about how an isolated free-market country such as New Zealand could be used by a big multinational company to experiment with human genes . . . How long will it be, she asks, until "you've got a child who has been completely grown from conception till birth in some sort of artificial womb"? Excited by the possibilities of the story, Mackay did further research, including exploring the ethics of exogenesis with experts at Monash University. She then planted the embryo of the story in the imagination of Mahy and waited for it to grow.'

Margaret took up the idea with great gusto, and what emerged, Mackay told the *Listener*, 'was a rather Gothic tale of intrigue about a multinational called Biobrite Corporation, which breeds perfect babies in a secret location in the South Island. When the head of the project is assassinated, agents from a rival corporation are sent to steal Typhon's research, and the New Zealand government has to deal with the fallout.'

In retrospect, Margaret says that the idea (that people can be manufactured) is much less fantastic now, when 'it's thought that cloning has apparently taken place, though people deny it', than it was then. 'In script conferences they accused me of being too tied to the known facts about clonings. I'd say, well I don't think that could happen and they'd say we'll make it happen — and in film there's a certain amount of truth in that.'

Made with the help of some overseas money, and starring English actors Greg Wise and Alfred Molina, Australian Sophie Lee, as well as leading local stars John Bach and Miranda Harcourt, *Typhon's People* was a really successful series, Mackay recalls. 'We shot it into four one-hour slots; the theme was right up Margaret's alley and characters she invented were very futuristic, different, almost fantasy. Typhon himself was a man with lots of money, a voyeur of life, not a person who enters life physically himself. As someone who adores beauty, he gets the chance to create a whole series of people who are extraordinary — because he can. He'll cross animal and plant genes if he has to — and do it in remote New Zealand, in the mountains, underground, and suddenly spring it on the world. It was quite an intellectual puzzle.' *Typhon's People* was sold to a number of countries, including Britain.

Margaret told the *Listener*: 'It's a very complicated story, because it works in two different ways. It's making a reference to current advances in technology and yet, basically, it's still the Frankenstein story. It links into the sort of speculative story of the past, as well as making comments about the possibilities of the future.' She had read Stephen Hawking's *A Brief History of Time* and partly understood it, largely because she listened to the tape while driving round Christchurch. Was she personally opposed to genetic engineering? Not per se, she said, 'in an answer which ranged over Marie Curie's discovery of radium, the patenting of bulls in Holland and the dangers of commercial sponsorship of scientific research in universities', though she did worry about 'the irresponsible use of the techniques and the reduction in biodiversity as species are replaced by more "desirable" ones. "I think that's much more alarming than Frankenstein lumbering out of the cave. Some of these ideas were in the script, but they made it too long." She pauses. "Sometimes, when people ask me a question, I give great long answers. You can see what a disadvantage that is in a television script."'

Margaret Mahy was not, in writer Noel O'Hare's judgement, a natural TV writer. Her mind was too subtle and playful to turn itself easily to a medium that worked in broad brushstrokes. Yet she took a real delight in television and film, and according to Mackay, owned enough videos to start a rental shop, including such titles as *Robocop* and *The Terminator*. Margaret admitted to owning 'quite a lot of violent videos . . . but the violence is of a particular sort — not that anyone who's opposed to violence would find my arguments particularly convincing'. She did not worry too much about the violence in science-fiction horror stories, although she occasionally enjoyed the mock violence of the WWF *Superstars of Wrestling*. 'It was very funny. Every match had a story of its own. I suppose basically there was a feeling that nobody got hurt, which is something you don't necessarily find watching Olympic boxing.'

As well as her first trip to Japan (a three-week tour visiting Tokyo, Sendai and Hokkaido), 1989 brought the publication of *The Great White Man-Eating Shark*, one of four picture books to appear that year and often singled out as one of her favourites to read aloud.

She chose a special occasion to talk extensively — and hilariously — about the genesis of this gloriously wicked story of a plain but sharkish boy called Norvin: the prestigious 1989 May Hill Arbuthnot Lecture presented on 23 April at the University of Pittsburgh. Her address was subsequently printed in a collection of these prestigious Arbuthnot lectures and reprinted twice, in *A Dissolving Ghost* and the updated, third edition of Canadian Sheila Egoff's classic 1969 collection of essays on children's literature, *Only Connect*.

The Arbuthnot, presented annually by a distinguished author, critic, librarian, historian or teacher of children's literature, was instituted in 1969. Margaret, at her most exuberant, ranged over the sharkish Norvin, a searching examination of Noel Streatfeild's *Ballet Shoes* and her own novel *Memory*, the relationship between fact and fiction, and her background as the different bookish child who grew into a 'dis-located' writer. The opening few minutes provided a fascinating glimpse into how yet another childhood memory combined with an adult experience to produce a story.

'Two years ago it happened. I found myself in a motel swimming pool in New Mexico. I like swimming. I swim quite purposefully and I had the swimming pool almost to myself — not quite, however. At the shallow end of the pool stood a young man and woman passionately, indeed it sometimes seemed permanently, embraced. I didn't mind this while I was swimming away from them, but as I swam towards them I found myself filled with the embarrassment of someone who is intruding into a private space, a space which one has no right to violate. My shyness, my wish not to intrude upon this couple, alternated with something less charitable, self-righteous indignation. After all this was not a private space; it was a motel swimming pool and I was swimming backwards and forwards, which everyone knows is the proper thing to do in a swimming pool. Why should I be the one to feel intrusive and guilty? I felt like this swimming away from them. Then swimming towards them I began to think — ah, but am I jealous of their youth and passion and so on, (kicking regularly, surging to the other end of the pool). Yet who wants to be bothered with self-analysis when you are trying to shoot through the water like a silver arrow? As I swam backwards and forwards I began to dream of dressing up as a shark, and gliding, up the pool towards them. I could see myself soundless, menacing, and ruthless, my skin set with sharp close-set denticles, my silent crescent snarl filled with rows and rows of teeth. The lovers would suddenly see my dorsal fin approaching. They would leap out of the water screaming. I would have the whole pool to myself, free to be a silver arrow to my heart's content. It would all be *my* space, and deservedly so.

'After I left the pool, I found myself haunted, not by the lovers themselves but by the one who had wanted all the space in the swimming pool. This person usurping the primitive power of the shark, the fin cutting through the water, the huge mouthful of teeth rising up over the back of the boat — this temporary villain I had contemplated becoming, in order to have all the swimming pool to myself. It had in some ways been a tempting and empowering persona, and one I recognised, although I had never met it in that shape before. My temporary shark began to make other sharkish connections. Sharks have been part of my life for a long time. Though shark attacks are almost unknown in New Zealand, we all know the sharks are there. Parents sometimes warn their children, "Don't go out deep! There might be sharks!" Of course the children already know. Sharks!

'Once, dramatically, I saw a shark caught on a hand line pulled up and left to die on the sand. It was only a small one, but it was a genuine shark. I stood over it watching it drown in the sunny air of a remote North Island beach. When it began to rot away, someone threw it back into the deep water where smaller fish flickered around it for a while eating what was left, but even then its bones still glimmered mysteriously through the water if you knew where to look. It was the year I turned five. It was also the year I learned to swim. I couldn't write much in those days, but was already a slave to fiction. I talked aloud, waving sticks in the air, conducting unseen orchestras of stories remembered, recreated and invented, stories which I inhabited by temporarily becoming what I was inventing. That shark and the mystery and menace of the glimmering bones and what might have happened (that it might have been my bones glimmering there, I suppose) were part of those stories in those days. I was certainly part of the first nightmare I can ever remember having: that my little sister vanished under the water and after a second or two her sunbonnet came floating to the top. We were living in a caravan in those days. I woke up in the top bunk crying, and bewildered to find that something which only a moment before had seemed utterly real had dissolved into nothing. I think it was the same shark, flesh on its bones once more, that came out of the part to inhabit me and swim up and down the motel swimming pool. It's just as well I didn't have my shark suit with me.

'I like to swim in deep water. I like to be where I can't feel the bottom and I have always liked that from the time I was very small, but there is always the fear of the shark sneaking up from down below grabbing your foot. After you've been frightened of it for a while, you begin to tell stories about it, to take it over ... and in odd moments of life when you have a little go at being the shark yourself, you recognise something true in what you are doing ...'

'As I thought about my temporary sharkness, it suggested a simple story which I found entertaining to write. There are a lot of different sorts of sharks, many of them quite harmless but I wanted to evoke the most sinister of all, the great white man-eating shark ... Like most stories I write, I intended it primarily as a story to be told aloud, but it has been produced as a picture book, and tells the story of the villain, a plain boy who happens to be a very good actor and who dressed up as a great white man-eating shark, frightening other swimmers out of the sea so that he could have it all to himself. He acted the part so well that a female shark fell in love with him and proposed something approximating marriage. He fled from her in terror. His duplicity was revealed, and he was too scared to go swimming for a long time after. This is obviously didactic (but, I hope ironically didactic) and seems far from true, since we all know that in real life firstly people do not dress up as sharks, and that the figurative sharks often go undetected because they don't allow people to see their dorsal fins. But in another way I have told the children all the truth I know from personal experience. Kurt Vonnegut says in the introduction to *Mother Night* "We are what we pretend to be, so we must be careful of what we pretend to be." That turned out to be the hidden truth of my New Mexico swimming pool experience, but would that have been its hidden truth if I hadn't already read books like *Mother Night*, or if I didn't already know in a personal way that we become what we pretend to be ... But the story of the shark is a joke and that is how I expect it to be enjoyed, as a joke and only a joke. It is only in the context of this occasion that I am bothering to tell about the experience compacted in it, offering it as a joke at my own expense and also a part of a network, to a child who may one day read *Mother Night* or other books whose titles I can't guess at, and appreciate the truths in those books because they already know them. My own experience was real, funny, momentarily sinister and salutary, all at once, but someone else in that swimming pool on that day might have seen a different, a more anguished truth, might have realised that the lovers were saying goodbye, or that they were meeting after a long separation, or that they were honeymooners, or that the thought of being together without touching was unbearable to them. A thousand other stories were potentially there in the swimming pool with me, but my story was about the person who turned into a shark.'

The unexpected element of *The Great White Man-Eating Shark*, she said in a paper on 'incongruity, uncertainty and superiority' in humour in 1996, 'is not so much the final appearance of the real shark (a climax which theoretically should be, and generally is, anticipated even by very young children), but the fact that the shark turns out a female shark who, along with everyone else, fails to penetrate Norvin's disguise and makes ruthless and inappropriate romantic overtures. This leads to incongruity over and above expectation and, to a degree, at the expense of the traditional climax, so that knowing something of the probable climax ahead of time and then it present heightened with an unexpected modification should theoretically make the story funnier, since you have one tension in terms of an anticipated resolution crossed with a different tension between the expected ending and its modification. Of course this sort of speculation ruins the story, but you are here to have it ruined on your behalf.'

The following year, at another North American children's literature celebration, this time in Vancouver, Margaret shared the platform with her eminent American publisher Margaret McElderry, Canada's much-loved children's author Janet Lunn and Britain's award-winning illustrator Shirley Hughes. Between them, they represented 120 years of devoted experience to books for the young. Mahy's novels, it was stated, were among the finest anywhere being written for teenagers, although McElderry didn't down-play the problems inherent in the young adult genre, with even Margaret's novels not doing as well as they should in an unpredictable market.

If, from the mid-1980s, Margaret had been accepting an increasing number of invitations to such international events, this activity was not at the expense of her personal commitment to New Zealand readers, either at children's literature seminars, in schools or in interviews, such as writer/director Keith Hunter's for a major TV documentary in 1987 and Sue Kedgley's for *Our Own Country*, an important and frank 1989 book that placed Margaret in an A-team of eight New Zealand women writers.

In 1990 she was chosen by *North & South* magazine as the only woman of four 'Living Treasure' writers, along with playwright Roger Hall, poet Allen Curnow and novelist and broadcaster Ian Cross, who were asked to share 'their vision of the nation and the 90s'. ' "I make my stories out of what New Zealand has offered me. And what New Zealand offered me as I was growing up was an enormous concentration of English imagery. It's a paradox, but it's the New Zealand paradox."

'When she was growing up, anything made in New Zealand was supposed to be second rate . . . Growing up in the 40s and 50s, when we thought we had everything right, and now finding we didn't leaves Mahy with mixed feelings . . . "We are living in times when the New Zealand dream is not only under threat, but can be shown to be fallible . . . Somehow or other an ideal that looked as if it was working during the 40s and 50s has become increasingly inoperable. Institutions, including government, have come so much more hard-nosed and pragmatic to the extent that the ideal seems to have gone.

'"Where once one felt a degree of certainty and optimism, one feels much more anxiety and uncertainty now. But despite all the changes, one doesn't feel that we're any closer to achieving the millennium than we were 20 years ago."

'Perhaps not, but Margaret Mahy is making her contribution towards it. She takes a moral stance, in her words, in favour of goodness and kindness. She uses humour as her weapon.

"'I think humour is an innovative thing. It enables us to confront sensitive problems and not be too crushed by them. I try to joke about a lot of things. It's a way of coping." But it too, she adds, has its limitations.

'And what about the 1990s? "They look . . . all right," she says very tentatively, then laughs.'

During the productive 1980s Margaret's successes were celebrated by the growing number of children's writers and illustrators in New Zealand, who saw her as their guru, mentor, champion and friend.

She may have been published mostly in Britain and the United States, but she has always been very much part of the New Zealand writing community, and arguably one of the main reasons for a sudden expansion of New Zealand children's publishing from about Maurice Gee's *Under the Mountain* in 1979 onwards. The establishment of the children's book awards in 1982, and their growth from a modest sponsorship by Government Print to a handsome corporate funding, by AIM toothpaste in 1990 and New Zealand Post in 1997 (even though Margaret's books were not, through the 1980s, eligible), undoubtedly owes much to her high public profile and leadership.

Her generosity among writers is legendary, from offering the use of the central Christchurch apartment, to attending book awards armed with a heavy bag of shortlisted copies for their authors to sign, paying her own fares to functions around New Zealand where she knew the organisers were good people on tight budgets, to her famous late-night stamina (she is often the one who insists on paying any bill and among the last to leave) at after-awards and conference parties. ('Adult' writers have not been neglected, especially at many a Governors Bay party, whether for the New Zealand Society of Authors or unofficial gatherings.)

Margaret's assessment of this community has always been typically down-to-earth, and aware of its shared problems, such as finding an authentic New Zealand voice and editing for overseas editions. From her earliest years as a picture book writer, she had plenty of experience of editors wanting to diminish or eliminate the subtleties of her New Zealand voice. 'This certainly is different to the English voice. Vanessa was a wonderful editor in a lot of ways, but she had a supremely English voice and there were times when I felt that she would try and edit out not exactly slang or idiom, but a certain sort of Kiwi accent which I had and which sometimes I wanted, though I wouldn't argue about it . . .' For books being published in New Zealand, but seeking overseas markets, maintaining the integrity of indigenous storytelling was an ongoing worry.

She said, in a candid assessment to an Australian audience in 1985, that '. . . the New Zealand children's book community is a small one and not particularly self-critical. In a way it is still at a stage where any one person's triumph is everyone's triumph . . . We all tend to know each other — or of each other and my feeling is that Australia is more diversified, more critical and probably more innovative . . . It is probably enough to say it is a lively, optimistic, rather insecure, but very alert scene, and making unabashed use of a cliché, is establishing its own identity at last and in doing so, is, at least to the present, not uncritical but supportive of its writers . . .

'A writer like myself does not always straddle the voice between "small-local" and "big-international" all that easily. On the one hand I want to be part of my writing community. Though an essentially solitary experience, writing draws reinforcement from many places and passes it on too. At one level, at once superficial and important, a writer does not really want to abandon success and this tends to involve overseas publication. Yet the American market in particular is anxious about idioms that are not immediately familiar and local custom which they say their public will not understand or accept. People in Australia and New Zealand reflect with irony and even indignation that, for years, their children have adapted satisfactorily to books from GB and the USA but of course the situation has been they have had to adapt and this does apply in the USA. It is a huge and desirable market and sets its own rules. In my picture book *Jam*, mention of pikelets and scones and steam pudding (all useful ways of using up jam) was too idiomatic for the American market . . . Lynley Dodd had trouble with English editors over the mention of the "possum" at the end of *The Apple Tree*. They felt British children would not recognise a possum. The American publishers worried about the violence of the language . . . the possum who eats the apples is described as "a mean old rotten old possum", which I find quite verbally satisfying from a child's point of view. For my own part, I compromise. Others seem to me to be dictated by the conservatism implicit in power, by a certain humourless subjection to whatever society is choosing to be didactic about at the time and sometimes by lack of faith in the material and the children it is intended for. Alterations in accordance with the demands of these important markets do tend to eliminate the very local elements that teachers and critics in one's own immediate surroundings are longing to find. Some of them look very sternly at any compromise. Nevertheless, in any sort of bridge-building, there are two banks and one has to adapt one's bridge to various configurations.'

And yet — 'Will and good intentions alone do not create an indigenous children's literature. Though the desirability of writing "New Zealand" children's books has been discussed for over a hundred years, it took more than simply writing set in New Zealand to produce books that *felt* like New Zealand books and even as late as twelve years ago, people were submitting manuscripts to Oxford New Zealand in which New Zealand children played in the snow at Christmas, so I am not the only person with the fault line, though I think it is vanishing and certainly New Zealand is now as partisan about its own children's books as anyone could wish.'

She was also well aware of the increased pressures on authors, especially children's writers, to perform and, slightly ruefully, of the inevitable consequences of creating her own very singular and powerful public persona.

'It is increasingly expected of writers to stand up and be seen in New Zealand . . . "In a way, I'm not sure how fair it is for someone to talk about their own books, although I've enjoyed hearing other writers. Of course, we all want to be read, but then you experience the paradox of being commercial." Mahy wants to escape both the commercial side of publication as well as stereotypes surrounding children's authors. "It used to be that people didn't take you seriously if you were a children's writer. That has changed, but now and again it is a bit disconcerting to find that people remember the wig and find that the most interesting thing about you."'

Some time in the early 1990s she decided on a change of image, as noted by *North & South*.

'Even the fact that the chuckling, largish woman you see inside book jackets, usually sporting a dreadfully comic wig, has been replaced by the comparative wraith on the sofa before me has a prosaic explanation.

'Mahy had got to the point where she had to decide whether to stay uncomfortable, buy new clothes or lose weight. She chose the latter. "With a long, thin face, losing weight isn't necessarily the most flattering thing you can do and one or two people did say, oh dear, you do look thin but . . . they were usually people who were quite a lot heavier than I was. Walking up the hill and getting in and out of cars are easier," she adds. She has been interested to note people's reactions to her changed appearance. To a writer, everything is interesting.'

By around 1990 it was fairly common knowledge among children's book people that Margaret had dissuaded colleagues eager to put her name forward for recognition as, at the very least, a Dame Commander of the British Empire. Apart from her strong (some felt well overdue) claims for a high civil honour, there was something deliciously apt about the notion of the storyteller, the wise and wacky word magician, becoming, at the touch of a silver sword, Dame Margaret.

She was, however, perfectly happy to lend her name to a new

prize, the Margaret Mahy Medal and Lecture Award, instituted in 1991 by the New Zealand Children's Literature Foundation (later the Children's Book Foundation of New Zealand, now the Storylines Children's Literature Foundation of New Zealand). With Margaret as the first recipient for 'a distinguished contribution to New Zealand literature for young people', the award immediately became the country's most prestigious honour in the field, in subsequent years annually honouring lifetimes of service and distinction in writing, illustration and publishing.

The inaugural awards dinner, held in Auckland and attended by 200 people, was notable for the display, determinedly mounted by the librarians on the organising committee, of nearly every single one of Margaret's books. As probably the only time anyone has tried to gather her entire output physically in one place, trade *and* educational books, this display stunned even those familiar with the scope of her work.

Margaret's speech, entitled 'Surprising Moments', was packed with a typically glittering and, at times, highly comic array of literary, political and scientific allusions, beginning with the incongruity of reading 'not the most profound statement she'd ever read' about 'imagination' penned by L. Frank Baum, author of *The Wizard of Oz*, on the side of a packet of herb tea ('an adventurous blend of real strawberries and fruity herbs'.)

'Story and fantasy have many functions in our lives, but one of the functions is to mediate between us and naked existence, to nudge us back into a state of astonishment from which we can also easily retreat, as well as providing places to stand, strong places in an overwhelming world. And when, pushed by no matter what sort of force from outside, we fall into the cracks in the structure, we immediately start to compose stories to bridge the crack or fill it in so we can walk out of it safely. Of course, not all the cracks are profound ones. Some we experience as jokes, which brings me back to the quotation on imagination and the tea packet . . . It is odd to think that possibly more people have read Baum's thoughts on imagination on tea packets than in his original essay.

Governors Bay as seen from the Port Hills' Summit Road, with the jetty close to Margaret's house and the Manson's Point peninsula (bisecting the picture) running out into Lyttelton Harbour.

The sea-facing frontage of the house at Governors Bay.

A serene corner of the patio.

Living area and sea views at Governors Bay.

Work station, with many treasures.

The librarian's ladder and the astronomer's telescope are features of the large book-filled area which serves as both office and sleeping quarters.

THE VITAL SIXTY-SOMETHING — as fans at a signing session see her, July 2000, World Reading Congress, Auckland.

AT A STORYLINES FESTIVAL IN AUCKLAND — signing a young fan's cast and in performance mode.

Famous Mahy animal images, perfected over decades, on countless personally signed books, autograph books or even shyly offered scraps of paper.

MARGARET MAHY
PERSONAL COLLECTION

ABOVE: At the Storylines Festival, 2003, with Prime Minister Helen Clark.

RIGHT: Preparing for the marathon Harry Potter read-aloud session at Storylines 2003.

BELOW: Famous names in New Zealand children's literature at the annual Margaret Mahy Day, 2002. Left to right: Joy Cowley, Dorothy Butler, Margaret Mahy, Maurice Gee, Lynley Dodd, Ann Mallinson, Tessa Duder.

Margaret Mahy and the 'skull and rose' tattoo, 2005.
ALAN KNOWLES

'What others do with such ripe and fruity incongruities I don't know, but I do know that I make use of them in inward and outward ways, and the outward way is often a story, and often a fantasy. In New York in late January I saw a painted permanent sign that read, "Ears pierced. With pain or without pain — your choice!" For a fraction of a second, mid stride, I thought the message was not about ears being pierced but something much more metaphysical . . . the power we have to choose pain or to refuse it, the way some stories often give pain romantic status, and allow it to have power over us while other stories allow us, ultimately, to have some sort of power over pain. With these thoughts I climbed up out of the crack, lived through the ambivalent moment, finished my step, took another and another, went on to a lunch appointment and went on beyond that to write a story built around that sign, though it not a children's story [*The Illustrated Traveller's Tale*]. Statements often suggest their own audience. These moments are real enough, but they are fantastic too, and link one into fantasies so vast so profound they seem to be speculations about our own nature and the nature of the world . . . seem to be myths, seem to be mysteries, seem to be the source within ourselves, which we feed with stories and out of which stories come, directing us towards astonishment, even as we develop some sort of a technique for coping with the perpetual surprise of living in the everyday world.'

Part Five

The Doctor of Letters
— 1993 to 2005

The highest civil honour in New Zealand is the Order of New Zealand, instituted in 1987 and modelled on Britain's Order of Merit. Ordinary membership is limited to 20 living people: when one dies, a new member is appointed. A handful of additional members may be appointed to mark important royal, state or national occasions.

Two writers, already recipients of the CBE, were made additional members during the country's 1990 sesquicentenary celebrations: poet Allen Curnow and novelist Janet Frame. Three years later Margaret May Mahy, not previously decorated in any way, became the only New Zealand writer ever to be appointed an Ordinary Member of the Order of New Zealand. Other current members include Sir Edmund Hillary, the Maori Queen, Te Arikinui Dame Te Atairangikaahu, singer Dame Kiri Te Kanawa and two former Prime Ministers, David Lange and James Bolger. Others come from the legal profession, architecture, art, medicine, academia, politics and business. Apart from recognising Margaret's own life and works, the 1993 honour was a direct acknowledgement that a major contribution to the culture of children — their entertainment, their education, their well-being and their place in society — is as worthy an achievement as any other.

It was a good year, 1993. A second high official honour was bestowed, appropriately by her alma mater, the University of Canterbury. Flying in to the graduation ceremony from one of her overseas commitments, Margaret was presented with a citation conferring on her an honorary Doctorate of Letters by the head of the English Department, Professor David Gunby, who said that her 'underlying optimism about the human condition' and 'an innate capacity for growth and love' were 'always being affirmed in her work'. Margaret, in typical style, told a reporter afterwards that while she was happy to be affirmed by her former university, she felt she had 'cheated a little bit' by receiving a degree for which she had not had to sit examinations.

Nineteen ninety-three was also the first year of the now

acclaimed Storylines Festival of New Zealand Children's Writers and Illustrators in Auckland. In the long Easter weekend of the previous year, Joy Cowley (by now the internationally esteemed writer of many hundreds of school readers and a body of fine novels for both adults and children) had hosted the first ever gathering of children's writers and illustrators at her beachside home in the Marlborough Sounds, with Margaret and Joy honoured by their peers as the undoubted doyennes of the 32-strong group.

From this weekend came an idea, enthusiastically picked up by the Children's Book Foundation in Auckland, which materialised as the first Storylines Festival in June 1993. Centred for nearly a decade on the Auckland region, it has since spread to include Wellington, Christchurch and other centres, with Margaret making a loyal and (though this is not a word she would use) regal appearance nearly every year, reading and signing her books for lengthy queues of fascinated and patient children. If a single paid director backed by volunteer organisers have been able, by sheer hard work and passion, to nurture this five-day festival into probably the world's biggest children's literary festival — in 1993 it drew about 20,000 and now the free family days, writers' school tours, workshops, seminars and a national literature quiz attract around 50,000 — then it is due in large part to sponsors' recognition of Margaret and Joy's leadership of children's writers and publishing.

Approaching sixty, Margaret was now occasionally given to announcing herself as one of the 'oldest' writers in New Zealand, and getting 'older and tireder' by the year, although the spate of books, travel commitments and work on ongoing projects continued undiminished. In 1989, along with *The Great White Man-Eating Shark*, there had been three other publications; in 1990, three, including the lovely *Seven Chinese Brothers*. The following year saw no fewer than five, among them *Dangerous Spaces* (her first serious novel since *Memory* four years earlier) and at last, *Bubble Trouble*, that memorable patter song and favourite performance piece, enjoyed frequently by audiences and now committed to paper. The American edition featured her own illustrations and the British edition those of the highly esteemed Tony Ross. Another novel, *Underrunners*, appeared in 1992, and then two shorter novels, the jolly gang stories of the *Good Fortunes Quartet* in 1993 and the comic knockabout 'pirates and librarians' tale of *The Greatest Show off Earth* in 1994.

Interesting and dramatic novellas, *Dangerous Spaces* and *Underrunners* arguably suffered from coming after the great surge of award-winning novels. For instance, they rate only passing mention in reference book summaries of her work, such as *The Cambridge Guide to Children's Books in English* or *The Oxford Companion to New Zealand Literature*. No writer, even or especially those as prolific as Margaret, can keep on 'topping' their work, and a critical plateau, or even some fatigue on the part of booksellers and readers (if not the writer), was perhaps inevitable.

After more than ten years with J.M. Dent, the 1991 ghost story *Dangerous Spaces* was Margaret's first book with Hamish Hamilton. The imprint page states that this is 'A Vanessa Hamilton Book': her long-time editor Vanessa Hamilton (no connection to the publisher) had become principally Margaret's agent, working from her home, a converted stable in West Sussex, where she lived with her husband, the writer Noel Simon. Vanessa edited and 'packaged' the picture book manuscripts with a chosen illustrator for chosen publishers, and edited and advised on longer manuscripts.

The reasons for the change to Hamish Hamilton were, as often in publishing, convoluted. As the 1993 *North & South* profile explained, Dent had been taken over by Weidenfeld & Nicolson five years earlier, and Vanessa Hamilton was invited to join the new board. 'After "one year of intense frustration", she left to set up as an independent literary agent, presenting Margaret with a dilemma: to stay with Dent, where she almost felt like company property, or go with Vanessa with whom she'd had a happy professional relationship for 15 years. "I had been with Dent for almost

20 years but so many of the original people had gone it was almost as if its identity had dissolved. I chose to go with Vanessa."

'It was not the wrong choice. Hamilton takes up the tale: "As soon as it was known that I was representing Margaret, I was approached by most of the major groups in the UK. She and I decided to hold an auction for her first post-Dent novel, *Dangerous Spaces*, and we invited five publishers to bid, including Dent of course. The Penguin group [of which Hamish Hamilton is part] made an outstanding offer for world English language rights, the first time they had done so for a children's book."

'That "outstanding offer" was £30,000 and with it Hamish Hamilton became Mahy's mainline publisher in both hardback and paperback. "Suddenly," says Mahy, "I became rich in authorly terms."' As *North & South* reported, 'Based on royalties of Mahy titles currently in print, one New Zealand publisher estimates her annual income would be about $300,000. That would be about right, she agrees mildly, though it goes up and down and she doesn't think it would be as much this year. A far cry from 1976 when, still relatively new to the business, she got landed with an income tax bill for $10,000 and had to sell her car. She has an accountant to monitor these matters now.'

For the rest of the 1990s, Margaret was published mostly by Hamish Hamilton, though there was a long backlist with Dent, which still existed as part of the Orion Book Group.

Pleased as she was to be with Hamish Hamilton, Margaret looked back nostalgically to the 'calm' early days with Dent. 'Simple decisions' seemed to have vanished. 'The days when an author wrote one novel a year for the same publisher have gone. A lot of authors today apparently operate between several companies, no doubt playing one off against the other to a certain extent. I don't feel at ease with this, although I seem to have wound up doing it. Even if through an agent. I miss the familial relationship I used to have [with Dent] and find it harder to come to truly fair decisions. Dent still does very well by my backlist and yet I can never quite ally myself with Dent in the simple way I used to.'

Margaret enjoyed a long, grateful and unusually close relationship with her agent, maintained by technology and her own visits to Sussex, although Vanessa never made the journey to New Zealand. The pair talked and faxed at length over ideas and, later, editing possibilities. 'At times I think she becomes irritated with my lack of incisiveness,' Margaret told *North & South*. The fax machine was 'a wonderful way of getting in touch with Vanessa', but it had its disadvantages. 'I used to send stories away by mail and they'd take five days to get there, a day or two to read, then a few days to come back. Now she can get back in touch much more quickly. There is no time for a break.'

Published in 1992, the second Hamish Hamilton novel *Underrunners* earned Margaret her fifth Esther Glen Medal in New Zealand and enthusiastic reviews in Britain. Jan Mark, who had had reservations about *Memory*, found *Underrunners* 'sympathetic, unsentimental, effortlessly funny, this is high quality Mahy'. A contemporary story about family violence and the vulnerability of children, it was, more than any other of her books to date, a Lyttelton story. The background came from a time when Margaret was doing domestic work at a home for disturbed children.

During a promotional tour in Australia, she told an interviewer: 'In my story there is a child who escapes from a home like that. She gets out because she knows her father is looking for her and she believes the authorities will think what a nice man he is and actually she's scared of him — he's quite a violent person. At the end of the story he kidnaps her and the boy through whom the story is told.

'I had a version where at one stage the boy is sitting across the table from this man and the man puts a gun in his own mouth.' (Rather than the only slightly less shocking act of pointing it at his head and 'squinting down the barrel'.)

'Emotion has carried him into this — he's sick of himself, he's sick of the world. And at one stage the boy says to the girl: He [her father] was going to kill himself. She says "I wish he had".' (The street-wise child Winola says, 'He didn't last time.') 'But in the end I think I backed off because I think I was being gratuitous, perhaps inappropriately putting the view of some aspects of the world that I have on to other people... I suppose the story of *Underrunners* is set up so that you think it's ideal for this girl to be adopted by the boy's father — that's the boy's idea anyway — so that she can become like his sister and be safe and away from this rather dreadful family that she has, the father in particular. But of course it doesn't happen — it ends up with her galloping over the peninsula on a wild horse . . . I wanted to put her up against some fairly formidable things in her life. I didn't want to suggest in the story that she comes out unscathed.'

The setting for *Underrunners* came from Margaret's awareness of 80 hectares of nearby waste land which people didn't know what to do with; she later ('as an imaginative act', she told her doubtful lawyer) purchased the whole peninsula of Manson's Point. She also had no idea what to do with it — 'it seemed to be a heck of a lot of money to spend on a place to walk the dog' — though before long she and the family embarked on an extensive tree-planting programme to hold back the erosion, and built a house there for the growing family of grandchildren and their parents. 'There's not a lot of water on it, which is partly why the ground cracks underneath and forms these tunnels or underrunners. I'd known about this for a while but somehow that word concentrated it and it seemed to me like a metaphor for a lot of things including family life which sometimes look very secure on the surface but has all sorts of mysterious tunnels underneath.' Here is the Manson's Point peninsula as described, with her very characteristic use of personification, in the first chapter of *Underrunners*:

> There, almost under his feet . . . lay the great rambling house where the Featherstonehaugh family had once lived. Beyond the house and its well-grown trees, Gideon Bay nudged a sly elbow of water and mud into the land, and on the other side of that rippling muscle of water lay a long, brown, barren, brooding peninsula, a giant, diving towards the mouth of

the bay, aiming at the open sea beyond. Tris always looked for this uncouth figure, back humped, shoulders twisted with inhuman muscles, steep sides eroded into ribs. The outstretched arms were welded into one powerful arm, but the weak fingerless hands dissolved into the sea. There, between those hands, you could see, if you knew where to look for it, a little grey box. The diving man was desperately holding treasure above the water, and looked, from where Tris stood, as if he were losing his grasp on it. The treasure that appeared to be sliding down a slope into the water was Tris's house.

Two picture books and the rollicking comic novella, *The Greatest Show Off Earth*, appeared in 1994, but this was also the year when two major television projects came to fruition. The four one-hour episodes of *Typhon's People* finally went to air in September 1994, followed by animated versions of four of Margaret's most popular stories: *The Boy with Two Shadows*, *The Witch in the Cherry Tree*, *Keeping House* and *The Three Legged Cat*. This quartet followed an earlier film of *The Great White Man-Eating Shark*, produced in 1991 by Wellington's Gnome Productions; after a well-received screening as a cinema short in New Zealand, it had won several awards in film festivals in New York, Ottawa and Birmingham. Requiring no fewer than 3400 drawings to faithfully reflect the book's tone and original illustrations, and with voice-overs by leading Wellington actor Ray Henwood, *Shark* cost $107,000. This was low-budget by world standards, but it was judged a high-quality product.

Work on the further four Mahy stories began in 1993. With a total budget of $500,000 projected, including $250,000 funding from New Zealand On Air and $150,000 from the New Zealand Film Commission, it was, according to producer Shaun Bell, the largest initiative of its kind to be undertaken in New Zealand, with markets expected in the United States, Britain, Canada and Europe.

Despite their eight-minute length, these four videos took around 23 people from Gnome and TOONZ Animation in Auckland — background and character artists, animation camera operators and sound engineers — some eleven months to produce. Some 3800 finished pieces of artwork were required for each story. For the director Euan Frizzell, the artistic challenge was to flesh out the illustrator's images to correspond to the narration. 'It's similar to directing an actor, in that the performance must be convincing . . . Mahy's sound, dramatic sense of structure makes her stories easy to translate into a film medium. She takes an ordinary problem, adds an imaginative element and comes up with an enchanting mix. It's satisfying for a director to deal with stories like that.'

Margaret's next major novel, *The Other Side of Silence*, appeared in 1995. Rose Lovell-Smith, commenting on the judges' decision to shortlist the novel but not award it the 1997 Esther Glen Medal nor the New Zealand Post senior fiction prize, would later write, 'perhaps by now it is hard for judges to keep assessing Mahy fairly. The temptation to judge her against the standard of her own best work must be very strong.' First readings can be deceptive, and may result in a real failure to do a book justice, 'especially likely, of course, if an author has changed ground or shifted focus and so does not meet established expectations'. As one British journalist wrote in 1995, reviewing *The Other Side of Silence*, 'In a brilliant series of novels from *The Haunting* to *Memory*, Mahy seemed always to be pushing to the limits what could be dared and what could be achieved in the young adult novel. Later books, such as *Dangerous Spaces*, *Underrunners* and now *The Other Side of Silence*, seem to have retreated in age level and ambition from the high water mark of the starkly uncompromising *Memory*.' Margaret herself recognised that with *Memory* she had reached a plateau and, until *The Other Side of Silence* in 1995, had stayed there for quite a while.

The book began as a novel for people of about fifteen; that she was 'encouraged to bring it down a bit' reinforces the unease and ambivalence about the young adult genre, and the constant urging by cautious publishers, and not only to Margaret, to write for the more traditional and predictable market of 'children' between, say, eight and twelve. But this 'traditional Gothic story', as Margaret describes it, and the only one of her novels told in the first person, is still a disturbing read in which the characters are taken right to the brink: the elderly Miss Credence is one of her most sinister creations. Consider what Margaret herself has called an 'absolutely ferocious moment in the story', one she remembers writing 'and thinking, although it's so casual, the implication of the years that had gone before is horrific'. Miss Credence, the bitter daughter of a famous professor who has kept her own mute, illegitimate daughter chained and locked in a tower since birth, tells the elective mute, the distraught Hero,

> 'I thought of killing her when she was born . . . all I would have had to do was to hold a pillow over her face for a few minutes, and it would have changed everything. I could have planted her out under one of the trees and no one would ever have known. But there you are. I was sentimental. I didn't do it. Well, not very often and never enough to kill her. Only now and then, to stop her crying. And so she lived.'

After a harrowing climax, Miss Credence lives on too, in hospital and utter silence, having, in volcanic anger, trashed the sitting room full of memorabilia of her father's powerful presence and shot herself (but not comprehensively enough) in the head with his gun. Hero, the child for whom silence was a weapon, her way of being famous in a famous, talkative, gifted family, now chooses to talk. Wiser than her ambitious mother, she destroys both the manuscript and the electronic version of her story of the dramatic events at Squintum House.

> 'If things were fair, all stories would be anonymous. I don't mean that the storyteller wouldn't get paid for telling. But

there would be no names on the covers of books, or interviews on television . . . just the story itself, climbing walls, sliding from tree to tree, and stealing secretly through the forests of the world, real, but more than real. Set free from the faults that go with its author's name. Made true! But of course things aren't fair. They never have been.'

Margaret speculates that, before she burned her book, setting that lion free, Hero 'had actually seen the lion. Now she and the story were, at some level, one and the same thing. Through writing and reading she had reached a point where she would never need to make up a story again, because she was now at one with the platonic form with which we continually dance, inventing one another as we whirl. Have I invented stories or have the stories invented me?'

The kernel of the story was reading an article by Russ Rhymer in the *New Yorker* about Genie, a closet child who had been kept tied to a bed in an upstairs room, until her mother, leaving home, took the almost completely mute child to Welfare. 'She had had an unimaginable life for about twelve years — I think she could say about three words. One of the interesting things which happened was that there was a great argument among academic people about who was going to study her.'

Margaret has described *The Other Side of Silence* as 'a movement forward', and its many deliberate references to other books as 'a dangerous thing to do'. Embarking on 'a story whose time had come', hearing later of Morris Gleitzman's *Blabbermouth*, the Jodie Foster film *Nell*, Jill Paton Walsh's novel *Knowledge of Angels* (to which she might also have added the New Zealand film *The Piano*), she was aware of the many influences at work: Genie's story, Gothic horror stories, anecdotes of the strange house in the wood, the child kept in solitary confinement in the locked room upstairs, *Jane Eyre*.

These became mixed in 'with my own beginnings . . . the childhood memories of picking my way from one tree to another along the lines of wattles and pines that defined the boundaries of my father's timber yard, talking to imaginary animals, but of course really talking to myself . . . I seemed to have acknowledged, at last, that puddle-drinking child I had been ashamed of for so many years, but I changed her into the cloudy, mysterious heroine who had also been with me for a long time. There they are, both of them in *The Other of Silence*, and along with the heroine's Mowgli-ish preoccupation goes an adult acknowledgement of what a wolf child like Mowgli, a human brought up with human language, might really have been like . . . the underlying story — the deep story – was never mine in the first place, but existed like some platonic form.'

In *New Zealand Books*, Rose Lovell-Smith carefully and usefully assessed not only the novel itself but its place in Margaret's output and career. She admitted her initial reaction: 'that Mahy had run out of ideas and was starting to recycle material'. The mysterious old house, the house always under repair, the large, talkative family, the flamboyant older sister, the black-cloaked old woman, the capable but insensitive mother, even those old pirates and memory itself (to which could well be added the secretive, observant teenage girl who is industriously writing her own book, who *will be a writer*) — all had appeared at least once before – so that 'the reader is invited into a delusion that Mahy has started to repeat herself, that she's rehashing old themes: in short that she's lost the old magic'.

But 'being invited so to think, the reader is as securely in the grip of the old witch as ever. The intentions of this book are self-reflective, even backwards-looking. A second, and related, point is that this book goes further into a pattern – already recognisable in earlier books for older children — of play with a Christchurch setting, play with things that might be known to readers (or guessed by them) about Mahy's own life story. Ideas are raised about famous mothers; mothers who wield power through words, stories, and books' evasive or missing fathers; daughters who want to be special or different; mothers who lovingly keep their daughters in cages; and mothers' memories of younger selves — those heavenly creatures who once wanted so much to fly like birds.'

The main theme of Hero as 'another daughter-victim' is explored through her beginning to believe 'partly from watching her mother Annie and partly from learning the story of Miss Credence and her famous father — that fame is always something which the famous steal from those around them . . .' (a recurrent Mahy concern). 'Mahy would probably prefer it that all stories were indeed anonymous, so that people would not read her books (as I've just read this one) with an eye to her private and professional life and how they might be being mythologised in a book. But self-reference and a local setting both direct the reader towards precisely this kind of reading. Yet Mahy is also pointing out, modestly, that a story is always a gift — partly from "real life", partly from the literary and dream worlds of "true life". It is not something she creates single-handed. She is merely the noisy one, it seems, among other gifted children who choose, as this book hints, not to lift up public voices and break their private silence.'

The Other Side of Silence, Lovell-Smith concluded, 'may be less compelling than some of her earlier books for young adults or older children precisely to the extent that it is more interesting as a mother's, and a mature artist's, reflection on a noisy life's work'.

The next major novel, *24 Hours*, would not appear for another five years. This was partly because Margaret was spending more time with her growing grandchildren, especially Penny's family of five, four girls and a boy, living in the new house on nearby Manson's Point. Added to the daily writing routine, the speeches and letters, were such grandmotherly duties as taking children to and from school, driving them to after-school lessons in Christchurch, going for walks with the black standard poodle (first Cello and then, and currently, Baxter) sessions of reading, dancing, drawing and singing — 'unrepentantly' — those old

George Formby and Arthur Askey songs of her youth, storytelling ('Tell me a story with your mouth!' she was once ordered), family meals and games.

Margaret is unequivocal about her grandmotherly role and the time she is prepared to devote to it: 'I, myself, want to be an active part of the lives of my grandchildren. I want to be part of their daily scenery and want them to be part of mine. I want them to remember me bending over their cots, mumbling as I change their napkins. I want to praise their advances into the world, applaud their first words, tell them stories and listen to them when they begin to tell their own. I want to pin pictures especially drawn for me on my walls. Of course there are elements of unconscious egotism in all this, for one's family represents part of self, but self successfully set free from self — detached, launched and independently at large in the word. And there are other possibilities implicit in the relationship — chances that I think my own grandparents must have totally missed out on . . . my days are often built around their necessities, but not in any self-sacrificing way. They are moving into a wide life from which I am currently retiring, and my retreat (I hope) somehow supports their advance. Any mention of retreat sounds negative, but this is not the case . . . For I may be stepping back, but my advancing grandchildren are not the only ones involved in self-exploration and growth. I find their presence in my everyday life part of a continuous process of realignment with the world at large. Apparently eternal verities are regularly revealed as much more relative and hesitant than one had supposed them to be. The world is flux, flow and fruitfully fermenting doubt.'

She has written movingly of their births. 'I saw the oldest child struggle out of her mother and into the outer world. I missed the actual moment of the second girl's emergence because she was born underwater in a small plastic swimming — sorry, birthing — pool that had dominated her family's sitting room for several weeks. I was in London to see the third child arrive, but, finally, in spite of his mother's [Bridget's] extended heroism, he was delivered by instruments and only his father was allowed to witness his birth . . . I have also felt helpless agony of behalf of my two daughters. It is so much harder for humans to give birth than it is for cats (part of the price, I understand, of evolving to walk upright, an evolutionary exercise which freed the hands for creative tool-using, but incorporated an inhibiting curve in the birth canal). One longs to intercede . . . to take on any weariness and anguish for a short while at least, and to give the struggling mother a break. But, no matter how many concerned people may cluster around the bed, the actual birth belongs with inescapable intimacy to two people only — the bearer and the one being born.'

She believes she is being reinterpreted and changed by the experience of being a grandparent, that it is not a one-way traffic. 'Literature tends to dwell on the imaginative development a good grandparent can bring about in a children's life, but there may be less emphasis on the possibilities for a reciprocal inner growth and alteration in the life of an attentive grandparent. The axioms of our own childhood become part of the relativity of age.' In the end, 'the 'remarkable thing about connection with grandchildren is living, moment to moment with what they are in themselves . . . [yet] I am part of a close family, but I am also outside the magical necessities that rule the most intimate circle of that family. There are times when I cannot comfort, no matter how passionately I long to do so . . . time when only a parent will do, because the parent has power beyond reason or will. I am not complaining about this, because of course there is freedom in being outside that intimate circle, and solitude has its own blessings.'

Despite the extensive time given to her family, Margaret's generous public life continued on through the 1990s. Asked to preside at the official opening of the first Christchurch Books and Beyond Festival, she sat down and concocted new words for Gilbert and Sullivan's 'I am the very model of a modern major general' from *The Pirates of Penzance*, then delivered it flawlessly at breakneck speed to an enchanted audience in the Great Hall of the

Christchurch Arts Centre. The only rough surviving manuscript of this spectacular *vers d'occasion* includes some unfinished fragments of several more verses, indicating that she could have continued in this vein for some time.

For the Opening of Books and Beyond

I have written many poems but I think this is the best of all,
A dithyrambic ditty to extol our city festival;
A dithyramb, for those who lack a vocab academical,
Is a Dionysian choric hymn, poetic not polemical.
And though some philistines may cry 'No! Bugger all!
    It's doggerel,'
All connoisseurs of poetry will gape and be a-goggeral.
Free verse is never quite as free as something with
    a rhyme to it,
If you're the sort of poet who'll devote a lot of time to it.
As form competes with chaos the explosions can be various,
Revealing Art as heavenly, hypnotic or hilarious.
Wake, wake then, Art! Bestow on us your blessings
    bright and aureate,
According to instructions from the local poet laureate.

As wintertime approaches other cities start to aestivate,
But in the Garden City we wake up and start to festivate.
The season which in other towns breeds angst and
    deep anxiety,
Fills everyone in Christchurch with a longing for variety.
Theatres, squares and galleries display our great diversity,
A balcony or bus stop can become a university;
A festival's explosive — there are some who think it facile,
But it's frolicking — it's rollicking, aesthetic razzle-dazzle.
And if there's any one thing over which the town
    can glory at
It's being told to 'Go it!' by a local poet laureate.

We go lurching, ever searching for the moment
    that translates us all,
The word, the note, the image that so strangely
    recreates us all . . .
We look for dissolution, the true instant of
    dumbfoundedness
When art conspires to face us and reveal its true
    unboundedness.
We flow into the universe and cosmic magic fills us all,
Our petty agitations cease as contemplation stills us all;
Though I'm the sort of laureate who tends to make
    a joke of it,
We've artists who exemplify the glory, pain and yoke of it.
It's like a wand transfiguring the long, the short
    and tall of it,
It's like a firework going off, illuminating all of us,
A truly thrilling flare-up is the underlying quest of all,
Go out! Rise up like rockets! And enjoy the city Festival.

Another occasion, in Whakatane, provided a rare public glimpse into a quicksilver mind, delighting the audience of 200 but greatly discomforting the three people sharing the stage with her. Unwisely agreeing to join Whakatane's favourite daughter and by turn improvise a story on the spot, author David Hill, illustrator Martin Baynton and the present writer soon had their worst fears confirmed: from Margaret, remembers a trembling David, who was sitting alongside and had to follow her, came a flood of 'astonishing and baroquely inventive ideas like one of those time-lapse sequences of flowers unfolding'.

We did not know, of course, of the days spent with Belinda Rotman in the Ohariu Valley talking only in rhyming couplets, but after her first two or three turns this is what happened, in spectacular, chuckling style. Not only wicked, off-the-wall twists to the story, but in verse. David was seen to turn white, rise to his feet and, to avoid the follow-on, treacherously move his chair to the other side of her, to the audience's gratification. The present writer was left with the task of picking up from verse worthy of Pope crossed with Ogden Nash, and by now reduced to nearly mute terror, remembers little of the rest, only vast gratitude when the MC, local librarian Nan Pemberth, stepped in and put us out of our misery. Rarely have three writers, none strangers to public speaking, felt so outgunned, or so convinced (we later consolingly agreed) that not a single stand-up comic in New Zealand, with the possible exception of David Lange in his heyday, could have matched her.

Four books, *The Other Side of Silence* and three picture books, appeared in 1995. She told one interviewer, 'I am 59 and I feel I am still looking for my identity. There are areas where I think I'm established, but watching my daughter with her children makes me re-interpret the way I brought up my own children, so even the past is not totally closed off. It's a lifetime search, trying to establish one's identity. Even when you're old and have lost large pieces of memory, you may still be searching for yourself . . . I think you never give up this search for identity, even when you know yourself, even when you have a definite job and a definite place in the family and feel in charge of your life.'

The acquisition of experience and knowledge, she thought, was not entirely a romantic blessing: 'It's certainly true that if you go out looking for a certain form of experience and certain form of information and you find it, then you can't really go back to what you were before, even if you discover, when you get what you were searching for, that you don't like it . . . It's the same with a lot of things, sexuality, for example. You can't forget experiences, you have to build up your identity in a way that accepts experience, and make as good a profit as you can out of those experiences . . . When you get cause and effect, you always get some sort of a message, even in a story just told for fun.'

An English conference in 1996, also attended by the illustrator of two of her books, Steven Kellogg, presented her with the rare opportunity to talk about the relationship between pictures and text, and between author and illustrator. Her initial experience back in 1968, with the five books published by Helen Hoke Watts, had set a lasting pattern: 'though published in the USA they were illustrated by English illustrators . . . people I had never met. We had no discussion about the relationship of text and picture, and indeed I would have been too frightened to ask, in case any assertion on my part might cause some bubble to burst and the magical chance to disappear.'

For all the many picture books in the 37 years since, she had put her faith in her editor/agent Vanessa Hamilton's judgement on the selection of illustrators and, on the whole, she had been very happy with the results. So it was something quite new to be 'able to sit down beside the illustrator and to discuss the text of the story I had written as it might or might not relate to the pictures he wanted to draw . . .

'Almost all stories begin in a sort of solitude, in that they depend on connections made in the crowded attic of a single head. Many picture books however are the result of co-operation between two imaginations and separate skills, and there is a general assumption, sometimes justified, that author and illustrator must have worked closely together. This is not necessarily true . . . indeed I know there are publishers who prefer to keep illustrator and author apart except perhaps for lunch after the book has been published. I haven't time to comment on this beyond saying that no publisher has ever had any difficulty in keeping me apart from my illustrators, for I live in one hemisphere and they live in another, and though phones and faxes theoretically break down that isolation, my first published stories were stories written for the ear, but produced, almost accidentally from my point of view, as picture books and I had nothing to say to the illustrators nor they to me.'

For *The Boy Who Was Followed Home*, Steven Kellogg and Margaret had some to-ing and fro-ing before they agreed whether pictures or text should have the final say (Margaret did, with the line, 'Robert was very pleased,' that met her expressed preference for words that said to the child, 'That's it! You may stop listening now'). Then Steven asked Margaret if she would consider changing the title for the next book, the story of a family picnicking on the slopes of a volcano, and escaping from lava flow by using one of Granny's pizzas to replace a car wheel.

'*The Escape from Volcano Mountain* [was] another domestic story, this time concerning the unreliability of old cars, something I know a great deal about. I have pushed more reluctant cars than any other children's writer in New Zealand and possibly the USA. To this day the sight of people pushing a car sets off a conditioned reflex in me. I stop my own currently blameless car, leap out and offer to help push. One of Steven's first contributions was a suggestion that the title should be changed, since that first title was a summary of the plot. Any reader would know, before they so much as began reading, what the story was going to be about . . . I agreed to change both the title and the name of the mountain (to Mount Fogg) though I always liked the idea of the reader feeling he or she knew something the characters in the story did not. However illustrators are treacherous. Almost at once Steven's pictures let the reader in on the secret the words no longer acknowledge . . . though Steven and I are working together to tell a story, there is an illustrator's tale separated yet merging with the writer's one . . . I am claiming that the landscape he thinks he has invented is my own, though I had to see it in the outside world to recognise it. For better or for worse we are both story tellers and both live in the landscape of story.'

Shortly before *The Rattlebang Picnic*, as it became, was to be launched, the publisher contacted Margaret with a new kind of problem. 'The Booksellers' Conference at which the book was due to make its debut was to be held in Los Angeles that particular year and Los Angeles had suffered a damaging earthquake in the recent past. Children's books are always subject to a singularly intent scrutiny by people anxious to detect insensitivity on the part of the author and it was felt that joking about earthquakes might be seen as unduly callous. Would I consider changing my reference to Earthquake Valley to Tornado Valley? The publishers did not demand this. They merely suggested it and left it to me.

'I agreed to change it, not so much because I was anxious about disadvantaging the book from the point of view of sales (after all, I had insisted in the case of a previous book *The Horrendous Hullabaloo* that a pirate must drink rum for breakfast not passionfruit juice though I had been warned that this alcoholic reference would automatically reduce sales, no matter how traditionally piratical) but because I was filled with anxiety on behalf of those who had suffered a really terrible earthquake and felt temporarily ashamed of my own levity. I do joke over disasters, my own as well as other people's, but when my right to do so is questioned I retreat and apologise and I am not sure to this day whether it is because of mere cowardice or belated sensitivity . . . I hope the latter. Anyhow, the strange thing was that the alteration of a single word — one word — changed the story far more than Steven's pictures from being a New Zealand story to being a story set once again nowhere. When I tell it or read it aloud, I find I still have to say Earthquake Valley . . .'

In 1996 Margaret was also given the chance to speak at length to the New Zealand Reading Association conference on a topic dear to her heart, 'taking humour seriously'.

'I joke with language,' she once said, 'because I think it makes it more entertaining for children and, after all, when things are entertaining they stick in our minds. Entertainment reinforces important events which we would not remember if we had not been entertained . . . I think laughter is very important . . . we are relieved by laughter, and when we are confronted with concepts we can't take in, one of the things we do is to joke about them. This enables us, in some way, to relieve the pressure and to absorb what we need from the experience without trying to rationalise it too much. I think one of the dangers of laughing at things is that we falsely feel we have power over them. We have to be aware and careful of what we laugh at and of *how* we laugh. But I laugh a lot and I make jokes about things — serious things. I laugh at disasters or semi-disasters in my own life, because it's a way I learnt to come to terms with them. Laughter helps me absorb and incorporate many contradictions — clashes between ego and objectivity, between desire and altruism.'

The 1996 speech's opening salvo, for what became an erudite examination of classical philosophers' support for various theories of humour — 'release and pleasure' (Freud), 'superiority' (Aristotle, Hobbes, Bain and Bergson) and 'incongruity' (Kierkegaard, Koestler, Schopenhauer and possibly Kant) — was a vintage Mahy anecdote.

'On one occasion I found myself at an afternoon party talking to someone I had never met before and this man began telling me a story. It seemed a friend of his, visiting a strange house, was invited to enjoy the facility of the host's swimming pool. Having climbed into an appropriate swimming costume the man came into the sitting room, looked out over the terrace and saw the swimming pool, shimmeringly replete with its promises of pleasure. Filled with sudden exhilaration he ran at increasing speed across the living room and burst onto the terrace planning to dive into the swimming pool. However, there were none of the defining spiderwebs . . . the streaks of dog's blood and mud . . . the smears of icecream . . . that usefully modify the clarity of glass in my own home, and the would-be swimmer did not realise that a sheet of plate glass in a sliding door extended between him and the terrace. He exploded through the glass. Badly gashed he fell to the ground while others raced to call an ambulance on his behalf. I listened with interest to this anecdote rather like an antelope watching from a safe distance as disaster falls on another member of the herd, and then, as the story had ended I heard myself say:

'"It would have been awful if he'd got out there and found there was no water in the pool."

'As I said this, the image of the lacerated victim spouting blood in all directions, diving out over the pool only to fall with a dull thud onto sloping concrete painted with that bright delusive blue paint that characterises many swimming pools, shot through

my mind. It immediately seemed like a metaphor for existence
. . . a tempting symbol of life itself. I had certainly made a joke of
someone else's painful and disfiguring misfortune.

'"It wasn't funny," said the narrator indignantly. I hastened
to agree in a small, shamed voice that of course it must have been
terrible — tragic — and to apologise for my joke at the expense
of the unknown sufferer — probably permanently scarred.
My attempt to seem nice was of course too late. At some level,
I had been entertained by the image of the accident and later I
wondered just why I had had that immediate reaction. And since,
like all speakers on occasions like these, I want to present myself
in a good light, I suppose that in telling you this story I am acting
on the assumption that a significant number of people here today
will have had similar experiences and suffered similar confusion
at realising they have been caught out, laughing at someone else's
misfortune. If I thought you were all going to be disgusted at
my lack of sensitivity I would obviously have kept this story to
myself.' Despite the success in life of many humourless people, she
thought humour did 'add to our prospects of survival as a species
. . . Laughter thrives with practice, but one's ability to laugh in a
totally light-hearted way may mutate. I laugh just as much as I
ever did, but my laughter becomes increasingly less carefree as
I grow old and I have to cope with the increasing complications
imposed by time, age, experience, the accumulation of knowledge
while understanding, at the same time, that what I know will never
be enough, and the problems of trying to integrate all information
— all instinct, all judgement — into some harmonious system.'

The Five Sisters was one of two books published in 1996.
Margaret described it as a mysterious book for younger readers
and was uncertain as to whether it would actually get published.
'Do you know the game where you fold up a piece of paper, then
you draw the shape of a child on it and cut it out? When you
unfold the paper you have several figures all holding hands. The
story is about five sisters who are cut out of a piece of paper, all of
them holding hands. However, only the first one has a face. They

get blown away by the wind, but they didn't fall to pieces; they persist in holding hands, and every now and then someone finds them, and slowly different faces are drawn on the blank figures. Eventually they all have different faces; so, in a way, the story is actually about how each sister gets a face as an identity. What I intended to was to suggest that everybody who gives a sister a face is not only giving a face but receiving something in return. In the end, the sisters look a little bit frail but are still together. The child who finally finds them is the daughter of the woman who drew them in the first place. In the final chapter you're told what happened to the other people who had drawn the faces. The sisters are all differently drawn or painted — one is scribbled, another is very carefully drawn, one has eyes drawn and a face which is completed by somebody else. Later an artist turns a mark into a tear, so that this sister is drawn to cry, while the final one is drawn to laugh. It seems to me you can use a story like this to say some interesting things about the world without having to write a young adults story. I have no idea of just what set of readers I'm writing for with a story like this. When you write a story, as you probably know, you write with the idea that the people out there are the sort of readers that you are yourself, and that they will live with the story in the same way you do. You pass the story you've received on to them. *Five Sisters* is an introspective kind of story, but at the same time there's a lot of adventure in it.' The story, dedicated to her old friend Belinda Rotman, was handsomely published in hardback, with jacket cover artwork and charming, subtle illustrations by the English artist Patricia MacCarthy. Three years later, Margaret would read extracts from this story to an audience of about 400 at the first Auckland Writers' Festival. She had been rather reluctantly included on a panel of 'Scary Marys' alongside more familiar feminist writers — novelist Rosie Scott, health activist Sandra Coney and Australian poet Dorothy Porter — but it was Margaret's reading which quietly stole the show, causing one young woman to rise to her feet and thank the festival organisers for the opportunity of hearing a 'feminist' writer previously unknown to her. To most in that audience except the children's writers, Margaret's contribution was a revelation.

At 62, Margaret set off on a journey that rivalled even Rider Haggard's African adventures — ten days in the Antarctic. She was the first writer sent under the new Creative New Zealand Artists in Antarctica scheme; a friend had encouraged her to apply. 'It was the most mysterious place I've ever been in . . . You land at Scott Base and there's all this human activity in the foreground but behind that is the silence of the continent . . . it's not a natural place for humans to be . . . you're there because of the technology.'

Typically, her novel take on the experience, *The Riddle of the Frozen Phantom*, was to combine two highly improbable elements: the Antarctic as a place of mysterious history, and scientific research with children. When explorer Boniface Sapwood is abandoned by his housekeeper Daffodil, who leaves to pursue her career as a dancer, he decides to take his three children, Sophie, Edward and little Hotspur, south with him. Add Corona Wottley, an ambitious female penguin expert, the ghost of a murdered captain awakening like the Sleeping Beauty from a long nap, a colony of albino penguins, and various villains with names like Rancid Swarthy seeking cheap thrills with explosives and the good ship *Riddle*'s clues to a stash of diamonds, and you have mainstream comic Mahy. Closer reading, however, reveals a good knowledge of 20th-century Antarctic exploration, Scott, Shackleton *et al.*, and her own direct experience, in such details as the webbing seats in the Hercules aircraft, the necessary polar clothing and the timeless landscape:

> [Boniface Sapwood considers] there is something wonderful about spinning out across Antarctic snow and seeing mountains ahead of you, beautiful as dreams yet somehow truer than dreams. Once you have seen those dreams there is no waking up from them. They are in your head for always. As for Edward and Sophie, they were both now staring across a stretch of dark beach. Summer winds had beaten the

snow back, revealing black sand and stones, curving away towards a distant headland. Embraced by this beach was yet another long curve (of broken ice this time) and beyond the ice, the sea spread like a great blue plain. *Olð! Olð! Olð!* that Antarctic sea whispered to Sophie while, in the distance, on the other side of the sea, far, far beyond the black stones and the broken ice, Sophie could make out another distant blue-and-white shoreline marked with valleys, peaks and glaciers.

'It's like being on another planet,' said Edward again.

'It's cold enough to freeze your nose off!' said Sophie. Indeed the cold was so fierce it seemed as if you should be able to fling your arms around it and wrestle with it, as you might with a bear.

The Riddle of the Frozen Phantom, she has said, 'is a book in the tall story tradition, full of impossibilities but set in a possible, indeed an accurately described setting. Possibility and impossibility emphasise one another. [It's] essentially a tall story but family life intrudes. I imagined some explorer like Scott or Shackleton setting out to do some classical Great Exploration and being suddenly deserted by his baby-sitter. What if someone like Scott or Shackleton had had to take his kids to the Antarctic along with his polypropylene waistcoat and his [polar boot] mukluks?

'Of course there is more to the story than jokes about family life. I was in Antarctica as a part of a writer's fellowship. It is an astonishing place. There is a feeling of purity about it and you don't want that purity diluted in any way. You can feel that people should not be there but the paradox is that you are there yourself. *The Riddle* is set in that landscape and needs to be truthful to that landscape: a vast whiteness and black rock.

'On one of the trips outside Scott Base I stayed for a few days at Cape Bird adjacent to a colony of 30,000 Adelie penguins and one day, looking out over all these penguins and penguin nests I saw a single white penguin weaving its way through all the others like a great penguin ghost. In my story I have stretched that single bird out into a whole colony of albino penguins. Once again real life and imagination twist around each other.'

The one book published in 1998 gave Margaret particular pleasure, and not only because it won her the Picture Book Award and her first Supreme Award in the New Zealand Post Children's Book Awards the following year. This was *A Summery Saturday Morning*, beautifully illustrated by a young English-trained artist, Selina Young, who also lived in the volcanic crater of Lyttelton Harbour. Her representation of the area's distinctive headlands, inlets and bare and golden hillsides matched by superb design and production turned some of Margaret's slighter verses into a small gem of a book. She told an Australasian conference held in Christchurch: 'There is no way I can adequately tell you how delighted I have been by these pictures. It has almost been like being forgiven and taken back into a family, even though my strange sort of alienation was not my fault, and of course there have been times when it has been an advantage that I am not denying or regretting, since I have been only too happy to exploit it. Nevertheless, looking at *A Summery Saturday Morning*, I do feel I have come home at last, and am truly one of the New Zealand writers and illustrators who have discovered their own country both for themselves and for children too.'

The story was based on an incident 'in which two dogs are taken for a walk, chase a flock of geese, only to have the geese turn around, flap and hiss and begin to chase the dogs. The reversal seems fictional but was a real event. I did see my two dogs chase retreating geese, only to see the geese suddenly irritated beyond all measure turn around and begin chasing my dogs. Of course the story reads like invention. It is told in rhyme with repetition and a one-line chorus. The dogs begin their rascally adventures by chasing a boy on a rattling bike and then a cat before they chase the geese thereby meeting their comeuppance. The story has taken on a classical structure where a certain kind of event is repeated three times, changing dramatically on the third.'

Although delighted with that feeling of homecoming to what was now a well-established and lively children's literature scene, Margaret has always been prepared to sound notes of caution about disturbing trends in publishing and achieving a balance for New Zealand children between their enjoyment of overtly indigenous stories and those from other countries.

'In choosing to develop our new local literature, which of course we should do, it may be we sacrifice our connection with the marvellous books from other places. And perhaps there isn't the time — the reading space in the life of modern children — to be both a local and a universal reader, alone with taking swimming lessons, playing with others kids, and keeping up homework (as well as carefully chosen TV programmes and videos). My granddaughters both read extensively, but they have many other things that take up their time, and my impression is that at a time when the number of books is increasing, the time available for extensive reading is less than it used to be. My impression is also that children's editors have a difference pressure on them from editors of 30 years ago. I certainly know of cases when the dominating pressure to accept or reject a book has come from the sales department, rather than the editorial one and certainly in two cases that I know of, a literary editor, on retirement, has been replaced by someone from the Sales Department — the book being interpreted more purely as saleable project, rather than literary art.'

As the millennium approached, Margaret was asked to contribute to two special publications to mark the event. One was a special supplement of the *Sunday Star-Times*, published on 2 January 2000, which included commissioned essays from a range of established and newer New Zealand writers; the other was a thoughtful and surprising piece on her chosen key literary moment of the 20th century for the literary journal *Landfall*, along with novelist Witi Ihimaera and essayist Denis McEldowney.

Her irreverent *Sunday Star-Times* piece, a fantastical, quirky and welcome breath of fresh air among some more portentous offerings, shared the Margaret Mahy — writer, of Governors Bay — with her alter ego, 'the old witch who lives somewhere in the back of my head . . . I hear that voice every day.'

'"Millennium-Millooonium!" exclaims the old woman, but I can't tell if she is making fun of the coming occasion, or of me, trying to sound significant about a senseless subject. "It's talked about everywhere these days," she adds, cackling and throwing up her heels . . . she's right, of course. It is everywhere . . . Millennial moments on television — Millennium promises, prophecies, prognostications and possible profits . . ."Two thousand years . . . but since what?" she cries . . .

'What we are *really* going to celebrate, she tells me, is not so much the changed date, but the changed *look* of the date . . . that "2" . . . almost a question mark . . . (but a question mark ruled off before the question had been properly asked, perhaps) is going to crowd out the "1" — that straight number which stood sternly to attention in front of all the years any of us can remember. And that "2" — that half-question — will be followed by a line of "0"s . . . three round windows through which we may try squinting into the future.

'Or are those "0"s three *eyes* staring back at us? The thought of it seems to make some people uneasy. Disasters are being predicted. We may be about to enter on a time of revelation and disaster. Or, according to other theories we may be on the edge of new hope . . . new optimism. Either way we like the idea of a party of some kind, but what we are celebrating is the different look that next year's calendars will be taking on.'

As for the momentous day itself,

'. . . though I like the idea of a party, my own wishes for the Millennium are small scale, intimate and ironical. And there is a sort of pleasure in the thought of missing out on it altogether — of going to bed (just as usual) in one Millennium and waking up (just as usual) in another. Missing the actual Millennium moment might actually help me to feel the occasion all the more closely. I imagine myself getting up, feeding the dog and cats, and making myself a cup of tea (if the power is off due to computer failure I am quite capable of boiling a billy on the woodstove) and thinking with a sort of quiet pleasure that the new Millennium would be a subtext to the day — something both significant and irrelevant . . . a huge joke that is only partly a human joke. After all, why shouldn't the universe have a sense of humour?

'Anyhow of this imaginary first morning I would glance at the calendar . . . and I would see the new year looking back at me . . . that curling "2" hanging on its forehead like an unruly forelock, and then those three eyes staring back at me. If I ever look into them directly I know they will be round, innocent and empty enough, but the woman tells me that, once I have turned my back on the date, the year will begin winking ironically, pulling secret faces. Its "0" eyes will narrow . . . will stretch sideways, will reduce themselves to dots, to hyphens and dashes, hastily rounding themselves out again to meet the suspicious gaze I will no doubt be shooting uneasily backwards across my shoulder from time to time. "Oh sure —," the year will be saying. "I've started! Here I am. But am I what people say I am? Am I the Golden Age? Fata Morgana? Or am I a different sort of farter — the year of the Great Raspberry?"

'"It could be the year of the Apocalypse!" the old woman reminds me slyly. 'Doom could fall . . . or even DOOOM! Capital letters with three eyes looking out of the middle of the year. There they are again — the eyes of the year using a different peephole this time. "Did you notice", interjects the old woman, "that when I called it 'the Milloooney-um' back then, I stretched out the middle of the word?"

'"Three eyes?" I suggest.

'"Three '0's," she answers. "Oh! Oh! OH! Get it right."'

Her choice of key event for *Landfall* would have surprised many readers, not so much for her consideration of a children's book but for the very compelling reasons she gave for suggesting that, with his fine 1994 novel *The Fat Man*, Maurice Gee had produced a important work of 'literature', not a children's novel valued more for its entertainment or educational worth. *The Fat Man*, she thought, was a 'quite different sort of book, on dangerous ground because of people's expectation of what a book for children or even young adults should be like'.

In the controversy about *The Fat Man*'s placement, for the purposes of the 1995 New Zealand Post Children's Book Awards, in the junior rather than senior fiction category, and again with the outcry over Paula Boock's *Dare Truth or Promise*, a novel about a lesbian relationship which won the 1998 Supreme Award, it was noticeable that few who involved themselves publicly in the debate spoke about the books as, simply, successful works of *literature*.

'Every so-called key event in New Zealand writing seems to me to be not so much a single event as an intensification — a tangle — of other winding circumstances. Anyhow I am choosing . . . the publication of *The Fat Man*, a young adult book by Maurice Gee which is both a single event and the exemplification of a 20th-century process which allows children's books to be taken seriously as literature.

'When Maurice Gee wrote his first book for children, *Under the Mountain*, he had recently become a full-time writer and was exploring the possibilities of making a living. Books for children often generate more income than books for adults for reasons irrelevant in this context. Having said this, Gee was not exploitative of the genre. He took writing for children seriously, and wrote with imagination and concern. Yet one does not feel in *Under the Mountain* the same central necessary that one feels in his adult books. It is, however, a considerable leap from *Under the Mountain* and *The Half-Men of O* to *The Fat Man* which won the New Zealand Post Book of the Year award, and, in doing so, alarmed some truly knowledgeable and caring children's book people. It was declared by some to be "a book without hope", and children, it was maintained, should not have hopeless stories imposed on them.

'As it happens I think all human beings, including children, need the reassurances of hope, and, though the word 'realism' often suggests misery, happy endings are not necessarily unrealistic. True reporting on life, however, demands that certain implacable stories be made available to a range of readers, including young adults (and I must add here that, personally, I do not think that *The Fat Man* is a story without hope). However, when submitted for the award, *The Fat Man* was classified as a junior book. I subsequently puzzled over this remarkable classification, and was told that it was based on the hero's age — he was aged eleven — which does not seem to me an adequate reason.

'Anyhow, Gee is telling a story which, like many of his adult books, draws on complex and sometimes dark themes, but he writes with truth, including truths that children's writers are generally expected to avoid or symbolise, since appreciation of these truths calls for a perception that most children have not had a chance to develop. And I think that, with *The Fat Man*, Maurice Gee's writing for young readers becomes one with his most central adult writing. One feels the author is engaged in a primary way.

'Books for young adults have moved beyond being children's books, yet they are often classified with them, sometimes shelved beside them and are readily available to good child readers. As far as awards are concerned, books for young adults are essentially linked with children's books rather than with books for adults. I think the publication of *The Fat Man* was a challenging literary event because the book was written without imaginative reduction, and, though simpler than, say, *Loving Ways*, it seems to me to be as much a part of Maurice Gee's primary writing as *Loving Ways* or *Crime Story*, and I think it takes writing for young adults seriously as literature, rather than as peripheral entertainment or as a source of moral example.'

Margaret's abilities as a shrewd and particularly well-informed critic were also noticeable in a piece she wrote on the Harry Potter phenomenon for the *Listener* in 2000.

'Walk into any bookshop and there they are — the Harry Potter books — three titles prominently displayed alongside adult best sellers by the likes of Tom Clancy and Wilbur Smith, and the latest chapter in the career of Hannibal Lecter. And, according to gossip, only the indignation of intellectuals prevented Harry Potter from winning last year's Whitbread Award over the Seamus Heaney translation of Beowulf . . .

'. . . in the case of the Harry Potter books these venerable oppositions (folk tale, old-fashioned school story) are given a singular spin; for Hogwarts, the school Harry Potter attends, is a magicians' school . . . the traditional school morality is merged with the folk tale and the supernatural joke and, so far at least, good magic has been triumphant. The books contain a variety of traditional satisfactions, which, for all the freshness and the originality of the stories, are highly recognisable.

'That being so, just why have they been so very successful? I imagine I am not the only reader astonished not so much at their success, but at the degree of it. On the one hand there is enormous pleasure in seeing good books enjoy the sort of victory achieved up to now apparently only by books such as those in the *Goosebumps* series. But the Harry Potter books, whether one is a fervent fan or not, are books for competent readers. They tell active, entertaining, ironical stories, using sophisticated situations and language. Such books do have their recognised place in the reading world, but, unless they have been turned into films or a TV series, booksellers don't display them beside sure-fire bestsellers such as the latest Jackie Collins or Jeffrey Archer — so one must conclude that the Harry Potter books have become, not only stories to be read, but objects that it is desirable to possess and display . . .

'The Harry Potters are probably successful because of the happy combination of several interacting systems. First, the strengths of the stories themselves, reinforced by the publisher's willingness to back up its product and subsequent ardour when it came to capitalising on success. The right publicity generates a momentum that in turn fuels more ambitious publicity. Children in the playground discuss these books, and recommend them to one another. Parents and teachers begin to read and enjoy them, too . . .

'Yet, in spite of everything, there is still something enigmatic about Harry Potter's success. Perhaps some sort of intangible element of luck comes into the equation. Successful formulas along with lively individual variation, exciting stories, humour and strong publicity are all part of the phenomenon. But they also seem to have been the right books for the right moment. Why not? In the end one can only rejoice that good books are enjoying such success and are being read so enthusiastically. Long may it last!'

Her own next book, published in 2000, marked the beginning of a new publishing relationship. HarperCollins UK emerged as the successful bidder in a Vanessa Hamilton auction for Margaret's first serious novel in five years, a decidedly contemporary and teenage work set firmly in urban Christchurch. Like *The Other Side of Silence*, *24 Hours* was shortlisted for the New Zealand Post awards, even designated an 'Honour Book', but was edged out as a winner, reinforcing Rose Lovell-Smith's concern that any Margaret Mahy novel was now possibly being judged primarily against her own best work.

For an Internet 'teen read' site, she wrote: 'There is nothing directly autobiographical about this story. All the same, there have been times when I have gone out to visit friends and progressed from one party to another and have had a similar feeling of timelessness to the one that Ellis experiences along with a feeling of space and adventure. In a matter of a few hours I would experience exhilaration, join in with cheerful conversations, see people in the process of falling in love and witness great arguments and fights (I've never actually been a fighter myself — fighting tires me out and I'm not an efficient fighter anyway — but I have certainly seen other people have great complicated goes at one another). By the time ordinary life asserted itself once more, I would feel I had already lived for a while in some other lifetime, that I had even taken over someone else's life. I am not recommending this sort of experience, but that in writing this particular story I was remembering the quality of it all.'

The research for *24 Hours* had been unusual and curious, including 'some research into the work an undertaker does. I talked to undertakers and asked them a lot of questions and I read one or two books. I soon had more information than I either needed or used. On the whole, the stories I write do not involve me in a great deal of research, since I am inventing the story and can set my own rules to a considerable extent. Still, one has to make anything one writes as convincing as possible, and there are times when research is essential.'

Then there was the tattoo, which caused some surprise, amusement and media comment. 'It's just a small tasteful tattoo on my shoulder. I had it done while I was working on my new book *24 Hours*. The lead character, Ellis, is tattooed at one point and I wanted to know what it felt like, so I could write about it more accurately. My stories come mainly from my imagination, but I like to get things right. So I'm prepared to do a bit of research, particularly when I want my characters to have experiences I haven't had myself. People looking at my tattoo will probably assume it's a stick-on. But it's the real thing. I've suffered for my art.'

Car chases, however, like the one over the Port Hills vividly described in *24 Hours*, were a step too far. 'I've never been in a car chase,' she reassured one interviewer. 'But I've driven over those hills many, many times, sometimes quite quickly — especially when I've been in a hurry to catch a plane at Christchurch Airport. And, of course, I've watched many films with car chases.'

24 Hours abounds, as always, in folklore references and literary allusions (the hero comes to think of himself as 'Ellis in Wonderland'), reinforcing her insistence that no writer works in isolation. 'There's a romantic notion of the writer as a singular, solitary essence. But I've always regarded myself as part of a wider network of writing. I've been influenced by everything I've read and I enjoy making references to other books.

'When I began *24 Hours* I called the hero Doyle. Then I became intrigued by the Lewis Carroll parallels. In the flats of university students I've known there's often been an element of Carroll-like craziness or surrealism, with odd characters coming and going at all hours. A tumbledown motel seemed quite an amenable location for my novel.'

In 2000, too, Margaret's developing secondary career as an essayist and speech-writer received due recognition, when Wellington's Victoria University Press (not, significantly, either of the universities she attended) decided to publish *A Dissolving Ghost — Essays and More*, as part of an intermittent essay series begun with James Bertram, Ian Wedde, Bill Manhire and Greg O'Brien. Four of her major international speeches were included, along with Murray Edmond's 1987 *Landfall* interview, an adult short story of the magic realism, post-modern kind (*The Illustrated Traveller's Tale*) and her memorable contribution to Marilyn Duckworth's anthology on sisters. Curiously, none of the essays was attributed to a date, place or audience, and others, such as her 1989 *Signal* 'Joining the Network' piece or the 1991 'Surprising Moments' speech in Auckland or the after-dinner speech at Harvard University in 1996 were regrettably absent.

'Has anyone,' asked David Hill in his *Listener* review, 'summarised Mahy's work as well as Mahy? . . . I don't think I've ever read a selection of explorations/explanations where the writer's voice comes through so clearly. The rhythms and cadences of these sentences are Margaret Mahy speaking: wondering and sometimes wandering, enthusiastic and delighted, making discoveries, connecting, connecting, connecting.

'So it's not surprising that she goes on a bit. Several of these pieces are 8000–10,000 words long. Through them, Mahy whizzes like a proton in a particle accelerator, shooting off, whirling about, inhabiting three places at once, disappearing then reappearing nearby. Just occasionally, you wish she'd stay still for a second, so you can get a good look at where she is. Zip — she's onto a favourite 1910 kids' book. Flick — she's discussing the semantic significance of "Levin". Ping — she's making simultaneous reference to mini-black holes and creationist science.

'Right from the Foreword, she has so much fun.'

Reviewer Greg O'Brien, writing in *New Zealand Books*, was unequivocal about his enthusiasm for a volume 'in which Mahy's intelligence explodes in the brilliant black and white of her prose. It's a book full of wisdom, as just about any paragraph taken at random would prove:

"We build ourselves as we grow. Our physical structure is the basis around which we extend a mental and spiritual structure, of which imagination is a vital part. Structure is the key word here, for suppose that imagination, so far from being the shapeless, vague and dreamy cloud we often feel it to be, has a potential beautiful, intricate and possibly unknowable structure of its own . . ."

'*A Dissolving Ghost* hints at art's paradoxical nature as something inherently structural yet also, by necessity, shapeless and free form.

'Mahy's tone and manner in the book are, generally, speculative . . . Needless to say, [she] is frequently, brilliantly funny and has an ever-vigilant eye and ear for the right word or phrase which, just once in a while, can open up elusive areas of experience like a magic key. She can be magnificently incisive and impassioned at the same time . . . she tackles with humility and aplomb such big themes as faith, loss, memory and truth . . . Unfailingly, she avoids the essayist's trap of staring admiringly into their own mirror and the pitfall essay-writing novelists often fall into of sounding like they are grooming themselves for their imminent Booker Prize acceptance speech.

'Mahy is certainly scholarly in the thoroughness of her attentions, but mercifully she doesn't conform to Anne Carson's definition of a scholar as "someone who takes a position . . . who knows how to limit himself to the matter at hand". Mahy is a thinker of the perambulatory, discursive kind. With the intelligence (as well as the personable nature and poise) of a cat in a tree, she leaps from branch to branch.

'My only reservation is that I wanted the book to be bigger. As it is, it certainly doesn't feel like it has exhausted or defined the outer boundaries of Mahy's creative territory — in fact the book sticks pretty much to Mainstream Mahy: her unfailingly wise utterances about story, character, language and the imaginative life. The points she makes are crucial — but now that she has made them, she should be encouraged to range more freely in whatever direction she feels inclined.

'At the conclusion of *A Dissolving Ghost* I found myself making a list of the essay topics I would like Mahy to get on with: pirates, the regional landscape, the body in children's literature, the use of trees, the art of librarianship, snow, Christchurch, the South Island, the mass media.

'In fact, all the above subjects do surface in the assembled essays. But maybe if the audience wasn't sitting so expectantly in front of her — as they were on the occasion of so many of the pieces in this book — then we would see Mahy stretching out more.

'"We build ourselves as we grow." Mahy as a writer is still, happily, in a state of construction, building and growing a body of work of paramount importance to both children and adults. She is one of the line of New Zealand geniuses that also includes Janet Frame, Rita Angus, Katherine Mansfield and Frances Hodgkins. She is a *makar*, in the truest sense. A person of vision. A gem.'

Early in 2001 the Children's Literature Foundation, organisers of the Storylines Festival, decided to nominate Margaret for the world's most prestigious prize for children's writers, the Hans Christian Andersen Award, often known as the 'Little Nobel'. This had not happened before because nomination required membership of the organising body, the Swiss-based International Board on Books for Young People (IBBY). For a volunteer organisation this came at a hefty price — around $3,700 annually to join IBBY, and about $1,500 to cover nomination fees and preparation, packaging and posting of nine sets of the required books and documentation.

In 2001, however, a consortium of Margaret's New Zealand publishers (HarperCollins, Penguin and Scholastic), plus the New Zealand Book Council, the New Zealand Reading Association and two anonymous donors was put together, beginning an ongoing and increasingly involved membership of IBBY, which is the only global children's literature organisation. International president

Dr Peter Schneck, from Austria, visited Auckland for the 2004 Storylines Festival and in 2007 the foundation will be hosting International Children's Book Day. Because of Margaret, New Zealand's status in the organisation was assured from the start.

The 2002 Hans Christian Andersen Award went to British writer Aidan Chambers, and the 2004 award to Irish writer Martin Waddell, but the foundation is committed to a third nomination for 2006. It is aware that Margaret's nomination might never overcome a possible Eurocentric and American leaning, but there are still major benefits from the IBBY involvement in general exposure of New Zealand children's writing generally, and Margaret specifically, on the world stage.

In recognition of her growing reputation as an essayist, Margaret was appointed judge of *Landfall*'s 2002 essay competition. Her judge's report was in itself a meaty mini-essay on the art of essay writing:

'There is something both necessary yet fundamentally unfair about competitions. They work so well in some ways. They focus attention on areas that might otherwise be overlooked or even ignored, and there is value in comparing one contender with another, even if, at the same time, one knows that true comparison is often impossible. Some of these essays just ought not to be compared with others. Their intentions are entirely different. Some give lucid accounts of people and events. They do not intend to define or speculate. Their value lies in what they record, which sounds rather flat except when the record also elucidates, as it often does. However the basis of other essays is speculation — an attempt to put both the writer and reader in charge of feelings that have, until writing or reading the essay, been obstinately obscure. The essayist directs speculations not only to the outside world but back into a puzzled self, and the essay becomes the means by which the writer achieves inner power of some area of his or her own thoughts that possibly had been rather nebulous until then.

'The finalists for the *Landfall* competition seem to divide into two approximate categories. There are essays in which some sort of direct account of an event or a person is given, then there are essays that are concerned with the deciphering of some human enigma.

'Any judge has personal vulnerability when it comes to judging. Personally I value the straightforward accounts that add to one's understanding and general knowledge, but at the same time I can be most deeply touched by those essays that draw one into more mysterious mediations on human beings and their troubled discernment. These essays, when well written, can command more intensity than the objective account. Of course from a reader's point of view, both the account and the speculation, serving (as they do) different purposes, can be equally valuable. As a judge, however, one finds oneself shuffling backwards and forwards, frowning and mumbling, and trying to evaluate elements that probably should not be compared in the first place. Some of the essays are appropriately objective, yet, unfairly enough, I am aware as I write this that objectivity and accuracy sound flat words of praise when compared with the more passionate responses one has to the more passionate essays. And, at the same time, part of what makes the passion most potent is a recognisable accuracy of observation . . . something with which the reader needs to concert before branching out to consider new and possibly startling possibilities . . .

'Having emphasised the differences in intention that haunt the various essays submitted for this competition, one must pay necessary tribute to the form that unites them — a form that creates an accessible space in which a specialised meditation may take place. The essay form demands less of a reader's valuable reading time than does a novel, but may be equally rich in ideas. Indeed the relative brevity of some essays intensifies their focus and brings a precise enlightenment initially, one imagines, to the writer but in due course to the reader as well.'

Two sharply contrasting books appeared in 2002, the seriously spooky ghost story *Alchemy*, and the comic picture book *Dashing Dog*, about a dog 'who spends a lot of his time looking like a long legged sheep'. Any newcomer to Mahy's work would be astonished to be told they came from the same pen.

Dashing Dog, with its sixteen patter song-style verses packed with alliteration and off-the-wall rhymes requiring a nimble tongue and supple lips, began life as an idea about a dog's adventures to be told in pictures with a text of just three words. '"Good dog", it would say, while the pictures showed the dog as beautifully groomed though a trifle bewildered. The next few pictures would all have the caption "Bad dog" as the dog had a variety of linked and destructive adventures.

'But in my story the dog hero would finally perform an act of traditional heroism, totally destroying what was left of his grooming but causing the unseen narrator to exclaim "Good dog!" once more. I liked the idea of the very simple text, and even said the illustrator could have most of any money the publisher was prepared to pay, which I think is proof of deep sincerity. However, the publisher and my agent both said that these simple captions were not what I did best and that I should tell the story in a fuller form. I agreed to do so ... and was interested, when I came to actually write this fuller version to find that it presented itself, not only in a rhyming form but complete with verbal convolutions and tongue twisters that, once considered, became somehow necessary, and which meant that the final book would be a long way removed from what I had had in mind in the first place.' As Margaret herself has said, 'The voice of the poem is not what I had in mind in the first place, indeed it was what I was trying to avoid, the writer's voice tending to push in before the parent's, but there it is. Somehow my particular voice insists on games with alliterations and rhymes even when that is not my intention. My voice, though acrobatic at times, will remain a reasonably classical one for all that.'

> Dashing dog! Dashing dog! Oh, what a sight to see!
> Cleaned up and curlicued — what a delight to be

Walking a dog who is brushed-up and downery
Dare-devil-daring and Dog-about Townery.

Down on the sand, gulls perambulate pondering
Keeping one eye on whatever comes wandering
OFF goes the dog, keen to catch every quill of them
UP go the gulls, every feather and bill of them.

And when, his immaculate grooming quickly destroyed by running
through seaweed and bracken, Dashing Dog sees the wind blow
a baby off the jetty:

Run! How we run! But a comet goes ripping past
Rushing and racing and skilfully skipping past.
Diving and dipping where Betty is floundering
Saving our girl from the danger of drowndering.

Hurrah for the hero who swims, full of cheer to us
Bringing back Betty so precious and dear to us.
Out on the jetty we're towing then tugging them,
Petting and patting, and holding and hugging them.

Coat in confusion, his hairy tiara gone
Dipping and draggling — but oh! what a paragon!
Look at the wagging tail — wet every bend of it
But he's our HERO — and that is the end of it.

'This story is a joke — a primitive fantasy with its basis in everyday
life. I do have a dog — a large standard poodle — and poodles in
themselves are fantasies made actually according to human desires
rather than any desire on the dog's part. Originally they were
hunting dogs, but nowadays they exist as dogs reduced to human
accessories. Of course this is not how poodles see themselves. They
think they are simply dogs and that is that. Anyhow every so often
I take my dog to be groomed and tided up (poodles grow wool

instead of traditional dog hair and don't shed it. I don't have him cut in patterns or anything like that, but some people do which is imposing an even more exaggerated human fantasy on the dog). Anyhow for a brief time my dog looks smart and urban according to some human judgement, which the dog himself does not share. (Of course he hasn't shared the expense either.) Immediately we leave the dog grooming parlour entropy swings in. My dog Baxter has no vanity and is disinterested in his appearance. He behaves like a dog . . . drinks from puddles dangling his carefully brushed ears in them (after all his ears are simply his ears) and his expensive ordering immediately begins to collapse. Though I have paid good money to achieve this appearance a more subversive part of seeing this disintegration fulfils my observing life. This underlying truth is fantasised in this story. Practically every event in the story . . . chasing gulls, leaping up after a Frisbee, scruffling with other dogs, pursuing a cat . . . is a real event though they don't necessarily happen in the same walk. My dog has never saved anyone from drowning — poodles are waterdogs and have webbed paws, but Baxter thinks his webbed paws are not enough and he deeply mistrusts water. However the idea of noble dog saving a child from drowning is deeply entrenched in traditional story and seems to me at least to flow out of the story I have just told quite naturally.'

With *Alchemy*, also published in 2002, many felt that Margaret returned to the subtle, chilling and challenging complexities of *The Changeover* and *The Tricksters*. There are the similar Christchurch settings, similar fairy tale good versus evil elements; similar clever, articulate but troubled teenage protagonists challenged by, in this case, a sinister fairground magician named Quando who inhabits Roland's childhood dreams and, reappearing unpleasantly in his life, seeks to steal the teenagers' powers, in a prolonged struggle culminating in what is possibly Margaret's most eerie and terrifying fictional climax. *Alchemy* studies the idea that love and hate can both release powerful energy, and, in the perilous transformation of the gifted but self-absorbed Roland into a young man of greater self-knowledge and empathy with others, warns of the dangers of denying one's true nature.

Alchemy was another instance of strong publisher recommendation, almost insistence, to lower the age of the main character. 'I started writing about someone who was 19 and the publishers quickly came back and said no, that's too old for a YA book, pull the age down. It's to do with all sorts of categorisations, and to do with wanting the character to be the same age as the reader — which isn't necessarily a true thing at all.' To Margaret's admirers in New Zealand, it came as no surprise that *Alchemy* swept away the opposition for the 2003 New Zealand Post Senior Fiction Award: it was widely seen as vintage Mahy, as intricately layered and compelling as any of the 1980s novels.

Always, as the century of the three '0's' settled down, there was international travel, and major speeches and essays to write: in 2000, for the 7th World Congress of the International Reading Association held in Auckland; in 2002, for the Auckland College of Education as the first recipient of their Sylvia Ashton-Warner Fellowship; in 2002 a keynote speech for the Australasian conference organised by Centre for Children's Literature of the Christchurch College of Education. In 2003, her essay, *Notes of a Bag Lady*, was acclaimed as one of the very best of the new Montana Estates Essay Series, published in attractive mini-book format by editor Lloyd Jones and credited with reviving interest in the essay as a literary form in New Zealand. It was a fascinating short take on her life and influences, the 'drinking from puddles' story and Allan Quartermain and all, in a necessary but often very funny shorthand, her unmistakeable voice clearly chuckling.

> I could easily have been an alcoholic, though as things stand I can only lay claim to the lesser title of binge drinker. Sometimes I think, a little wistfully, that I might still make it, but really I have missed my chance, for the days when alcoholism seemed a necessary confirmation of one's artistic capacity are over. And these days I am mostly too tired to be bothered. Still, I

remember drinking for the first time and the seductive feeling of being at ease with the world, I remember the clarity and fluency that comes with the first two drinks. Above all, the huge relief. The world is still there in all its searing wonder and horror — one can still acknowledge its complexity, name its features, but somehow one is no longer trapped by it all.

I am, therefore, fascinated by the way in which people try to present that drinking is a matter of good taste and nothing to do with getting drunk. Recently I have listened, amazed, to BBC connoisseurs enlivening the early hours of the television morning by discussing the flavour and scent of wine, have even leaped from bed to write their comments down so that I can frown over them in the more rational light of day. 'It smells like an embrocation for tired muscles . . .' said one expert tasting one particular wine, 'like very ripe pineapples. It tastes sweet but floral — not sugary.'

'Get your nose in!' commanded yet another expert, speaking poetically and being heard on the other side of the world by someone who, having no judgement herself, was naturally sceptical of the discernment of others. 'It smells like grapefruit and that bobbly grass. It smells silky — a lovely lissom wine.' None of them once mentioned the possibility that the wine might smell of grapes. In an article on New Zealand white wine published in the *New Scientist*, one author, presumably a person of taste and judgement, mentioned (apparently intending it as a compliment) that our wine tasted of apples and cat's pee. Could I ever, even with the most single-minded dedication, have developed such delicacy of recognition? I don't think so. I have rarely been anything but brutal where wine is concerned.

The years of 2002 and 2003 were clouded by first, the unwelcome news from England of her agent Vanessa Hamilton's illness, and early in 2003, her death from cancer at just over 60. Vanessa had been editor, agent, adviser and friend for 30 years; the dependable, methodical and assertive administrator of Margaret's literary affairs, her most ardent, loyal admirer. It had been her deepest desire to see Margaret awarded the Hans Christian Andersen Medal, and she was instrumental in helping the New Zealand organisers put together the elaborate documentation for the first 2002 nomination. However, she passed on to Margaret's new London agent, Mandy Little, a strong hope that Margaret's fantasy trilogy, long sidelined by her advisers in favour of her shorter trademark 'realistic stories with fantasy elements,' would now come to fruition.

This lengthy manuscript, with the working title of *Heriot*, has been intriguing listeners for two decades when mentioned in conversations, talks and interviews. 'The shortest book I have had published is nine words long and the longest is two hundred and sixty-five pages. The longest book I have *written* is over 800 pages at present [1987] but when I mention this, which I do with a mixture of pride and uneasiness, my daughter tells me I am off on mathematics not literature. I can't help being secretly impressed with it, a carry-over from childhood, I suppose, when the excellence of a book was equated with its length.' In 2002 she told a Christchurch audience that 'about four years ago I had a novel turned down on the grounds that the voice underlying the story, as well as its central preoccupation, was too adult'. In 2004 the trilogy has risen again as one of her major projects with still 'a heck of a lot of work to do' and publication (in a market now crowded with such works) still some way off. It is, she admits, 'tremendously dear to me'. As far back as 1987, when discussing the long book with Murray Edmond, she admitted that when she was writing it, she would 'quite often work all night'. She has described its setting as an 'elsewhere', vaguely European, requiring a lot of research on the towns of the pre-Renaissance period, 'a sort of pre-industrial world. I suppose it is approximately the same as early Tudor times. Printing has been established. There are quite a lot of sophisticated reactions towards art and the world of ideas.

'The hero is a young man with long hair who, having had a supernatural power detected in him, is removed from his home, becoming (like Barney in *The Haunting*) very passive; the heroine a feisty girl who dresses as a boy, who's been sexually abused and finds herself a child on the streets. At the same time, there's a parallel story about a prince of the city who also is a damaged character, but wants in a romantic way to be not just a king, but something more, a magician of power and standing, plus another involving a tomboyish princess from an outlying kingdom who feels much reduced by her father's wish to have a son as his heir. It's for young adults, more at the sixteen to seventeen level than twelve, and possibly even an adult fantasy at the same time.'

'This novel', she says, 'has transposed all the supernatural elements of my other books to a more conventional supernatural setting, in that it's an imaginary world where it's possible to envisage the sort of energy people like Laura (in *The Changeover*) and Troy (in *The Haunting*) have, being able to go. As long as you keep it in the domestic, realistic setting, it becomes very difficult to think of some ways, somewhere for that energy to go . . . giving the individual who possesses it [energy] something I would like to have myself — a wonderful, pure insight into the structure of nature. Which is not too different from what I was doing when I was a child and wanted to talk to the animals. So I do a lot of repetition of what I did when I was a child, but I hope it's a spiral repetition rather than purely circular.'

Scheduled for publication in 2005 and 2006 are one very short children's novel, *Zerelda's Horses*; reissues of *Shock Forest* and *The Very Wicked Headmistress*; the famous performance piece *Down the Back of the Chair* as a picture book illustrated by Polly Dunbar; and another short novel, *Portable Ghosts*. In 2004 Margaret was also working on a war story for a Michael Morpurgo anthology of war stories, a biographical entry on Gavin Bishop for an encyclopaedia, and picture book stories were always 'lurking around'. Despite assertions that she's 'got older and tired so it's not possible to work through the night in the way that I used to', this is still a writer who finds it difficult to turn down work or resist ideas which strike out of the blue.

Before all of these, however, are two projects that venture boldly into new territory: her first novel and TV series written simultaneously, and the first novel 'for children edging on young adult' with a Maori title. *Kaitangata* refers to the story's setting on an island in Lyttelton Harbour, 'one of other kaitangata in New Zealand, places where Maori people have eaten other Maori people'. The story has some Maori references — the children's mother is half-Maori — and echoes of a much earlier true Governors Bay controversy stirred up by an American developer who wanted to subdivide Manson's Point, known locally as Kaitangata and now owned by Margaret.

She has little sympathy for the contemporary notion that only Maori can have a spiritual feeling for the land. 'I don't think that's true, it's up to individuals.' Nor does she believe that Maori storytellers should have a monopoly on Maori themes: 'I think that people should be allowed to write what they want, provided that if they get it wrong they don't mind being told. But I'd be too shy myself to write a book about Maori people — except, I suppose, if they were like my nephews and nieces who are part-Maori and live European lives'. The Maori elements of *Kaitangata* include the cannibalism of the title, 'a natural part of history . . . which never really seems all that terrible — killing people seems terrible, but what you do with them afterwards never seems as terrible to me as it does to other people. Well, they lived in a country where there wasn't an abundance of protein like there was in Europe, with plenty of cattle; and of course there's the whole symbolic thing, that you have eaten people and beaten people — in my story the island is capable of taking on this consuming atmosphere and finally consumes the villain.' In editing discussions with Margaret about the book before she died, Vanessa expressed concern that the villain, though unpleasant, 'came across as a more attractive character than the children's father, a rather obsessed man'. Subsequently, Margaret tried to make the villain 'a bit less attractive . . . though I have to say I quite liked him the way he was, and now of course they come back and say he's too unattractive — just one of those ironical things that happen in editing, having to correct what was seen as a fault!'

The 'spooky thing' about *Maddigan's Fantasia*, says Margaret, is that it's a quite new sort of project — a book springing out of a TV series — 'there's a lot more interest from publishers because of the TV connection . . . I've never done anything quite like that before and I don't quite know how it's going to turn out.' It is some years since she was first approached for the concept; finance proved difficult, but 2004, with a charter in place indicating better times ahead for family television drama, brought a sudden revival by its producers, South Pacific Pictures, in partnership with the BBC. The script conferences, involving Margaret, producer John Barnett and two or three scriptwriters, were 'quite a disconcerting experience for me because they talk very quickly about things whereas I tend to think, hang on a moment, I need to *think* about that, and by that time they've jumped on to the next story'. Also, any grand ideas about having a whole circus, with horses, had to be modified for reasons of cost and scale. Margaret provided the storyline, backstory and characters of the thirteen-part series, about a travelling circus playing in various isolated areas of post-apocalyptic New Zealand, and then it was suggested that 'it would be a good thing if I wrote a book based on the story to come out more or less at the same time'. The book appears — unusually, *before* the TV series — in May 2005, and the television series, to be shot in Auckland, sometime later in the year.

The post-apocalyptic New Zealand setting of *Maddigan's Fantasia* came about because she liked the idea of creating a series of strange communities set up after war, each remade community different but tied together by government and one or two big cities. Some are reasonably well established, some are really struggling. Into this fantasy she has woven time travel, suggesting echoes of the travelling Punch and Judy puppet shows in Russell Hoban's 1980 cult book *Ridley Walker*, one of her great favourites.

These days Margaret gives the impression of someone in enviable harmony with herself, her family, her many loyal and protective friends, her career and the physical surroundings of rambling, book-filled home and mature garden she has worked so hard to create. Solitude she regards with the serenity of long habit and preference: 'the basic human condition is one of loneliness — yes, and it also surprises me how consistently we try to break down our solitude. I think that all the people we love and feel very close to and who love us do, of course, break down our solitude to a big extent. But in the end, if you had a child in pain you can't take the pain over yourself. The child is alone with that pain, no matter how you love him and how passionately you want to help him; this is true of a lot of human situations. In the end we are locked in a particular skin, a particular nervous system, a particular set of memories; you may share those memories with other people, but they are still particularly your own. Talking with my brother and sisters about memories of our childhood, I realised how much memories of the same incident are affected by our place in the family.'

She would like to cut down her travelling, to write a bit less and to read a great deal more. For her, reading has never been something done for relaxation at the end of the day, but an intellectual, consciously creative act. 'Reading gives you a subtle range of interpretive capacities; it seems to me that if you live with books, you live with real life as opposed to the relatively primitive approach of those who discard books for "reality". Books themselves are not sacred objects, but what they've got in them can become so.'

Concerned friends, hearing of occasional bouts of indifferent health in recent winters — 'the asthmatic hay fever thing is very tiring' — are assured that it is nothing: oh, the voice will always be croaky. Her storytelling passion and inventiveness remain as fierce and compulsive as ever. A 2000 profile stated: 'She can't envisage a time when she'll retire from writing, it's too big a part of her. But she says, "I'd like to go back to a more playful phase.

Writing can become a terribly serious business when it's your means of making a living. But that's eased off now.'"

The need for stories in the troubled, post-9/11 age, she believes, is greater than ever. Her essential optimism allows her to regard the future without too much gloom. 'I think the world is alarming because it's always been alarming, but the alarm shifts and changes and sometimes we concluded wrongfully that we overcame alarming things — but they come up again because of human limitations. One of the alarming things is that people use stories and believe in them and use them passionately in very destructive ways. So I'm not suggesting for a moment that all stories work desirably on the lives of people — stories that demonstrate a return to less complicated and less destructive lives would be a very good thing, but of course a bit of an over-simplification. While I'm an enthusiast about stories, I don't think I've ever suggested that stories have a necessary morality about them, but I suggest they are a necessary way that people structure their experience. When you think of the wide variety of possibilities that get offered to people through education and so on, people often structure some story about them. Of course, some people structure their stories about things that other people disapprove of a great deal — so I don't want to sound as if I'm saying that it's a story, so it must be good.

'I don't think there's been a time in history when there's been more impulse towards good; a lot of people want to *do good*. I also think that when you listen to the news, disaster after disaster, despite the tremendous number of people who've done good – – it's just that good news radio is not all that interesting. There's something within human beings that responds to alarm rather than to serenity — they are trying to live their lives by serenity, do good and kind things, but they don't want to listen to good news. For example, people working for Greenpeace, who struggle to express positive and good messages and make people aware of the dangers, don't get the attention they deserve or the good responses from those that they help.'

She is not easily alarmed or repelled by horror stories, ghost stories or action movies. 'I've read lots and lots of horror stories. Bridget and I used to watch the Friday night horrors together, and I've got quite a few horror films on video. I think it's possible you can exhaust your power to be frightened, though I suppose a realistic story in which people domestically do very cruel things to one another would probably shock me a great deal. I don't believe in ghosts or vampires or anything like but I do believe that people . . . can do horrible things to one another. I've never had a ghost experience but spoken to people who have — yes, people I respect have told me about supernatural experiences. I like the symbolism of human experience — the spiritual meaning, say, of Cape Reinga — of course I'm prepared to give it some sort of symbolic respect, but I haven't had that sort of experience myself.

'I don't think I believe in afterlife, but I do believe that the *energy* that a person represents goes back into the world and takes on other forms; I don't think death is the end. Human beings are creatures that form a continuation that goes on, in some way we find it very hard to tie it down as something that's familiar to us. The emergence of a particular baby we know whose personality is uniquely theirs — over and beyond the energy of conception, there's some sort of flow of energy, which you could call spiritual, that a person generates during their life, some of which is innate and some which is chosen. That whole thing about environment and inheritance and free will represents some sort of mysterious energy which we don't really understand.

'Philip Pullman's daemons [in the *His Dark Materials* trilogy], the twin souls, forms of energy and perception over and above the individual person — that was a very good idea, as a coming of age, with truthful resonances about a way of finding out about yourself. I don't think death is utter, except because of human limitation that familiar progress has been interrupted and something else has taken over. Existence is just hugely mysterious — of matter, of consciousness and all the various sorts of awareness and everything we've got which is so intricate and so wonderful, and also mysterious because it's got its limitation. Although human beings have understandings about themselves and their situations, so far as we know no other species has, and in the end somehow or other we have to cope with those limitations. Some people cope by denying that they exist at all, but it doesn't seem to me that they do cope with the idea that we're not an infinite species and that we do use all sorts of things like symbolism and metaphor and things beyond language in order to make some sort of contract or entry into the mysteriousness that surrounds us.'

Margaret has never ruled out the possibility that an adult novel could be an interesting challenge. 'People say to me, of course, you've moved on to older books because your children have got older. I wouldn't want to cut that out as an influence, but I tend to react against it a bit. People see anyone who writes for children as writing out of a response to their own children, rather than writing out of a response to a particular set of reading experiences children's books give. Or, of course, out of a response to the author's own childhood. Which often tends to be the dominating thing.' But she always hastens that she would not write an adult novel 'because I think I'd be doing a superior thing, but because I'd be able to make use of a different range of experiences and language and everything like that. Maybe sometime in the next twenty years, sooner if I have the time, but I rather suspect I won't have the time.'

Queried about the shining characteristic of her language, the sparkling dialogue, the quirky metaphors, that unrivalled zest and energy which Julia Eccleshare says has the unusual quality of actually charging up the reader, Margaret says, 'Well, if that's true I suppose it comes from a response to the world, wanting metaphors to be fresh, but also wanting them to come out fairly readily from an individual way of looking at the world. The extent to which you're successful you don't really know about until the reader comes back; the reader completes what the writer began. As a reader, as I've got older, I find it harder to make those connections. It's harder for me to be taken by surprise.'

So-called 'good writing', she thinks, is both a gift and something that can be learned. 'If it was some sort of gift I wouldn't have bothered to learn it, I suppose, and you never learn enough, you never learn it to the extent that you are totally satisfied.' Writers she particularly admires among a wide range of favourites are not unexpectedly Angela Carter, Russell Hoban, Charles Dickens, 'for their caricatures, their jokes, their seriousness'.

Everything in the course of ordinary days seen, heard, touched, tasted, smelled and felt is possible grist to her inexhaustible storyteller's mill. 'Yesterday, for instance, I was in a car park and found myself in a knot of cars — a situation where one car couldn't move until another car moved but that other car couldn't move until a third car moved, and so on. I found I was automatically imagining a story for very young children about a series of people, all anxious to get home by a certain time. I began telling myself this story and explaining that the green car couldn't move until the red car moved, and the red car couldn't move until the blue car moved . . . and then I realised that, in real life I was confronted with something even more remarkable. The five cars in the complicated knot (including my own) were all silver — a fashionable colour it seems. Memories of previously existing stores and picture book illustration had somehow taken over the way I was considering a real life situation. Since then I have thought of this knot of silver cars in the supermarket parking lot and have imagined the owners getting out of their cars to argue with each other, and then getting back into the wrong cars and driving away. The possibilities seem endless. Of course I like to think of my stories as original, but I know they are part of a network of stories which support one another as they are linked in a reader's mind.'

But the possibilities are not only direct personal experience. 'Writers are very treacherous people; they will readily take over other people's stories. They can move in quite cunningly and take possession of other people's experiences, and then they transform them in certain ways . . .

'Certainly in a lot of cases, writers bear witness by breaking the peace. I myself am not an abrasive or peace-breaking writer, though I think that some of the ideas I speak about are quite challenging and question peace to a certain extent. For instance, I often assert, in *The Tricksters* . . . that the peace should be broken provided we reassemble it in a better form . . . a lot of writers, because of ego or other grandiose reasons, sometimes think they are the ones chosen to tell the stories. To think you are the one at the expense of other people may be dangerous, but I think there are those moments where it's not self-assertion but just perception of the naked power of the self.'

Imagination, she says, is clearly a creative force for good, 'but we can't pretend that only good people have imagination. There is plenty of evidence of nasty people having imaginative power and using it in horrifying ways. There's a character who crops up from time to time in my books — the older brother of the three brothers in *The Tricksters*, for instance, is rather demonic. He's a very frustrated character, because, no matter how crowded the world is with wonderful things, it's never going to be wonderful enough for him. He wants continuously to be the transforming magician, the persona at the heart of everything; his ego is such that there is never enough fulfilment. He always feels something beyond; he feels he deserves more . . . These characters feel the world owes them something. Their discontent is one of the things wickedness comes from.

'There is a character in a fantasy I once wrote who stands in his inherited kingdom but despises it because it's just not enough; he doesn't want to be just king — he wants to be something more marvellous still. He has, in effect, an insatiable imaginative demand which makes him wicked, it makes him a dangerous person to be around partly because he gets particularly jealous when he sees somebody who seems to have access to the power or insight he covets.'

Every family, she believes, has its storytellers, 'some more professional than others, perhaps, but if listening to stories is a human function so is telling them, and children are often more thrilled by family stories than they are by the most polished stories in books. "Tell me about when I was little and was tossed by the cow . . ." the child demands. "Tell me about the time I rode my tricycle to the shops and got lost." They listen intently as these pieces of their identity are rescued from the past and part of their lives is restored to them. For the most part parents, telling these stories, give them some sort of shape and drama. It is an essential human thing to do.'

Questioned by one interviewer about specific messages that she wanted to convey through her stories, Margaret replied: 'I suppose I have some main themes about the capacity of any individual to be transformed by poetry, art, or imagination. Ordinary people have as much access to the power of imagination, transformation, as the "extraordinary" people, writers or artists, who make quite a big statement about their transformation. I don't think that in terms of any sort of morality; I do have a very high opinion of people who, for one reason or another, manage to get the better of an incident from which they have suffered, and move on into a position of forgiveness — either forgiving other people or forgiving the world or forgiving themselves. I think that's a very fruitful state to be in — to be the person who offers true forgiveness. If you do find you can't be as perfect as you want to be, what you do is to acknowledge your own imperfections and laugh about it to some extent; but the important thing is: don't let it turn into any sort of revulsion towards yourself or to the world.

'It's a hard thing to ask, but in many of the stories I've written there is a moment where a person has a chance to discharge resentment and overcome it . . . We should do our best to be right according to what has been given to us, but we shouldn't agonise over being wrong past a certain point — just forgive yourself or try to do better if you think you've really done wrong. However, I don't see any point in punishing yourself; that's where I think a lot of useless guilt comes from. There's a point in life where guilt may have a creative function, because it actually makes you behave differently and work better as a human being. But when you've passed this certain point, guilt tends to be self-indulgent; people who go back and feel uselessly guilty for past events that they can't change don't do anything constructive at all, either for themselves or for anybody else.'

She sees her writing as an act of subversion, although what really interests her is the tension between order and anarchy, and that 'so much thought is directed towards imposing order. But once one has pinned down some sort of ideal in a framework of words, then some of the anarchy of the original idea escapes — energy has escaped. That's why I tend to give very long answers to questions — as I answer, all sorts of things seem to me to be escaping, so I rush round like a sheepdog trying to herd it all in to make it reasonably complete. The exercise of being truthful is so complicated and wearying and in the end sometimes so inadequate and unsatisfactory that it fragments and drifts away round the edges as mine is doing right now . . .'

Childhood, she says, was for her 'a time of receiving extremely concentrated bursts of information; the extent to which you spend the rest of your life deciphering that is a matter of personal choice — consciously or unconsciously. I've chosen to spend my time disentangling that and simultaneously writing about it quite seriously while joking about it. I like to think I write the sort of story someone can begin to enjoy in childhood and can continue enjoying in a variety of ways as they get older.'

To the question 'What is your *favourite* book that you have written?', one of the three questions invariably fired at authors in classrooms (the others are 'How many books have you written?' and 'Where do you get your ideas from?'), Margaret has always replied that it is the one not yet written, the exhilarating, *perfect* story that is in her head, because no story ever turns out to be as good as she first imagined it would be. 'I always start writing a story with a lot of optimism; that this time I have a really good idea. Then towards the end I start to lose confidence.'

'As both reader and writer I expect to be changed by a story. Somewhere there is a wonderful story, a platonic *form* of a story which, as I read it will complete me. It will become an indissoluble part of me forever, and yet as I read it again and again will always surprise or deepen me or change me in some way. I may not ever quite find that story, but I can discern its presence in other stories. That is one of the main reasons I read. In a way I hope to write it, and though it is not a realistic expectation, it is real enough to be a starting place for whatever I write. All the time I look for signs that the story is passing by, not only in books, but in the shadows of clouds or words overheard in the street. It leaves clues, omens, promises in the stains on a kitchen bench, in letters from children, in the entrails of mice the cats leave on the new rug, the way in which the old volcanic cone in which I live has been invaded by water and become a harbour, in lotteries and rocking horses. And of course it leaves its traces in stories by other people, and it makes lots of jokes to distract me.'

To summarise the work of a writer of such accomplishment, variety and range is testing. If there is one author 'whose work belies the old critical adage that children's literature cannot sustain serious critical examination', it is Margaret Mahy, 'something of a phenomenon in New Zealand and international publishing', according to leading British academic Peter Hunt. 'It can be very persuasively argued that although Mahy seems to use conventional forms, her work is resolutely postmodern, frequently (or perhaps pervasively) feminist, and continually deals in margins and eccentricities, mirroring the conflicting expansions of adolescence.' Her writing is 'prolific and erratic . . . genuinely child-centred . . . [and] contains highly suggestive, interwoven levels of complexity that are increasingly regarded as a challenge to serious critics'.

The first specialist in children's literature appointed to a professorship at a British university, Peter Hunt includes Margaret in a stellar list of 38 great 19th- and 20th-century children's writers in English, from Lewis Carroll to Kipling to Beatrix Potter to Dr Seuss to Philip Pullman. Apart from Margaret, the only other 'colonial' is the Australian Patricia Wrightson, born in 1921. Hunt cites a characteristic passage which has been declared by Jack Lasenby, among many others, as one of the most memorable, poetic and vivid of Margaret's many images: the naked Angela, wakeful on a hot summer night in a bedroom 'infected with disturbing silver', drawn to the window in the opening chapter of *The Catalogue of the Universe*.

As she stood, simply feeling grateful, [Angela] heard for the third time, beyond all doubt, a sound outside, a sound so soft that it would have been possible to think it out of existence again, except that this time she really *knew* she had heard it, a sound as gentle as a hand brushing down a velvet curtain. It made her curious but it did not alarm her, for she was used to many different sounds in the night, living as she did up above the city, in a wild place close under the sky. She went to her window and looked out, and there in the bright moonlight she saw her mother Dido in the centre of the square of grass half-contained in the right angle made by their odd home (a home that had never quite got as far as being a proper house). It took a moment to realise what Dido was doing, but that rhythmic and dreamy sway was familiar — Dido was scything the grass by moonlight. Angela could see the entranced, semi-circular swing of her shoulders, heard the whisper of the keen steel and the sigh of long grass bowing down before her. Everything around her was drenched in a light so clear and so intense it seemed as if it must have more substance than ordinary light. It was the very light of visions and prophecies.

Resting on the shank of her scythe, Dido turned her head and looked straight over at Angela, but the slumberous lid of the verandah was half-closed over the small eye of Angela's bedroom, and besides, Angela could plainly see that Dido's own eyes were so flooded with moonlight that she was radiantly blind, a fairy-tale woman who, having lost her own sight, had been given pale, shining eyes of silver . . .

Watching Dido scythe in the moonlight like Mother Time herself, Angela found herself thinking of the road, and wondering at the same time if Dido might not be just a little crazy. Like the road, Dido had a dangerous edge and sometimes she went right out to it and danced, apparently challenging it to crumble away under her. Angela feared for such a reckless dancer, though by now she knew that she, too, had an inside road as well as an outside one, and dangerous edges of her own. Still, sooner or later, she confidently expected to find wonderful happiness in life. But whatever Dido challenged by dancing on dangerous edges was no sort of happiness Angela could recognise. Dido scythed on, leaving a swathe of shadow behind her . . .

A *Washington Post Bookworld* writer noted that, for intelligent adolescents, Margaret writes 'with all the force and precision and richness of a poet'; another that her books for young readers 'are full of linguistic pyrotechnics . . . as well as plenty to eat'. Indeed, the duality of Margaret's prodigious storytelling gifts has often been spoken of: the wacky and whimsical stories for young children, the compelling and suspenseful novels for teenagers.

Throughout all her work, she deals with opposing concepts of reality and illusion, truth and imagination, the fabulous in the ordinary, the fantastic in the domestic. The many witches, wizards, clowns, robbers and pirates challenge, often with humour but sometimes in darker tones, the commonplace and the respectable; she 'uses fantasy as a light to illuminate aspects of our so-called ordinary lives'. In her YA novels she 'often takes a realistic theme within a family setting and supercharges it with fantastical or supernatural elements'. Her resolutely non-sexist perspective is often noted: she 'continually pushes at the boundaries of [fairy-tale conventions]' and 'roots out the sexism that used to be integral' to fiction for young readers. And shining through everything she writes is her conviction in 'the power of love and the power of the imagination to enhance and redeem our world'.

Yet she also writes unflinchingly of starkly contemporary and universal philosophical issues. 'The double aspect of things — man and beast, [good] and evil, young and old intrigues Margaret Mahy,' wrote Sarah Hayes in the *Times Literary Supplement*. David Rees has drawn parallels in Margaret's work with the Dracula story, that metaphor 'for the basic human fear of being (or desire to be) changed into somebody or something else. It questions the very concept of having an identity... one recurring theme from *The Haunting* onwards is that our ancestors have power over us whether we like it or not; we resemble them physically, they bequeath us certain characteristics and there is little we can do to escape from this inheritance. They are to some extent spirits moulding our lives . . .'

And among the many critics who have drawn attention to the inherent *sexiness* of her narratives is the award-winning English writer Francis Spufford. In his elegant memoir of childhood reading, Spufford singles out an American and a New Zealander from the many authors who appeared in the 1980s with novels 'designed to lead "young adults" gently out of children's books by offering them the certainties of a children's book narration, only applied to the lives of those who had entered the Age of Acne.' As an 80s teenager, he 'could have read Cynthia Voight's extraordinarily tough, and sparely beautiful, series of novels about the Tillermans . . . or the New Zealand novelist Margaret Mahy's terrific Bronteesque supernatural thrillers, *The Changeover*, *The Haunting* and *The Tricksters*. Mahy did family life with an elegant, witty realism that made you feel you were getting a leg-up to being an altogether more noticing kind of person; simultaneously, she understood how inchoately sexy magic is, at a point in your life when real sex is still three wishes away, and gleams with as much mixed fascination and alarm as if it were truly a spell.'

It is surely timely, that in 2005, as Margaret approaches her 70th birthday, her 45th year as a published story writer and her 25th year as a novelist, there should be a new resource on her work available to scholars, beside the general American and

British reference books and studies by leading international commentators such as Jack Zipes, Sheila Egoff, Maurice Saxby and Christine Wilkie-Stibbs. A major collection of essays is imminent: *Marvellous Codes: The Fiction of Margaret Mahy*, edited by two expatriate Kiwis Dr Elizabeth Hale, of the University of New England, New South Wales, and Dr Sarah Winters, of the University of Toronto. Published by Victoria University Press in Wellington, it features contributions by American, English, Australian and Canadian academics; the New Zealand contributors are Diane Hebley, Claudia Marquis, Lisa Scally, Anna Smith and Kathryn Walls.

Given the paucity of academic comment on any children's writing in New Zealand, these studies will provide a new assessment of Margaret's work both as a 'New Zealand' writer and a 'universal' one for both younger and older children.

Thus Diane Hebley and Claudia Marquis produce ample evidence to refute English assertions since the 1980s that Margaret's novels have little or no New Zealand flavour, even those written after her own affirmation of 'homecoming' from *The Changeover* onwards. Hebley concludes, 'Clearly, in all her YA novels, Mahy shows extraordinary power in drawing imagery from her own environment to empower her fictional concerns. She is outstanding among her compatriot writers for releasing through her sense of place . . . a "special country of the mind right for this tale". Thus she contributes to a valuable sense of national identity for New Zealand readers. Recognisable seascapes and landscapes, and the fault lines in association with distinctions between truth and illusion, reality and imagination, establish her perception of human experience in this land . . .' Claudia Marquis, too, touches on *The Tricksters'* narrative which 'insistently attaches itself to local circumstances at many points', and ultimately challenges us 'to construct — or reconstruct — the fantasy of adolescence, a fantasy that for none of us is unimaginably distant'.

Elizabeth Hale's introduction states: 'That a writer working in such traditionally marginalised, or non-canonical, genres as children's and young adults' literature, and fantasy literature, to say nothing of her consistent representation of marginalised people such as single parents and the elderly, should be one of the foremost writers of a nation marginalised by its size, population, and location, is pleasingly appropriate. Mahy is not wholly a realist, she does not write canonical forms, she does not write the "Great New Zealand novel", and she does not place New Zealand-ness front and centre in her writing, having deliberately set her sights on an international marketplace. But in writing within marginalised, rather than central forms, she has been incredibly successful, and, I think, has been instrumental in reframing the possibilities of this country: bringing a kind of wild magic into New Zealand writing, blending European, Maori, and other literary traditions in her work.'

In another forthcoming publication on the Gothic in children's literature, Auckland academic Rose Lovell-Smith convincingly defines Margaret's use of the beach in *The Tricksters* as a Gothic site, 'a place where violent and significant events and encounters are common now, and were common in the past. For a long time, the beach was the place where you met the other . . . where Maori and Pakeha met . . . where they talked and translated and traded and fought, where animals and goods were imported and exported, where ships were wrecked, and travellers drowned . . . Beaches therefore seem an improbable Gothic site only until second thoughts reveal them to be the parts of New Zealand with the longest histories. These are some of our most haunted landscapes.' *The Tricksters*, she claims, with its story played out around the beach and the rambling, wind-lashed and above all isolated family holiday home beside the Lyttelton harbour beach, 'modifies symbols derived from 200 years of Gothic novel-writing in Britain.'

And if the trickster brothers 'themselves are, as Felix puts it, "tied to that strip of beach", clearly it is their national culture that tied them there. Mahy, an author often accused of writing like a foreigner, shows an accurate sense of her local heritage in thus relocating her haunting from family home to that elemental yet domestic meeting place, the beach.'

But as the many facets of her reputation continue to grow, that mischievous Millooonnium witchy voice is never far away.

'Astonished, amazed, confused,' she told a teenage magazine's readers in 2001, asking her to describe herself in three words. She worked in her bedroom in a state of siege, surrounded by books that climbed her walls, hid themselves in odd corners and shouted out mockingly from under her bed. She had been writing for 57 years and two little known and closely guarded facts about her were that 'I have an elegant though menacing skull tattooed on my right shoulder. It has a rose clenched in its teeth. I had it done when I was 63 so it isn't a youthful mistake. If people see it they usually think it's a transfer but it isn't. And I know more about the history of sewerage (and have more direct contact with it) than any other children's writer in New Zealand and probably the world.'

Quick questions: *What kind of person were you at school?* A chattering liar — but I believed many of my own lies. *What are the best things about being an author?* Being swallowed and digested by a story. *What are the worst things?* Being spat out by a story (which then runs off laughing). *Which book did she most enjoy writing? The Great White Man-Eating Shark*.

Her ideal day out? Sleep in. Breakfast. Reading, take the dog for a walk, come home, reading, dinner, more reading, more reading and bed. *What would you most like to change about yourself?* Be able to sing in tune. *Least enjoyable job ever done?* Finding and clearing out blockages in a drain from a lavatory.

If not a writer? I would be a much-loved children's librarian. *Writer's writer?* Russell Hoban. *What makes you laugh?* Practically everything (but I sometimes laugh out of horror and despair). *How do you relax?* I go to sleep (occasionally while driving). *Advice for aspiring writers?* Be persistent! Work hard! Be tough! Read! Read! Read!

The party question — you're at a party and someone finds out what you do. What is the question they invariably ask? And how do you answer them? Are you still writing? (Then they tell me what they would have written themselves.)

What is the most important lesson life has taught you? I am still working it out. I can't help being suspicious of the answers so far.

By way of a coda, it seems entirely suitable that this narrative should finish with a brief poem which closed one of her earliest speeches, on the theme of building bridges between inner and outer landscapes, delivered to a reading teachers' conference in 1973.

'When it comes to the end of a talk I always like to contribute something of my own — a story or a poem . . . I couldn't think of any story that was appropriate but on the way here I wrote something down. It's written on a bag that has printed on it "Please fold here after using". (It was on the back of the seat in front of me on the aeroplane.) I don't know if this poem actually illustrates very lucidly what I have been talking about, except that in a general way everything I write or do illustrates something . . .

When I am old and wrinkled like a raisin
I will dance like a kite on the bucking back of the wind.
I won't look ahead at the few bright days I am facing
Or look back at the years trailing out like streamers behind.

Everyone else will be gone. The silence will seem
    to be mocking,
But I will dangle and dance in the bright and clear air
    of the day
Kicking my old stick legs in their red striped stockings.
An old leaf wrinkled and brown but golden and gay.

Dance, dance, little old feet. Spin on your halfpenny
    of time.
Roar little old lion in your meadow of cobwebs and rust
Till you burn with the fiery power of the dance
    and the rhyme
And fall back to the earth in a sprinkle of golden dust.

Notes

Guide to Notes

Archival and research sources

Introduction

12 **Two minutes later, he says** DH/TD, 2004.

15 **She's eminently quotable** David Hill, *NZ Listener*, 8 April 2000.

17 **somehow detached from literature** MM/TD, 2004.

18 **a powerful hierarchy of genres** Sturm, Terry, ed. 'Introduction' to *The Oxford History of New Zealand Literature in English*, Auckland: Oxford University Press, 1991.

19 **an international leader** Gibbons, Joan. 'Family Relationships in the Stories of Margaret Mahy', *Papers — Explorations in Children's Literature*, Vol. 5: No. 1, April, 1994.

19 **the amount of useful and extensive critical commentary** Hebley, Diane. *The Power of Place: Landscape in New Zealand Children's Fiction, 1970–1989*, Dunedin: Otago University Press, 1998.

19 **in every way, a serious writer** O'Brien, Greg. *Moments of Invention: Portraits of 21 New Zealand Writers*, Auckland: Heinemann Reed, 1988.

19 **Frame is a poet in all of her work** Williams, Mark. 'A variety of voices,' in *Under Review: A selection from New Zealand Books 1991–1996*, edited by Lauris Edmond, Harry Ricketts, Bill Sewell, Christchurch: Lincoln University Press and Daphne Brassell Associates, 1997.

20 **a great deal of this taped** Edmond, Murray, 'Interview with Margaret Mahy, *Landfall* 41(2), June 1987.

20 **suggested that this rather slim** O'Brien, Gregory. 'Imagine the imagination: Margaret Mahy's Dissolving Ghost', book review 'Branching Out' reprinted from *NZ Books*, August 2000, in *After Bathing at Baxter's: essays and notebooks*, Wellington: Victoria University Press, 2002.

20 **I wouldn't be backward** Dunlop, Celia. 'The stranger ghost', *NZ Listener* 128 (2651), 14 January 1991.

21 **but she's an exquisite writer** Sarti, Antonella. *Spiritcarvers: interviews with eighteen writers from New Zealand*. Cross/cultures Series, Amsterdam: Rodopi, 1998.

21 **I imagined these two figures** O'Brien, Gregory, op. cit.

24 **Who wants all that old** MM/TD

24 **talked a lot** MM/TD

Part One

28 **a collapsed caldera type of crater** MM, 'A New Zealand Writer Speaks', in *Brave New World: International Understanding through Books*, ed. by Wendy and John Birman, Western Library Studies, 11, Proceedings of the Combined Conference on Youth Literature, Perth, 1985, Perth: Curtin University of Technology, 1988.

29 **I spent thirty-seven** ibid.

29 **a beautiful damaged country** MM speech, c. 1995, unpublished. (MM Files)

30 **looking energetically inwards** MM, 'Looking inward, exploring outward', Foreign Correspondence in *The Horn Book*, March–April, 2004.

30 **the warmest and most vivid evocation** Fitzgibbon, Tom with Barbara Spiers. *Beneath Southern Skies: New Zealand Children's Book Authors and Illustrators*, Auckland: Ashton Scholastic, 1993.

32 **cry 'Earthquake!'** Gilderdale, Betty. *Introducing Margaret Mahy*, Auckland: Viking Kestrel, 1987, Puffin 1988.

32 **the ground twist** MM, 'A Place in the World: the impact of childhood reading', c. 1992. (unpublished, MM Files)

32 **sometimes you can swim in the river** Sarti, Antonella, op. cit.

32 **Her overwhelming memories of** MM, '"I'll say this bit"' in *Grand Stands: New Zealand writers on being grandparents*, edited by Barbara Else, Auckland: Vintage, 2000.

32 **terribly keen to have a** MM, 'Beginnings', *Landfall* 193, Autumn, 1997.

33 **perhaps with some justice** MM, Else, Barbara, op. cit.

33 **He wrote letters to** Kedgley, Sue, ed. *Our Own Country: Leading New Zealand writers talk about their writing and their lives*, Auckland: Penguin, 1989.

33 **His voice speaks** MM, Else, Barbara, op. cit.

33 **Dear Little Margaret Mahy** Gilderdale, Betty, op. cit.

34 **it now seems as receiving a *written* greeting** MM, 'Beginnings', *Landfall* 193.

34 **literary in an academic way** MM, 'A Place in the World'.

35 **rather patronised by her children** MM, Else, Barbara, op. cit.

Notes

35 **automatically meant that she** MM, *Notes of a Bag Lady*, Montana Estates Essay Series, editor Lloyd Jones, Wellington: Four Winds Press, 2003.

35 **a homemaker in an interesting way** MM/TD

35 **a respectable one** MM, 'A Place in the World'

35 **My father was actually a bridge builder** MM, 'A New Zealand Writer Speaks', in *Brave New World: International Understanding through Books*, ed. by Wendy and John Birman, Western Library Studies, 11, Proceedings of the Combined Conference on Youth Literature, Perth, 1985, Perth: Curtin University of Technology, 1988.

36 **I did watch bridges appear** MM unpublished speech c. 1995. (MM Files)

36 **We used to travel round** Sarti, Antonella, op. cit.

37 **a natural philosopher** MM/TD

37 **Wartime introduced the young** MM/TD

38 **a fairly plain childhood** Kedgley, Sue, op. cit.

38 **I was always the little red hen** MM, 'Beginnings', *Landfall* 193.

38 **You be Stan Kerr** ibid.

39 **At the Regent Theatre in Whakatane** MM, 'Taking humour seriously', in *Reading Forum NZ* 2, New Zealand Reading Association, 1996. Paper presented to 22nd NZ Reading Association Conference on Reading, New Plymouth, 1996.

39 **I was a child strongly affected** MM, *Surprising Moments: The Inaugural Margaret Mahy Award Lecture*, Auckland: New Zealand Children's Book Foundation, 1991.

40 **There she vividly remembers** Introduction, in *Fabulous and Familiar — Children's reading in New Zealand, past and present*, Wellington: National Library of New Zealand, 1991.

40 **People didn't believe** MM/TD

40 **I once got the strap** NZ Book Council website, Author files.

40 **I used to play by myself** Kedgley, Sue, op. cit.

41 **odd battles with truth** MM, *Surprising Moments*.

41 **I didn't have friends** Chamberlain, Jenny. 'Margaret Mahy: Word Witchery', *North & South*, November 1993.

41 **become astonishing, not only** MM, *Notes of a Bag Lady*.

42 **rather more dangerous** ibid.

42 **instantly and profoundly envious** ibid.

42 **I began telling** ibid.

43 **with scrupulous care** ibid.

43 **obsessively — initially in** ibid.

43 **placed heavy emphasis** MM, 'Joining the Network', *Signal* (UK) No. 54, The Thimble Press, 1987.

44 **You're dumb** Stirling, Pamela. 'Things that go bump on the page', *NZ Listener* 118 (2489), 31 October 1987.

44 **But really, the only thing unusual** ibid.

44 **when pencil was** MM, unpublished speech, c. 2003.

44 **My mother saved that first** Barley, Janet Crane. Essay by Margaret Mahy in *Winter in July: Visits with Children's Authors Down Under*, The Scarecrow Press, Metuchen, NJ & London, 1995.

45 **on the whole, pleased with** MM, 'Beginnings' *Landfall* 193.

45 **writing was something that I** ibid.

45 **what interests me is that there is a curious** MM, unpublished speech to teachers (incomplete), c. 2002. (MM Files)

46 **I did have one friend called Margaret** Stirling, Pamela, op. cit.

46 **I published early** MM, unpublished speech, 'The Bubble', c. 1987.

46 **The Friday after I had** MM, 'Beginnings', *Landfall* 193.

47 **Anyone who had a poem** MM, Barley, Janet Crane, op. cit.

47 **I remember opening the issue** ibid.

47 **The sources of my inspirations** MM, 'Beginnings', *Landfall* 193.

48 **filled with agony** ibid.

48 **unite two systems** ibid.

48 **for what that means** MM/TD

48 **I can remember my father** MM/TD

49 **coming to it** MM/TD

49 **My exposure to these books** MM, 'A New Zealand Writer Speaks'.

50 **in the drama of** MM, 'Joining the Network', *Signal* 54.

50 **reading them over and over** ibid.

50 **she recalls as nearly physical** ibid.

50 **that the stories I enjoyed** *ibid*

50 **fairly resilient about fear** MM/TD

50 **Some children like** MM/TD

51 **many of the stories** Stirling, Pamela, op. cit.

51 **There were only a few** MM. 'The School Journal', *Fact Magazine*, March 1982.

52 **they were very often modest, even clumsy** MM, 'The Bubble'.

52 **to crush Maori folklore** MM, 'A New Zealand Writer Speaks'.

52 **Since the Maoris had** ibid.

53 **Culturally as well as geographically** MM in 'A Place in the World'.

53 **had once been a fiery ball** MM, *Surprising Moments*.

54 **When the original copy** MM, *Notes of a Bag Lady*.

54 **When I was about eight years old** 'Margaret Mahy on *King Solomon's Mines*', Early Reading (New Zealand writers describe books that impressed them in their childhood), *Education*, c. 1975. (NF)

54 **for I could not bear to think its heady** ibid.

56 **Once, as I was running away with my two children** MM, *Notes of a Bag Lady*.

56 **though you understand I'm** MM/TD

57 **I come from a family** Duckworth, Marilyn. *Cherries on a Plate: New Zealand writers talk about their sisters*, Auckland: Random House, 1996.

57 **a very worrying thing** MM/TD

58 **So I got a hiding** MM/TD

58 **partly because being done by wives** MM, *Notes of a Bag Lady*.

58 **who just had no time** MM, Else, Barbara, op. cit.

59 **filled with astonishment** MM in *Sound Ideas*, Vol. 6, No. 2, University of Canterbury School of Music, May 2003.

60 **My connections with music** ibid.

61 **as the mother of five** MM/TD

61 **probably extremely irritating** MM/TD

61 **If at that time** MM/TD

61 **Once when I was ten or eleven** MM in 'A fantastic tale', *Opening the Book: new essays in New Zealand writing*, edited by Mark Williams and Michele Leggott, Auckland: Auckland University Press, 1995.

63 **In Standard Three I once** MM, *Notes of a Bag Lady*.

63 **probably being less sexist** ibid.

64 **Even as a child** Kedgley, Sue, op. cit.

64 **At some time during my standard** MM, 'Favourite Teachers', *NZ Education Review*, July 15, 1998.

66 **to people like T.S. Eliot** Dunlop, Celia. 'The stranger ghost', *NZ Listener* 128 (2651), 14 January 1991.

66 **treated their parents** Gilderdale, Betty. *A Sea Change*, Auckland: Longman Paul, 1982.

66 **For the first time, perhaps.** MM, 'A New Zealand Writer Speaks'.

67 **I remember going down** ibid.

67 **verbal jazz** MM in *Sound Ideas*.

67 **because I don't know The Grand Duke** ibid.

67 **A Bay of Plenty listener** ibid.

68 **Of course my more profoundly** ibid.

68 **only partly consciously** ibid.

69 **The Apolloni Quarto** MM/TD

69 **Yes, I was rather self-consciously** MM/TD

69 **what's going to be** MM/TD

69 **an unusual girl with a zany** Dunlop, Celia, op. cit.

69 **I thought it was vastly** ibid.

69 **That she'd even heard** ibid.

70 **quieter and a little more** ibid.

70 **but of course in a lot of good fiction** MM/TD

70 **I think she would have done** Dunlop, Celia, op. cit.

70 **an extraordinary breadth** ibid.

73 **forced alarming truths** MM, *Notes of a Bag Lady*.

73 **I saw compassion** MM/TD

73 **Other nurses and nurse aids** MM, *Notes of a Bag Lady*.

73 **miles better at** MM/TD

73 **never before or since** MM, *Notes of a Bag Lady*.

73 **the whole question of academic** MM/TD

74 **a bit of a self-indulgence** MM/TD

74 **Auckland wasn't then a great** MM/TD

74 **a general feeling that when poets** MM, *Notes of a Bag Lady*.

75 **When I went to university** McCracken, Jill. 'Margaret Mahy's Magic', *NZ Listener*, 3 May 1975.

75 **even then had the whole story** JL/TD, 2004.

76 **who suffered terribly** MM, unpublished speech, c. 1982.

76 **I absolutely loved it** MM/TD

76 **it was always very primitive** MM/TD

77 **Classical philosophy** MM/TD

77 **longed for fantasy** MM, 'Joining the Network', *Signal* 54.

77 **searching, I suppose, for** ibid.

77 **When I look with apprehension** 'Emblems and Journeys: The Power of Story in the Imagination', in *Readings in Children's Literature*, ed. by Brian Murphy, Proceedings of the Second National Seminar on Children's Literature, 1978, Frankston, Victoria: Frankston State College, 1980.

78 **At the time I was growing up** MM, Williams, Mark and Leggott, Michele, op. cit.

78 **which generated a very different** ibid.

78 **I have previously speculated** MM, 'Fantasy: Flights of the Mind', *The Inside Story*.

79 **I began to imitate this particular** MM, 'Joining the Network', *Signal* 54.

79 **I had always known I was** MM, 'Fantasy: Flights of the Mind', *The Inside Story*.

79 **I was writing stories at this time** MM, 'Joining the Network', *Signal* 54.

80 **whereas reading it now** MM, Williams, Mark and Leggott, Michele, op. cit.

80 **a very ordinary degree** MM/TD

81 **The idea of the adventurous life** MM, *Notes of a Bag Lady*.

81 **Only a few days ago I saw** ibid.

Part Two

85 **sat down and wrote** MM, Kedgley, Sue, op. cit.

85 **intensely thrilled and vindicated** ibid.

86 **I remember that I had sent** MM, 'One Great Frolic with Words,' question and answer interview, *Education*, Vol. 22, No. 6, 1973.

86 **One I wrote for myself** Schur, Maxine. 'The Magic of Margaret Mahy', *NZ Bookworld*, No. 31, December 1976.

90 **It's not the sort of thing** McCracken, Jill. 'Margaret Mahy's Magic', *NZ Listener*, 3 May 1975.

90 **romantic and compelling love affair** MM, Kedgley, Sue, op. cit.

90 **my own particular** ibid.

90 **at the time I don't think I contemplated** Brett, Cate. 'Horrakapotchkin!', Family Ties (interviews with Margaret, Penny and Bridget Mahy), *North & South* 115, October, 1995.

90 **a rather falsely romantic view** MM, Kedgley, Sue, op. cit.

91 **It was the most carefree, lovely time** van Dongen, Yvonne. 'Wit and work in the fey world of Margaret Mahy', Sunday profile, *New Zealand Times*, 18 November 1984. (NF)

92 **writing like a** MM, *The Catalogue of the Universe*, 1985.

93 **above all other sums** Gilderdale, Betty. *A Sea Change: 145 years of New Zealand junior fiction*, Auckland: Longman Paul, 1982.

95 **very monogamous on** Stirling, Pamela, op. cit.

95 **As a child I assumed** MM, Kedgley, Sue, op. cit.

96 **were women who imitated men** ibid.

96 **as an adventure, and I still** ibid.

96 **that realisation enabled me** ibid.

97 **there were times when she** Stirling, Pamela, op. cit.

97 **One evening when my two** MM, 'A Place in the World'.

99 **Things became more frantic** Brett, Cate, op. cit.

99 **a workaholic** ibid.

100 **is of course a wonderful** ibid.

100 **be damaged but is not easily** Gibbons, Joan. 'Family Relationships in the Stories of Margaret Mahy', *Papers — Explorations in Children's Literature*, Vol. 5: No. 1, April, 1994.

100 **as being a leader amongst** ibid.

101 **were a bit like psychic** Edmond, Murray. 'Interview with Margaret Mahy', *Landfall* 41 (2), June 1987.

101 **family life is** ibid.

101 **a leader amongst writers** Gibbons, Joan, op. cit.

101 **ambitious, courageous** ibid.

101 **focus for their activities** ibid.

102 **They wrote me notes** MM, Kedgley, Sue, op. cit.

102 **I was enthusiastic about** ibid.

102 **I'm still puzzled** ibid.

103 **I knew her stories pretty well** (and following) JL/TD, 2004.

Part Three

110 **Who wrote that?** Gilderdale, Betty, *Introducing Margaret Mahy*.

110 **Too much money** ibid.

110 **No one likes to think** MM, 'A New Zealand Writer Speaks', in *Brave New World: International Understanding through Books*, ed. by Wendy and John Birman, Western Library Studies, 11, Proceedings of the Combined Conference on Youth Literature, Perth, 1985, Perth: Curtin University of Technology, 1988.

110 **like Cinderella** MM, 'Authorzone', c. 2002.
110 **within seconds** MM, 'Seeing the Lion,' speech given at *Endings and Beginning: The Shape of Story*, CLNE at Harvard University, Cambridge, Massachusetts, 1996. (MM Files)
110 **I opened it — read it** MM, Barley, Janet Crane, op. cit.
111 **servile in its enthusiasm** MM speech in UK, c. 1996.
111 **a transmutation that I had imagined** MM, 'Seeing the Lion'.
111 **I always had that feeling** MM, Kedgley, Sue, op. cit.
111 **When she first got in touch** MM/TD
112 **less lost and anonymous** 'Cinderella Transformed: Multiple Voices and Diverse Dialogues in Children's Literature, proceedings of the Conference on children's literature, Centre for Children's Literature (Christchurch College of Education) and Australian Children's Literature Association for Research, 2003.
112 **made it plain** ibid.
113 **it is hard for** ibid.
114 **notably well-dressed** MM/TD
114 **does not pass unnoticed** Steincamp, Jacqueline. 'A house with running water', *New Zealand Woman's Weekly*, 1969.
114 **she was carrying quite a lot of** MM/TD
114 **On the one hand I found** Chamberlain, Jenny, op. cit.
114 **My God they don't** MM/TD
114 **I was carrying** MM, Barley, Janet Crane, op. cit.
115 **this was never quite** MM/TD
115 **went over a lot of material** *The Press*, 'Chance Visit Lucky For Author', c. June 1969.
115 **She stayed at the local** MM/TD
115 **Helen was to launch** MM, Barley, Janet Crane, op. cit.
116 **The number of words on** MM, 'Cinderella Transformed'.
116 **I would describe *The Procession*** MM, '*Tragedy's Wild Twin: the mixed nature of humour*, Sylvia Ashton-Warner Fellowship Lecture, Auckland: Auckland College of Education, 2003.
117 **for the most part** Gilderdale, Betty. *A Sea Change: 145 years of New Zealand junior fiction*, Auckland: Longman Paul, 1982.
117 ***A Lion in the Meadow* is a very simple** MM, *Surprising Moments*.
118 **basically about the same thing** Edmond, Murray, op. cit.
118 **Sometime after I had become used** MM, 'Seeing the Lion'.
120 **a bit of a stark ending** Lafferty, Fiona. 'Magic and Mystery: an interview with Margaret Mahy', *Children's Books*, June, 1986.
120 **A story is seldom published** MM, 'Seeing the Lion'.
122 **In moments of exhilaration** 'The Lion, the Magician, the Hero, the Witch: Thoughts about Magic and Reality', *Children's Literature Association Yearbook*, 1976.
123 **I wrote a story, *Pillycock's*** Gunby, Penny. 'The "total involvement" world of writer Margaret Mahy', *NZ Bookworld*, c. 1975.
124 **because they changed the quality** 'One Great Frolic with Words,' *Education*, Vol. 22, No. 6, 1973.
125 **tallish, strongly boned blonde** Steincamp, Jacqueline, op. cit.
126 **of great familiarity and affection** MM/TD
126 **No summary of Mrs Mahy's talk** Reed, Constance. 'The magical world of Margaret Mahy', *Books for your Children*, March 1974.
126 **the very circumscribed nature** 'Report on overseas visit', to School Library Service, Christchurch, 1973. (CCL/MMA)
127 **an incredible experience** ibid.
127 **ritualised by repetitions** ibid.
128 **I'm sure that Brian Froud's** Scott, Bruce. 'Searching for truth — and art of telling stories', Bruce Scott's People, Lifestyle, *The Press* or *Christchurch Star*, c. 1976. (NF)
128 **Every working day I get up** 'Meet our Author Margaret Mahy,' *Cricket*, Vol. 5, No. 3, 1976.
128 **I used to think it didn't matter** McCracken, Jill. 'Margaret Mahy's Magic', *NZ Listener*, 3 May 1975.
128 **I suppose every writer** ibid.
130 **If there is any area in the literary** 'Educating the Imagination', on women as writers, 'Women in 1975'. (NF)
134 **Her tousled, bright green wig** Bell, Terry. 'To Magic and Mystery in a Green Wig', *New Zealand Woman's Weekly*, 15 November 1976. (NF)
134 **Dressing up for me** Duggan, Sally. 'Wizardry with words,' Tuesday Morning, *NZ Herald*, September 8 1987.
135 **A bit of an exhibitionist** 'Authorgraph No. 24,' *Books for Keeps*, No. 24, January 1984.
135 **Margaret Mahy minus** Pickles, Veda. Children's Literature Association Yearbook, 1981.
135 **Kids were very entertained** Chamberlain, Jenny, op. cit.
135 **realised she'd got a bit** *ibid*
136 **it was hot inside this penguin** Gilderdale, Betty. *Introducing Margaret Mahy*.
136 **Mahy said the underwhelmed** Waldren, Murray. 'Margaret's magical Mahyhem', Features, Review, *The Weekend Australian*, 6–9 June 1991.
136 **Working does cut time** Gunby, Penny. 'The "total involvement" world of writer Margaret Mahy', *NZ Bookworld*, c. 1975. (NF)
137 **She has often been criticised** Scott, Bruce, op. cit.
138 **Not a great deal because** MM, 'One Great Frolic with Words'.
141 **was soon called on to make some statement** MM, 'The Lion, the Magician, the Hero, the Witch'.
144 **Perhaps we are all born with witches** ibid.
144 **I am a New Zealander** 'Building bridges between our outer and inner landscapes', in *Reading is Everybody's Business*, ed. by W.B. Elley, Selected Proceedings of the Fourth New Zealand Conference, May 1973, Wellington: IRA, Wellington Council, 1973.
150 **if only by showing how** Williams, Mark in *Under Review, a Selection from New Zealand Books*, eds Lauris Edmond, Harry Ricketts, Bill Sewell, Christchurch: Lincoln University Press and Daphne Brassell Associates, 1997.
151 **I increasingly became addicted** Lafferty, Fiona, op. cit.
154 **Language seems at times** 'Intuitive Aspects of Language', in *Children and Language*, the 1974 Lectures, Wellington: Association for the Study of Childhood, 1975.
154 **I once had an aunt** ibid.
157 **But the abiding memory everyone** Chamberlain, Jenny, op. cit.
159 **What has she got against the poor** Lafferty, Fiona, op. cit.

159 **They simultaneously have** ibid.

159 **Jorges Luis Borges was** MM, unpublished speech to FOL (incomplete), November 1988. (NF)

160 **Human beings are driven** MM, *Notes of a Bag Lady.*

160 **Do you have anything on disasters** 'Children's Libraries Are For Parents Too,' *Press or Star,* c. 1979. (NF)

162 **I am a solo mother aged** 'Emblems and Journeys: The Power of Story in the Imagination', in *Readings in Children's Literature,* ed. by Brian Murphy, Proceedings of the Second National Seminar on Children's Literature, 1978, Frankston, Victoria: Frankston State College, 1980.

165 **divided my interior landscape** 'On building houses that face the sun', in *A Track to Unknown Water,* Proceedings of the second Pacific Rim Conference on children's literature, edited by Stella Lees, Melbourne: Melbourne State College (Victoria), 1980. (NF)

165 **in their building imagination** ibid.

167 **by New Zealanders** ibid.

167 **our local publishers** ibid.

167 **I find myself in an odd** ibid.

168 **Back then when I really was** MM, *Notes of a Bag Lady.*

Part Four

171 **gift of time** MM/TD

171 **Bridget agreed to spend** Brett, Cate, op. cit.

171 **a very scary thing** ibid.

171 **I was 44 when I finally** MM, Kedgley, Sue, op. cit.

172 **grown too long and somehow too** MM/TD

172 **rather different kettle of fish** MM/TD

172 **I didn't then and in many ways still** MM/TD

172 **I've lived in a family where** Lafferty, Fiona, op. cit.

173 **Suddenly everything that** Stirling, Pamela, op. cit.

173 **not the sort of person** ibid.

174 **We know Miss Mahy best** *Junior Bookshelf,* Vol. 47, No.1, February 1983.

174 **Here is an absolutely first-rate** Cart, Michael, *School Library Journal,* August, 1982.

175 **a plea for the liberating** Fitzgibbon, Tom with Barbara Spiers. *Beneath Southern Skies: New Zealand Children's Book Authors and Illustrators,* Auckland: Ashton Scholastic, 1993.

175 **a dazzling piece of writing** Nieuwenhuizen, Agnes. *Good Books for Teenagers,* Melbourne: Mandarin, 1992.

175 **Many people comment on** MM, 'A Place in the World'.

175 **straight ghost story was** Nettell, Stephanie, 'Afterword', *The Haunting* Puffin Modern Classic edition, 1999.

177 **diabolical** Steven Brownlee, Catherine Towers (students, West Denton High). 'Margaret Mahy Reads the World', *In brief,* September 1992.

177 **Bit prudish, unexpectedly moral** ibid.

177 **not quite as wishy-washy** ibid.

177 **Good editors can take the place** *Trouble in the Supermarket,* nine stories with background and comment, Melbourne: Thomas Nelson Australia, 1989.

178 **Aunty, I've won the** *Carnegie* MM/TD

179 **extreme delight and excitement** Plumpton, Frances, 'Bringing Margaret Mahy to Children', report of her first visit to Auckland, *Yearbook 1983,* Auckland: Children's Literature Association, 1983.

179 **It is to do with the difference** Edmond, Murray, op. cit.

179 **absolutely swept away** MM/TD

180 **The pleasure of being awarded** '1984 Carnegie Medal, *The Changeover* Margaret Mahy (Dent)', acceptance speech published in *Youth Library Review,* No. 1, Spring, 1986.

182 **One day when I was working** MM, 'The Bubble'.

183 **on the same level as** *The Haunting* MM/TD

183 **At this time Bridget** MM, 'Cinderella Transformed'.

184 **I was told as one so** MM, 'A New Zealand Writer Speaks'.

184 **Goodness for the life** van Dongen, Yvonne. 'Wit and work in the fey world of Margaret Mahy', Sunday profile, *New Zealand Times,* 18 November 1984. (NF)

184 **here was an author who insisted** University Chronicle (Canterbury). 'Writer in residence: Margaret Mahy's Plans', Vol. 9, No. 4, March 1984. (NF)

185 **Who would've expected such** MM, 'Authorgraph No. 24,' *Books for Keeps.*

185 **Well, any admirer of Margaret** ibid.

185 **about the whole human condition** Margery Fisher, *Growing Point.*

185 ***The Changeover* goes well beyond** *English Journal,* 4/87. (CCL/MMA)

185 **selected as an ALA** Hearne, Betsy. *Booklist,* November, 1985.

185 **Again as in** *The Haunting* *Kirkus Review,* Vol. 52, 1 September 1984.

186 **The double aspect of things** Hayes, Sarah. *Times Literary Supplement,* 13 July 1984.

186 **heady stuff then and Margaret** Hoffman, Mary. 'The Fabulous in the Ordinary — an Interview with Margaret Mahy', *The School Librarian,* 1987.

187 **a considerable difference** Rees, David. *What Do Draculas Do? — essays on contemporary writers of fiction for children and young adults,* Metuchen, NJ: Scarecrow Press, 1990.

187 **to reveal a unique place** ibid.

187 **make their own particular patch** ibid.

188 **But with Margaret Mahy** ibid.

188 **think it was** *The Changeover* MM/TD

188 **this was the first story** MM, 'Postscript' to *The Changeover,* Collins Modern Classic, 2003.

189 **And yet as I wrote the story** ibid.

190 **her habit of walking muttering** MM, 'Authorgraph No. 24,' *Books for Keeps.*

191 **Many of my books** ibid.

191 **It was a very transforming moment** Sarti, Antonella, op. cit.

191 **a love story of Angela** Fitzgibbon, Tom with Barbara Spiers, op. cit.

192 **have piled cliché upon cliché** Laski, Audrey, 'Test of Fire', *Times Educational Supplement,* 15 November 1985.

192 **Margaret Mahy is now** McVitty, Walter. 'Upside down look at the Young world', *The Age,* Melbourne, 2 February 1986.

193 **I couldn't work out** MM, 'On writing a longer book', with reference to *The Tricksters,* one page, typewritten fragment. (CCL/MMA)

193 **One day some years** MM, *Surprising Moments.*

196 **romantically involved with a ghost** Jones, Nicolette. 'Phantoms of teenage desire,' *Books & Bookmen,* Dec/Jan 1986/7.

197 **it would take very little** Madrigal, Alix, 'Ghostly Tale of Sexual Awakening', *The San Francisco Examiner-Chronicle,* 28 June 1987.

197 **both credible and incredible** Hebley, Diane, *NZ Listener*, 5 September 1987.

197 **Ms Mahy has proved she can** McKinley, Robin, 'Falling in Love With a Ghost', *New York Times Book Review*, 17 May 1987.

198 **The Haunting, The Changeover and The Tricksters aren't** Hoffman, Mary. 'The Fabulous in the Ordinary — an Interview with Margaret Mahy', *The School Librarian*, 1987.

198 **We like to test ourselves** ibid.

199 **Reading a manuscript all through again** MM, 'on writing a longer book'. (CCL/MMA, 429/6/5)

199 **I mean to answer** MM, van Dongen, Yvonne, op. cit.

199 **Even with a word processor** MM, 'Trouble in the Supermarket'.

200 **do you make of this one** van Dongen, Yvonne, op. cit.

200 **almost never turned down** Edmond, Murray, op. cit.

201 **despite a terrible temptation to** MM/TD

201 **There are books I have written** 'The theme of this conference, that of building bridges of understanding . . .' (unpublished speech), c. 1995. (MM Files)

202 **When I was first approached** 'Dissolving edges — Jokes and Passion in reading acquisition' (unpublished speech), c. 1991. (MM Files)

203 **We need to remember** 'Stories at home, stories at school — reading in the family and at school' (unpublished speech), c. 1989. (MM Files)

203 **So I begin my stories usually** MM, 'The Bubble'.

204 **who never ever doubted** MM/TD

206 **I'm very fond** Swain, Pauline. 'Taking inspiration from the odd', *Dominion*, 8 September 1987.

206 **very satisfying** ibid.

207 **most of which are** MM, 'Dissolving edges — Jokes and Passion in reading acquisition' (unpublished speech), c. 1991. (MM Files)

208 **I think I have made a lot of money** MM, *Trouble in the Supermarket*.

208 **The room where I write** ibid.

209 **Lately I've taken to thinking** O'Brien, Greg, *Moments of Invention*.

209 **She writes for long hours** Steven Brownlee, Catherine Towers (students, West Denton High). 'Margaret Mahy Reads the World', *In brief*, September 1992.

210 **If any story I have told** MM, 'A Dissolving Ghost: Possible Operations of Truth in Children's Books and the Lives of Children', *Journal of Youth Services in Libraries*, 2.4 1989. Arbuthnot Lecture, 1989, published in *The Arbuthnot Lectures 1980–1989* (Chicago: ALA, 1990), reprinted in *Only Connect*, ed. Sheila Egoff, 1996, *A Dissolving Ghost*, 2000.

211 **The support services were good** ibid.

211 **There's very little written** van Dongen, Yvonne, op. cit.

211 **When Bridget was working** Brophy, Cynthia. 'Nonsense, physics same to Margaret Mahy', *Panache — New Zealanders in the Visual and Performing Arts*, 1(1). November 1987.

211 **As long as she had her bankbook** Sarti, Antonella, op. cit.

212 **turned around and her mouth** Arthur, Garry. 'Memory of one who lost hers,' Features, *The Press*, Christchurch, May 4, 1988.

213 **if the story lacks the nastiness** MM, 'A Dissolving Ghost'.

213 **I don't wish to suggest that she** MM, 'A Place in the World'.

213 **the compressed ending** MM, 'Seeing the Lion'.

213 **magical encounter between** MM, 'A Dissolving Ghost'.

213 **I had an imaginary picture** Stirling, Pamela, op. cit.

214 **seen when I was driving home** MM, 'A Place in the World'.

214 **so close-grained and** Moss, Elaine, 'Rich pickings', *Observer*, 20 December 1987.

214 **strikes me as one of those few** Tomalin, Claire, 'The Judge's Tale', *New Society*, 18 December 1987.

214 **on the novel's overtly New Zealand** Anderson, Doug, 'A good anger', *Times Literary Supplement*, November 1987.

214 **only a churl surely** Mark, Jan. 'Children's Literature', *Times Educational Supplement*, July 1987.

215 **More recently, especially in** Eccleshare, Julia. 'Real and fantastic', *The Times Educational Supplement*, 6 June 1986.

215 **as a writer and as a person** MM, 'Authorgraph No. 24,' *Books for Keeps*.

216 **indefatigable and supremely** Edmond, Murray, op. cit.

217 **it appeals to the whims** Berkin, Adam. 'I Woke Myself': *The Changeover* as a modern adaptation of Sleeping Beauty'. *Children's Literature in Education*, Vol. 21, No. 4, 1990.

217 **exceptional intelligence which** O'Brien, Greg. *Moments of Invention*.

217 **Nabokov's notion that writing** ibid.

218 **now one of the oldest writers** MM, 'The Bubble'.

220 **an embarrassing daftness** Sullivan, Mary 'Tales of the Oppressed', *The Guardian*, 8 October 1988.

220 **all people should be dappled** Hoffman, Mary. 'Children's Literature', *Times Educational Supplement*, 30 September 1988.

221 **The bridge-builder's son** Dalley, Jan, 'Fantastical flights', *Times Literary Supplement*, 25 November 1988.

221 **a great deal of anxiety** MM, in 'The Margaret Mahy Pages', Christchurch City Libraries website.

221 **Some people have said** MM, *Trouble in the Supermarket*.

221 **Walter McVitty** MM/TD

222 **which makes me look like some sort** *New Zealand Woman's Weekly*, 1 August 1988.

222 **overall the young adult genre** Goedhart, Bernie. 'Serendipity builds solidarity among lovers of children's literature', Children's Corner, *The Gazette*, Montreal, 23 June 1990.

223 **I don't think I'm a born** Oomen, Monique. 'Watching the words', *Onfilm* 3(5), August 1986.

223 **the story's never your own** MM/TD

224 **Yes I probably have** MM/TD

224 **Cuckooland was** YM/TD, 2004.

224 **weird wacky loud** Linley Boniface, Gibson Group files.

225 **I remember Ned Beatty** YM/TD

226 **not a merry prank** *Variety*, 8 April 1987.

226 **The Haunting of Barney Palmer wasn't weird** 'The Haunting makes great TV', Children's Express, *Evening Post*, 26 November 1987.

226 **After the Haunting we** YM/TD

227 **spying, chases** Ford, Graham. 'New Season TV: Children: a Mahy mystery: Strangers', *NZ Listener*, 23 July 1988.

227 **Margaret's got a beaut** ibid.

227 **wonderful story** Reilly, Colleen, 'Strangers typical of our best', 'Television', *Dominion Sunday-Times*.

228 **about how an isolated** O'Hare, Noel. 'A question of breeding', *NZ Listener* 145(2838), 3 September 1994.

228 **was a rather Gothic tale** ibid.

228 **it's thought that cloning** ibid.

229 **We shot it into four** YM/TD

229 **It's a very complicated** O'Hare, Noel, op. cit.

229 **in an answer which** ibid.

230 **quite a lot of violent** ibid.

231 **Two years ago it happened** MM, 'A Dissolving Ghost'.

234 **is not so much the final** MM, 'Taking humour seriously', in *Reading Forum NZ* 2, N.Z. Reading Association, 1996. Paper presented to 22nd NZ Reading Association Conference on Reading, New Plymouth, 1996.

234 **were among the finest** Goedhart, Bernie, op. cit.

235 **I make my stories** 'Our Living Treasures: Margaret Mahy', *North & South*, January 1990.

237 **This certainly is different** MM/TD

237 **the New Zealand children's book** MM, 'A New Zealand Writer Speaks'.

238 **Will and good intentions** ibid.

239 **It is increasingly expected** Brophy, Cynthia, op. cit.

239 **Even the fact that the chuckling** Chamberlain, Jenny, op. cit.

240 **not the most profound** MM, *Surprising Moments*.

240 **story and fantasy** ibid.

240 **to write a story built** *The Illustrated Traveller's Tale*, in Soho Square, ed. Bill Manhire, Bloomsbury, 1991 and *A Dissolving Ghost*, Wellington: Victoria University Press, 2000.

Part Five

245 **underlying optimism about** Espiner, Colin. *The Press*, 1993. (NF)

245 **while she was happy** ibid.

247 **one year of intense frustration** Chamberlain, Jenny, op. cit.

247 **I had been with Dent** ibid.

248 **Simple decisions seem to have** ibid.

249 **At times I think she becomes** ibid.

249 **sympathetic, unsentimental** Mark, Jan, *Times Educational Supplement*, 1992.

249 **In my story there is a child** Hugo, Giles. 'Proving that there is strife after Grimm', Weekend Books, *The Saturday Mercury* (Hobart), 4 May 1991.

250 **as an imaginative act** MM/TD

250 **it seemed to be a heck** MM/TD

250 **There's not a lot of water** Steven Brownlee, Catherine Towers, op. cit.

251 **it was judged a high** Wakefield, Philip. 'Partners draw finny business', *Onfilm* 9(1), February 1992.

252 **It's similar to directing** Martin, Tamara. 'Moving tales', *Pacific Way* 79, December 1994/January 1995.

252 **perhaps by now it is hard** Lovell-Smith, Rose. 'A noisy life's work', review of *The Other Side of Silence* in *New Zealand Books*, March 1998.

252 **In a brilliant series** Neil, Philip, 'The other side of invention', *The Times Educational Supplement*, 10 November 1995.

252 **she'd reached a plateau** Sarti, Antonella, op. cit.

252 **encouraged to bring** MM/TD

253 **absolutely ferocious** Neil, Philip, 'The other side of invention', *The Times Educational Supplement*, 10 November 1995.

254 **she had actually seen** MM, 'Seeing the Lion'.

254 **she had had an unimaginable** Sarti, Antonella, op. cit.

254 **a movement forward** ibid.

254 **a dangerous thing** ibid.

254 **story whose time had come** MM, 'Seeing the Lion'.

254 **with my own beginnings** ibid.

255 **that Mahy had run out** Lovell-Smith, Rose, op. cit.

255 **the reader is invited** ibid.

256 **partly from watching** ibid.

256 **may be less compelling** ibid.

257 **I myself want to be an active part** MM, Else, Barbara, op. cit.

257 **I saw the oldest child** ibid.

258 **Literature tends to dwell** ibid.

260 **astonishing and baroquely** DH/TD, 2004.

261 **I am 59 and I feel** Sarti, Antonella, op. cit.

261 **It's certainly true that if** ibid.

262 **though published in the USA** MM, 'I tell this story ['Down the Back of the Chair']' UK speech with Steven Kellogg present (unpublished), c. 1996. (MM Files)

262 **be able to sit down beside** MM, 'I tell this story'.

263 *The Escape from Volcano Mountain* ibid.

263 **The Booksellers' Conference** ibid.

264 **I joke with language** Sarti, Antonella, op. cit. 1998.

265 **On one occasion** MM, 'Taking humour seriously'.

266 **Do you know the game** Sarti, Antonella, op. cit.

268 **It was the most mysterious** Greeks, Polly. 'Tattoos and skiddoos', *Evening Post* magazine, 8 December 2001.

269 **is a book written in the tall** Turton, Rayma. 'Talking with Margaret Mahy', *Magpies: talking about books for children* 17(1), March 2002.

270 **There is no way I can** MM, 'Cinderella Transformed'.

270 **in which two dogs** MM, 'From the time I was a small child . . .' speech to teachers (unpublished), c. 2002. (MM Files)

271 **In choosing to develop our** MM, 'Cinderella Transformed'.

272 **the old witch who lives** MM, 'Dissolving Millennium', *Sunday Star-Times*, supplement, 2 January 2000.

274 **quite different sort of book** MM/TD

274 **Every so-called key event** MM, 'Bookmarking the Century', *Landfall* 199, 2000.

275 **Walk into any bookshop** MM, 'Just Wild about Harry', *NZ Listener*, 15 July 2000.

277 **There is nothing directly autobiographical** www.teenreads.com, Author Profile: MM, 2003.

278 **some research into the work an undertaker** ibid.

278 **It's just a small tasteful** Sharp, Iain. 'Tattooed lady', *Sunday Star Times*, 29 October 2000.

278 **I've never been in a car chase** ibid.

278 **There's a romantic notion** ibid.

279 **Has anyone summarised** Hill, David. *NZ Listener*, 8 April 2000.

280 **a book in which Mahy's intelligence** O'Brien, Gregory. 'Imagine the imagination'.

282 **There is something both necessary** MM, 'Accounts and Meditations: A Judge's Report on the 2002 Landfall Essay Competition', *Landfall* 203, May 2002.

283 **who spends a lot of his time** MM, *Tragedy's Wild Twin: the mixed nature of humour*, Sylvia Ashton-Warner Fellowship Lecture, Auckland: Auckland College of Education, 2003.

284 **"Good dog", it would say** *Tragedy's Wild Twin: the mixed nature of humour*, Sylvia Ashton-Warner Fellowship Lecture, Auckland: Auckland College of Education, 2003.

284 **The voice of the poem** MM, 'Cinderella Transformed'.

284 **it was what I was trying** ibid.

285 **This story is a joke** MM, 'Fantasy: Flights of the Mind', *The Inside Story*.

287 **I started writing about someone who** MM/TD

287 **I could easily have been an alcoholic** MM, *Notes of a Bag Lady*.

289 **The shortest book I have ever** MM, 'The Bubble'.

289 **about four years ago** MM, 'Cinderella Transformed'.

289 **a heck of a lot of work** MM/TD

289 **quite often work all night** Edmond, Murray, op. cit.

289 **a sort of pre-industrial** ibid.

290 **The hero is a young man** MM/TD

290 **has transposed all the supernatural** Edmond, Murray, op. cit.

290 **got older and tireder** MM/TD

291 **for children edging** MM/TD

291 **one of the other kaitangata** MM/TD

291 **I don't think that's true** MM/TD

291 **I think that people should** Sarti, Antonella, op. cit.

291 **a natural part of history** MM/TD

291 **came across as** MM/TD

292 **a bit less attractive** MM/TD

292 **quite a disconcerting experience** MM/TD

292 **it would be a good thing** MM/TD

293 **the basic human condition is** Sarti, Antonella, op. cit.

293 **Reading gives you a subtle** Waldren, Murray. 'Margaret's magical Mayhem', Features, Review, *The Weekend Australian*, 6–9 June 1991.

293 **the asthmatic hay fever** MM/TD

293 **She can't envisage a time** Sharp, Iain, op. cit.

294 **I think the world is alarming** MM/TD

295 **I've read lots and lots of horror** MM/TD

296 **People say to me** Edmond, Murray, op. cit.

296 **because I think I'd be doing a superior** MM/TD

296 **Well, if that's true I suppose** MM/TD

297 **If it was some sort of gift** MM/TD

297 **Yesterday for instance** Turton, Rayma, op. cit.

297 **Writers are very treacherous** Sarti, Antonella, op. cit.

298 **but we can't pretend that only good** ibid.

298 **some more professional than others** MM, 'From the time I was a small child . . .'

299 **I suppose I have some main themes** Sarti, Antonella, op. cit.

300 **so much thought is directed towards** Waldren, Murray, op. cit.

300 **a time of receiving extremely** ibid.

300 **I always start writing a story with a lot** 'Authorgraph No. 24, *Books for Keeps*.

300 **As both read and writer I** MM, 'The Bubble'.

301 **whose work belies the old critical** Hunt, Peter. *Children's Literature*, Blackwell Guides to Literature, Oxford: 2001.

303 **with all the force and precision** Ward, Elizabeth, 'Space to Dream', *Washington Post Book World*, 12 October 1986.

303 **full of linguistic pyrotechnics** 'Sidelights', *Something about the Author*, Vol. 119, Gale, 2001.

303 **uses fantasy as a light** *Twentieth-century Young Adult Writers*, ed. Laura Standley Berger (MM essay: Bill Buchanan), Detroit: St James Press, 1994.

303 **continually pushes at the boundaries** Dalley, Jan, 'Fantastical flights', *Times Literary Supplement*, 25 November 1988.

303 **in the power of love** Watson, Victor, ed. *Cambridge Guide to Children's Books in English*, Cambridge: Cambridge University Press, 2001.

304 **The double aspect of things** Hayes, Sarah. *Times Literary Supplement*, 13 July 1984.

304 **for the basic human fear** Rees, David. *What Do Draculas Do? — essays on contemporary writers of fiction for children and young adults*, Metuchen, NJ: Scarecrow Press, 1990.

304 **designed to lead young adults** Spufford, Francis. *The Child that Books Built*, London: Faber & Faber, 2002.

305 **Clearly in all her YA** Hebley, Diane. 'A Fertility and Felicity and Ferocity of Invention', in *Marvellous Codes: The Fiction of Margaret Mahy*, ed. Hale, Elizabeth and Winters, Sarah, Wellington: Victoria University Press, 2005.

305 **insistently attaches itself to local** Marquis, Claudia. 'Ariadne "down under": Structures of Adolescent Fantasy in *The Tricksters*', Hale and Winters, op. cit.

305 **That a writer working** Hale, Elizabeth, 'Introduction', op. cit.

306 **a place where violent** Lovell-Smith, Rose. 'On the Gothic Beach: Margaret Mahy's *The Tricksters* and Gavin Bishop's *The Horror of Hickory Bay*', *Haunting the Borders: the Gothic in Children's Literature*, ed. Rod McGillis, Anna Jackson and Lisa Scally (forthcoming).

307 **Astonished, amazed, confused** MM, 'Margaret Mahy/Questionnaire/Bizarre Bits,' *AuthorZone*, c. 2001. (NF)

308 **When it comes to the end** 'Building bridges between our outer and inner landscapes', in *Reading is Everybody's Business*, ed.W.B. Elley, Selected Proceedings of the Fourth New Zealand Conference, May 1973, Wellington: IRA, Wellington Council, 1973.

Select bibliography and major sources

Books

Barley, Janet Crane. Talk by MM in *Winter in July: Visits with Children's Authors Down Under*, The Scarecrow Press, Metuchen, NJ & London, 1995.

Duckworth, Marilyn. *Cherries on a Plate: New Zealand writers talk about their sisters*, Auckland: Random House, 1996.

Dunkle, Margaret (ed.). *The Story Makers*, a collection of interviews with Australian and NZ authors and illustrators, Melbourne: Oxford University Press, 1987; MM page reprinted in *Reading Forum NZ*, journal of the NZ Reading Association, No. 3, 1990.

Fitzgibbon, Tom with Barbara Spiers. *Beneath Southern Skies: New Zealand Children's Book Authors and Illustrators*, Auckland: Ashton Scholastic, 1993.

Gilderdale, Betty. *A Sea Change: 145 years of New Zealand junior fiction*, Auckland: Longman Paul, 1982.

———. 'Children's Literature', in *The Oxford History of New Zealand Literature in English* (second edition), ed. by Terry Sturm, Auckland: Oxford University Press, 1998.

———. *Introducing Margaret Mahy*, Auckland: Viking Kestrel, 1987, Puffin 1987.

Hebley, Diane. *The Power of Place: Landscape in New Zealand Children's Fiction*, 1970–1989, Dunedin: Otago University Press, 1998.

Kedgley, Sue, ed. *Our Own Country: Leading New Zealand writers talk about their writing and their lives*, Auckland: Penguin, 1989.

Mahy, Margaret

———. *Trouble in the Supermarket*, stories with comment/background by the author, Melbourne: Thomas Nelson Australia, 1989.

———. *Surprising Moments: The Inaugural Margaret Mahy Award Lecture*, Auckland: NZ Children's Book Foundation, 1991.

———. 'Introduction', in *Fabulous and Familiar — Children's reading in New Zealand, past and present*, Wellington: National Library of NZ, 1991.

———. 'A fantastic tale' in *Opening the Book: new essays in New Zealand writing*, edited by Mark Williams and Michele Leggott, Auckland: Auckland University Press, 1995.

———. ' "I'll say this bit" ' in *Grand Stands: New Zealand writers on being grandparents*, edited by Barbara Else, Auckland: Vintage, 2000.

———. *A Dissolving Ghost, essays and more*, Wellington: Victoria University Press, 2000.

———. 'Introduction', *Kiwi Kids' Collection*, illustrated by Helen Humphries, selected by Fiona McRae, Auckland: Random House, 2001.

———. *Tragedy's Wild Twin: the mixed nature of humour*, Sylvia Ashton-Warner Fellowship Lecture, Auckland: Auckland College of Education, 2003.

————. *Notes of a Bag Lady*, Montana Estates Essay Series, ed. Lloyd Jones, Wellington: Four Winds Press, 2003.

Nettell, Stephanie. 'Afterword', to *The Haunting*, Puffin Modern Classic edition, 1999.

Nieuwenhuizen, Agnes. *Good Books for Teenagers*, Melbourne: Mandarin, 1992.

O'Brien, Greg. *Moments of Invention, Portraits of 21 New Zealand writers*, Auckland: Heinemann Reed, 1988.

O'Brien, Gregory. 'Imagine the imagination: Margaret Mahy's Dissolving Ghost', in *After Bathing at Baxter's: essays and notebooks*, Wellington: Victoria University Press, 2002.

Rees, David. *What Do Draculas Do? — essays on contemporary writers of fiction for children and young adults*, Metuchen, NJ: Scarecrow Press, 1990.

Sarti, Antonella. *Spiritcarvers: interviews with eighteen writers from NZ*, Cross/cultures Series, Amsterdam: Rodopi, 1998.

Wilkie-Stibbs, Christine. *The feminine subject in children's literature*, New York: Routledge, 2002. (Readings of 7 novels by MM and Gillian Cross)

Williams, Mark. 'A variety of voices', in *Under Review: A selection from New Zealand Books 1991–1996*, edited by Lauris Edmond, Harry Ricketts, Bill Sewell, Christchurch: Lincoln University Press and Daphne Brassell Associates, 1997.

Periodicals and conference proceedings

Berkin, Adam. 'I Woke Myself': *The Changeover* as a modern adaptation of Sleeping Beauty', *Children's Literature in Education*, Vol. 21, No. 4, 1990.

Edmond, Murray. 'Interview with Margaret Mahy', *Landfall* 41(2), June 1987.

Gibbons, Joan. 'Family Relationships in the Stories of Margaret Mahy', *Papers — Explorations in Children's Literature*, Vol. 5: No. 1, April, 1994.

Gose, Elliott. 'Fairy Tale and Myth in Mahy's *The Changeover* and *The Tricksters*', *Children's Literature Association Quarterly*, Vol. 16, No. 1, spring 1991.

Groeger, Tonja and Julia Brander. 'Astrid Lindgren and Margaret Mahy', *Reading Forum NZ*, No. 2, 2003, NZ Reading Association.

Hebley, Diane. 'A Fertility and Felicity and Ferocity of Invention', in *Marvellous Codes: The Fiction of Margaret Mahy*, edited by Elizabeth Hale and Sarah Winters, Wellington: Victoria University Press, 2005.

Hoffman, Mary. 'The Fabulous in the Ordinary — an Interview with Margaret Mahy', *The School Librarian*, 1987.

Lafferty, Fiona. 'Magic and Mystery: an interview with Margaret Mahy', *Children's Books*, June, 1986.

Lovell-Smith, Rose. 'A noisy life's work', review of *The Other Side of Silence* in *NZ Books*, March 1998.

————. 'On the Gothic Beach: Margaret Mahy's *The Tricksters* and Gavin Bishop's *The Horror of Hickory Bay*', *Haunting the Borders: the*

Gothic in Children's Literature, ed. Rod McGillis, Anna Jackson and Lisa Scally (forthcoming, 2006).

McVeigh, Janine. 'Myth and folktale in Margaret Mahy's young adult novels', *Talespinner* 8, September 1999.

Mahy, Margaret. 'Building bridges between our outer and inner landscapes', in *Reading is Everybody's Business*, ed. W.B. Elley, Selected Proceedings of the Fourth NZ Conference, May 1973, Wellington: IRA, Wellington Council, 1973.

———. 'One Great Frolic with Words,' *Education*, Vol. 22, No. 6, 1973.

———. 'Margaret Mahy on *King Solomon's Mines*,' Early Reading (NZ writers describe books that impressed them in their childhood), *Education*, c. 1975.

———. 'Intuitive Aspects of Language', in *Children and Language*, the 1974 Lectures, Wellington: Association for the Study of Childhood, 1975.

———. 'Educating the Imagination', 'Women in 1975.' (Nagelkerke Files, CCL)

———. 'Touchstones: The interpretation of adult experiences by the images of childhood reading', *Landfall*, 120, 1976. (Talk given at the NZLIA Conference, 1976.)

———. 'Meet our Author Margaret Mahy,' *Cricket*, Vol 5, No. 3, 1976.

———. 'The Lion, the Magician, the Hero, the Witch: Thoughts about Magic and Reality', *Yearbook*, Auckland: Children's Literature Association, 1976.

———. 'On building houses that face the sun', in *A Track to Unknown Water*, ed. Stella Lees, Proceedings of the second Pacific Rim Conference on children's literature, Melbourne: Melbourne State College, 1980.

———. 'Emblems and Journeys: The Power of Story in the Imagination', in *Readings in Children's Literature*, ed. Brian Murphy, Proceedings of the Second National Seminar on Children's Literature, 1978, Frankston, Victoria: Frankston State College, 1980.

———. 'Attitudes to Childhood in Early Australian and NZ Children's Books', in *Sharing*, ed. Jerelynn Emerson Brown, Proceedings from the First LAA-NZLA Conference, Christchurch, 1981, Sydney: LAA, 1981.

———. 'Countries of the Mind — Books and environment in childhood'. *Education*, Vol 31, No. 1, 1982.

———. '1984 Carnegie Medal, *The Changeover* Margaret Mahy (Dent)', acceptance speech in *Youth Library Review*, No. 1, Spring, 1986.

———. 'Joining the Network', *Signal* (UK) No. 54, The Thimble Press, 1987.

———. 'A New Zealand Writer Speaks', in *Brave New World: International Understanding through Books*, ed. Wendy and John Birman, Western Library Studies, 11, Proceedings of the Combined Conference on Youth Literature, Perth, 1985, Perth: Curtin University of Technology, 1988.

———. 'A Dissolving Ghost: Possible Operations of Truth in Children's Books and the Lives of Children', *Journal of Youth Services in Libraries*, 2.4 (1989), Arbuthnot Lecture, 1989, published in *The Arbuthnot*

Lectures 1980–1989 (Chicago: ALA, 1990), reprinted in *Only Connect*, ed. Sheila Egoff, Oxford University Press, 1996 and *A Dissolving Ghost: essays and more*, Wellington, Victoria University Press, 2000.

———. 'The long-shanked teddy', *Landfall* 44(2), June 1990 (short story).

———. 'Margaret Mahy', *Reading Forum NZ* 3, 1990.

———. 'The Illustrated Traveller's Tale', *Soho Square* 4, ed. Bill Manhire, Bloomsbury, 1991, reprinted in *A Dissolving Ghost*, 2000.

———. 'Part of the democratic pantomime', *New Zealand Books* 3(4), March 1994 (edited version of the 1993 Shelley Lecture).

———. 'Margaret Mahy', *New Zealand Official Yearbook* 1993.

———. 'The Writer in New Zealand: Building Bridges through Children's Books', *Bookbird* 34, No. 4, winter 1996.

———. 'Taking humour seriously', in *Reading Forum NZ* 2, NZ Reading Association, 1996. Paper presented to 22nd NZ Reading Association Conference on Reading, New Plymouth, 1996.

———. 'Beginnings', in *Landfall* 193, Autumn, 1997.

———. 'Books that shaped my life', column in *Booknotes*, journal of NZ Book Council, No. 127, Spring, 1999.

———. 'Bookmarking the Century', on Maurice Gee's *The Fat Man*, *Landfall* 199, 2000.

———. 'The child, the book and the future,' *Imprints* column in *New Zealand Books*, June 2000.

———. 'Two Trilogies and Mystery: Speculations on the Earthsea Stories', *Magpies*, Vol. 17, No. 3, July 2002.

———. 'Fantasy: Flights of the Mind,' *The Inside Story*, Storylines Children's Literature Foundation of NZ Yearbook 2002.

———. 'Accounts and Meditations: A Judge's Report on the 2002 *Landfall* Essay Competition', *Landfall* 203, May 2002.

———. 'Cinderella Transformed: Multiple Voices and Diverse Dialogues in Children's Literature', ed. John McKenzie, Doreen Darnell and Anna Smith, proceedings of the conference on children's literature, Centre for Children's Literature (Christchurch College of Education) and Australian Children's Literature Association for Research, 2003.

———. 'Margaret Mahy', *Sound Ideas*, Vol. 6, No. 2, University of Canterbury School of Music, May 2003.

———. 'Looking inward, exploring outward', Foreign Correspondence in *The Horn Book*, March–April, 2004.

Marquis, Claudia. 'Feminism, Freud and the Fairy Tale: Reading Margaret Mahy's *The Haunting*', *Landfall*, 162, 1987.

———. 'Principles pleasures: exploring fantasy in children's literature', *Antic* 7, June 1990.

———. 'Telling tales out of School: "Young adult" fiction in New Zealand', *Landfall*, 179, 1991.

———. 'Ariadne "down under": Structures of Adolescent Fantasy in *The Tricksters*', in *Marvellous Codes: the Fiction of Margaret Mahy*, edited by Elizabeth Hale and Sarah Winters, Wellington: Victoria University Press, 2005.

Pickles, Veda. 'A Tale of a Telethon', *Yearbook 1981*, Auckland: Children's Literature Association, 1981.

Plumpton, Frances, 'Bringing Margaret Mahy to Children', report of her first visit to Auckland, *Yearbook 1983*, Auckland: Children's Literature Association, 1983.

Sheahan, Robyn. 'The Use of the Supernatural to explore Realistic Issues in Margaret Mahy's *The Changeover* and *The Tricksters*, *Papers — Explorations in Children's Literature*, Vol. 2, No. 1, 1999.

Turton, Rayma. 'Talking with Margaret Mahy about imagination and writing and her latest book *The Riddle of the Frozen Phantom*', *Magpies*, Vol. 17, No. 1, March 2002.

Waller, Alison. '"Solid All the Way Through": Margaret Mahy's Ordinary Witches', *Children's Literature in Education*, Vol. 35, No. 1, March 2004.

Walls, Kathryn. 'True-seeming lyes' in Three Novels by Margaret Mahy, in *Marvellous Codes: The Fiction of Margaret Mahy*, edited by Elizabeth Hale and Sarah Winters, Wellington: Victoria University Press, 2005.

Worman, Ceri, 'From idealism to Capitalism: Margaret Mahy Talks About The Process of Writing and Her Recent Books', *Youth Libraries Review* (UK), 1997.

Newspapers and magazines

'Authorgraph No. 24: Margaret Mahy', *Books for Keeps*, No. 24, School Bookshop Association, January 1984.

Chamberlain, Jenny. 'Margaret Mahy: Word Witchery', *North & South*, November 1993.

Mahy, Margaret. 'Children's Libraries Are For Parents Too,' *Press*, c. 1978. (Nagelkerke file)

———. 'The School Journal,' Popular Books, *Fact Magazine*, March 1982.

———. 'Keep writing: the world needs you', Newspapers in Education (NIE), Star classroom, *The Star* (Christchurch), 4 November 1985.

———. 'Turning heads', *Listener* 121, 23 July 1988. (MM and other writers on books that have influenced them)

———. 'Favourite teachers', *NZ Education Review*, 15 July 1998.

———. 'Dissolving Millennium', *Sunday Star-Times*, supplement, 2 January 2000.

———. 'Just Wild about Harry', *Listener*, 15 July 2000.

———. 'Margaret Mahy/ Questionnaire/Bizarre Bits,' *AuthorZone*, c. 2001.

———. 'The Seventh Form,' socialisation in secondary schools, undated.

Thompson, Margie. 'A lion in our literary meadow', *New Zealand Herald*, 6 April 2002.

Margaret Mahy unpublished

'Report on overseas visit', to School Library Service, Christchurch, 1973. (Christchurch City Libraries, MM Archive)

'A Library Christmas Carol or The Consolations of Literature', written and illustrated by Margaret Mahy; 'The Library Advisor's Song'; 'The Branch Meeting'; 'An old music hall song of flowers'. (c. 1976–1979). (CCL: MM Archive)

On writing a longer book (*The Tricksters*), one page, typewritten draft. (CCL: MM Archive)

'In the beginning . . .' undated speech. (MM Files)

'Stories at home, stories at school — reading in the family and at school', undated speech on reading programmes, literacy. (MM Files)

'When I came seriously to consider . . .' speech, c. 1982, to teachers' gathering. (MM Files)

'The Bubble', speech, c. 1987. (MM Files)

'I am here to speak . . .' speech to Friends of the Library group (incomplete), November 1988. (Nagelkerke File)

'A Place in the World: the impact of childhood reading', speech, c. 1992. (MM Files)

'Dissolving edges — Jokes and Passion in reading acquisition', speech c. 1991 (incomplete). (MM Files)

'The theme of this conference, that of building bridges of understanding . . .' speech, c. 1995. (MM Files)

'I tell this story ['Down the Back of the Chair'] because it seems typical of many of the stories I write . . . fantastic yet essentially domestic . . .' speech, c. 1996. (MM Files)

'Seeing the Lion,' speech given at *Endings and Beginning: The Shape of Story*, CLNE at Harvard University, Cambridge, Massachusetts, 1996. (MM Files)

'From the time I was a small child . . .' speech to teachers, c. 2002. (MM Files)

Websites

www.bookcouncil.org.nz
NZ Book Council, writer files: MM entry includes Children's Questions for MM.

www.library.christchurch.org.nz
Christchurch City Libraries: 'The Margaret Mahy Pages', includes poem 'Down the Back of the Chair' and story, 'The Word-Eater', Q & A interview, 'In her Own Words'.

www.penguin.co.uk
Penguin Books (Authors: MM biography, quotes from reviews)

www.harpercollins.co.uk
Author Pages, MM entry includes Q & A interview with reference to *24 Hours*. (Also www.harpercollins.co.nz)

www.teenreads.com
Author Profile: MM Long interview 2003.

www.library.auckland.ac.nz
University of Auckland Library — LEARN/Margaret Mahy — extensive and useful select list of books and reviews; material by and about MM

Various on-line websites (including biographies, book lists/essays, references) available through subscribing libraries, e.g. 'Contemporary Authors Online', 'Writers for Young Adults', 'Junior Discovering Authors'.

General books on children's literature with references to Margaret Mahy

Children's Literature Review, excerpts from Reviews, Criticism and Commentary on Books for Children, Detroit: Gale Research Company, 1984.

Sheila A. Egoff, ed. *Worlds Within: children's fantasy from the Middle Ages to today*, American Library Association, 1988.

Saxby, Maurice and Gordon Winch, ed. *Give them Wings: the Experience of Children's Literature*, second edition (especially essays by Patricia Scott, Glenys Smith, Moira Robinson), Melbourne: Macmillan 1987 (2nd edition 1991).

Hobson, Margaret, Jennifer Madden, Ray Prytherch, ed. *Children's Fiction Sourcebook*, Aldershot UK: Ashgate 1992.

Twentieth-century Children's Writers, Tracy Chevalier, ed. (MM essay: Paul Heins), 3rd edition, Chicago, London: St James Press, 1989.

Twentieth-century Young Adult Writers, ed. Laura Standley Berger (MM essay: Bill Buchanan), Detroit: St James Press, 1994.

Hunt, Peter. *International Companion Encyclopaedia of Children's Literature*, (especially essays by Colin Mills, Julia Eccleshare, Betty Gilderdale), London/New York: Routledge, 1996.

Pringle, David, ed. *St James Guide to Fantasy Writers*, Detroit: St James Press, 1996.

The Oxford Companion to New Zealand Literature, eds. Roger Robinson and Nelson Wattie (essay: Kathryn Walls), Auckland: Oxford University Press, 1998.

Something about the Author, Vol. 119, Detroit: Gale, 2001.

Hunt, Peter. *Children's Literature*, Blackwell Guides to Literature, Oxford: Blackwell Publishers, 2001.

Watson, Victor, ed. *Cambridge Guide to Children's Books in English*, Cambridge: Cambridge University Press, 2001.

Children's Literature Review, Vol. 78, Thomson, Detroit: Gale, 2002.

Spufford, Francis. *The Child that Books Built*, London: Faber & Faber, 2002.

Margaret Mahy —
chronological bibliography

Entries are picture books, or as otherwise stated. All *School Journal* entries are for stories or poems; 'school readers' from educational literacy series have been indicated by (SR). Picture books reissued with new illustrations have been entered separately.

1961
'The Procession.' *School Journal* Part 2, no. 4.
'The Witch, my Sister.' *School Journal* Part 2,
no. 4. (Poem)

1962
'Guy and the Bears.' *School Journal* Part 2, no.2.
'The Birthday Party.' *School Journal* Part 2, no. 3.
'The Little Man Who Went to Sea.'
School Journal Part 2, no. 4.

1964
'The Old Bus.' *School Journal* Part 2, no. 5.

1965
'A Lion in the Meadow.'
School Journal Part 1, no. 3.
'The Adventures of Little-Mouse.'
School Journal Part 1, no. 3.
'The Clowns.' *School Journal* Part 1, no. 3. (Poem)
'Right-Hand Men.' *School Journal* Part 1, no. 3.
'Mouse Music.' *School Journal* Part 1, no. 3.
(Poem)
'Alone in the House.' *School Journal* Part 1, no. 3.
'A Witch in the House.'
School Journal Part 1, no. 3.
'Sailor Jack.' *School Journal* Part 1, no. 3.
'Christmas Day.' *School Journal* Part 1, no. 6.
(Poem)
'The Little Wild Woman.'
School Journal Part 2, no. 1.
'The Merry-Go-Round.'
School Journal Part 2, no. 5.

'Once Upon an Evening.' *School Journal* Part 2,
no. 5. (Poem)
'Mr Rumfit.' *School Journal* Part 2, no. 5.
'The Snail.' *School Journal* Part 2, no. 5. (Poem)
'The Playground.' *School Journal* Part 2, no. 5.
'The Road to the School.' *School Journal*, Part 2,
no. 5.

1966
'An Ordinary Family.'
School Journal, Part 1, no. 3.
'Green Needles.' *School Journal*, Part 2, no. 4.
The Wind Beneath the Stars,
School Journal Part 3, no. 3.
– collection of Margaret Mahy stories and
poems, illustrated by Jill McDonald:
'The Boy who Went Looking for a Friend'
'*Small Porks*'
'Pillycock's Shop'
'Mrs Discobobulus'
'The Ghastly Nightmare or
The Butcher's Dream' (Poem)
'When the King Rides By' (Poem)
'The Princess and the Clown'
'The Wind Between the Stars'
'The Witch Dog'

1967
'The Thinking Game.' *School Journal* Part 1, no. 3.

1968
'The Boy With Two Shadows.'
School Journal Part 2, no. 3.

1969

A Lion in the Meadow,
   illustrated by Jenny Williams. New York:
   Franklin Watts; London: Dent; Woodstock:
   Overlook Press (1992). (Revised edition
   with new illustrations and ending, 1986)
The Dragon of an Ordinary Family,
   illustrated by Helen Oxenbury. New York,
   Franklin Watts; London: Heinemann.
   (Revised edition, 1991)
Pillycock's Shop, illustrated by Carol Barker.
   New York: Franklin Watts; London: Dobson.
The Procession, illustrated by Charles Mozley.
   New York: Franklin Watts; London: Dent.
Mrs. Discombobulous, illustrated by Jan Brychta.
   New York: Franklin Watts; London: Dent.
   (Originally published as 'Mrs Discobobulus',
   School Journal, Part 3, no. 3, 1966)
'Mr Murgatroyd's Lodgers.'
   School Journal Part 2, no. 3.

1970

The Little Witch, illustrated by Charles Mozley.
   New York: Franklin Watts; London: Dent.
Sailor Jack and the 20 Orphans, illustrated by
   Robert Bartelt. New York: Franklin Watts;
   London: Dent.
'The Brown Man's Circus.'
   School Journal, Part 1, no. 1.
'The Stone Man.' *School Journal* Part 1, no. 4.
'Tai Taylor is Born.' *School Journal* Part 2, no. 1.
'Tai Taylor and the Sweet Annie.'
   School Journal Part 2, no. 2.
'Tai Taylor and his Education, Part 1.'
   School Journal Part 2, no. 3.
'Tai Taylor and his Education, Part 2.'
   School Journal Part 2, no. 4.

1971

The Princess and the Clown, illustrated by
   Carol Barker. New York: Franklin Watts;
   London: Dobson.
The Boy with Two Shadows, illustrated by
   Jenny Williams. New York: Franklin Watts;
   London: Dent. (Revised edition, 1987)

'Wonderful Me.'
   School Journal Part 1, no. 3. (Poem)
'Mike's Pet.' *School Journal* Part 2, no. 1.
'The Boy Who was Followed Home.'
   School Journal Part 2, no. 2.
'King of the World.'
   School Journal Part 2, no. 2. (Poem)
'Concerning a Little Woman and How She
   Won Herself a House and a Servant
   and Lived Happily Ever After.'
   School Journal, Part 2, no. 3.
'How the World Ended.' *School Journal*
   Part 2, no. 4. (Poem)
'The Railway Engine and the Hairy Brigands.'
   School Journal Part 2, no. 4.
'A Strange Old Man.' *School Journal* Part 2, no. 4.
   (Poem)

1972

Seventeen Kings and 42 Elephants, illustrated by
   Charles Mozely. London: Dent. (Poetry)
   (Revised edition, 1987)
The Man Whose Mother was a Pirate, illustrated by
   Brian Froud. London: Dent; New York:
   Atheneum (1973) (Revised edition, 1985)
   (Originally published as 'The Little Man
   Who Went To Sea, *School Journal*,
   Part 2, no. 4, 1962)
The First Margaret Mahy Story Book,
   illustrated by Shirley Hughes. London: Dent
   (Collection of 13 stories and 15 poems, most
   published first in *School Journal*)
'The Strange Case of Old Squashy.' *School Journal*
   Part 2, no. 1.

1973

The Railway Engine and the Hairy Brigands,
   illustrated by Brian Froud. London: Dent.
The Second Margaret Mahy Story Book,
   illustrated by Shirley Hughes. London: Dent.
   (14 stories and 4 poems)
'The Follower.' *School Journal* Part 1, no. 4.
'The Kings of the Broom Cupboard.'
   School Journal Part 2, no. 2.

'The Strange Adventure of Mr Pricker.'
  School Journal Part 2, no. 4.
'The Remarkable Birthday Party.'
  School Journal Part 2, no. 3.

1974

The Bus under the Leaves, illustrated by
  Margery Gill. London: Dent. (Short junior
  novel) (Originally published in *School Journal*
  under the title 'The Old Bus', *School Journal*,
  Part 2, no. 5, 1964)
Clancy's Cabin, illustrated by Trevor Stubley.
  London: Dent. (New edition illustrated by
  Barbara Steadman, Woodstock: Overlook
  Press, 1995) (Short junior novel)
Rooms for Rent, illustrated by Jenny Williams.
  New York: Franklin Watts; London: Dent
  (1975, under title *Rooms to Let*) (Originally
  published as 'Mr Murgatroyd's Lodgers', in
  School Journal, Part 2, no. 3, 1969)
The Rare Spotted Birthday Party, illustrated by
  Belinda Lyon. London: Franklin Watts.
The Witch in the Cherry Tree, illustrated by
  Jenny Williams. London: Dent; New York:
  Parents' Magazine Press.
Stepmother, illustrated by Terry Burton.
  London: Franklin Watts.
'The Little Witch.' *School Journal* Part 2, no. 5.

1975

*Ultra-Violet Catastrophe or, The Unexpected Walk
  with Great-Uncle Magnus Pringle*,
  illustrated by Brian Froud. London: Dent;
  New York: Parents' Magazine Press
Leaf Magic, illustrated by Jenny Williams.
  New York: Parents' Magazine Press;
  London: Dent (1976) (Originally
  published as 'The Follower,' in *School Journal*,
  Part 1, no. 4, 1973)
The Third Margaret Mahy Story Book, illustrated by
  Shirley Hughes. London: Dent.
The Great Millionaire Kidnap, illustrated by
  Jan Brytcha. London: Dent.
The Bus Under the Leaves, illustrated by
  Margery Gill. London: Dent.

The Boy Who Was Followed Home, illustrated by
  Steven Kellogg. New York: Franklin Watts;
  London: Dent (1977)
New Zealand: Yesterday and Today,
  illustrated by Jim Robins. New York:
  Franklin Watts. (Non-fiction, with
  photographs and line drawings)

1976

The Wind between the Stars, illustrated by Brian
  Froud. London: Dent.
Leaf Magic, illustrated by Jenny Williams.
  London: Dent; New York: Parents'
  Magazine Press (1977).
David's Witch Doctor, illustrated by Jim Russell.
  London: Franklin Watts.
A Lion in the Meadow and Five Other Favourites,
  illustrated by Jenny Williams, Robert
  Bartelt, Jan Brychta, Charles Mozley,
  and Brian Froud and Molly Lovejoy.
  London: Dent. (Collection of stories
  from *School Journal* published as picture
  books; with new illustrations)
'The Silly Song.' *School Journal* Part 2, no. 3.
  (Nonsense song)
'The New House Villain.' *School Journal*
  Part 3, no. 3.

1977

The Pirate Uncle, illustrated by Mary Dinsdale.
  London: Dent; Woodstock: Overlook Press
  (1994). (Junior novel)
Look under 'V', illustrated by Deidre Gardiner.
  Wellington: School Publications Branch,
  Department of Education. (Non-fiction/
  fiction)
'Trouble on the Bus.' *School Journal* Part 3, no 2.
'The Funny Funny Clown Face.' *School Journal*
  Part 3, no. 3.

1978

*The Great Piratical Rumbustification
  & The Librarian and the Robbers*,
  illustrated by Quentin Blake. London: Dent;
  Boston: Godine (1986)

Dry Days for Climbing George, illustrated by
Judith Trevalyn. Wellington: Department
of Education, School Publications.
'The Boomerang Rat.' *School Journal*, Part 2, no. 2.
'Ultra-Violet Catastrophe.' *School Journal* Part 3,
no. 2. (Published first as a picture book)

1979
Nonstop Nonsense, illustrated by Quentin Blake.
London: Dent; London: Magnet (1986);
New York: Margaret McElderry (1989).

1981
Raging Robots and Unruly Uncles, illustrated by
Peter Stevenson. London: Dent; New York:
Overlook Press (1993). (Junior novel)
'The Baby-sitter.' *School Journal* Part 3, no. 3.

1982
The Haunting. London: Dent; New York:
Athenaeum. (Junior novel)
The Chewing- Gum Rescue and Other Stories,
illustrated by Jan Ormerod. London: Dent;
London: Methuen (1984); Woodstock:
Overlook Press (1991)
Brrm Brrm! illustrated by Bob Kerr, Wellington:
School Publications Branch, Department of
Education. (SR)
The Crocodile's Christmas Jandals, illustrated by
Deirdre Gardiner. Wellington: School
Publications Branch, Department of
Education (SR) (Published as *The Christmas
Crocodile's Thongs*, Melbourne: Nelson, 1985)
Roly-Poly, with Joy Cowley and June Melser,
illustrated by Deirdre Gardiner. Auckland:
Shortland; Leeds: Arnold-Wheaton (1985).
Cooking Pot, with Joy Cowley and June Melser,
illustrated by Deirdre Gardiner. Auckland:
Shortland; Leeds: Arnold-Wheaton (1985).
Fast and Funny, with Joy Cowley and
June Melser, illustrated by
Lynette Vondrusha. Auckland: Shortland;
Leeds: Arnold-Wheaton (1985).
Sing to the Moon, with Joy Cowley and June
Melser, illustrated by Isabel Lowe. Auckland:
Shortland; Leeds: Arnold-Wheaton (1985).

Tiddalik, with Joy Cowley and June Melser,
illustrated by Philip Webb. Auckland:
Shortland; Leeds: Arnold-Wheaton (1985).
'The Great Stovie Transformation.'
School Journal Part 2, no. 3.
'The Alligator's Painting Day.'
School Journal, Part 3, no. 1.
'The Mad Puppet.' *School Journal* Part 4, no. 3.

1983
*The Pirates' Mixed-Up Voyage: Dark Doings in the
Thousand Islands*, illustrated by Margaret
Chamberlain. London: Dent; New York:
Dial Books. (Junior novel)
A Crocodile in the Library, illustrated by Deirdre
Gardiner. Wellington: School Publications
Branch, Department of Education. (SR)
Mrs Bubble's Baby, illustrated by Diane Perham.
Wellington: School Publications Branch,
Department of Education. (SR)
The Bubbling Crocodile, illustrated by Deirdre
Gardiner. Wellington: School Publications
Branch, Department of Education. (SR)
Shopping with a Crocodile, illustrated by Deidre
Gardiner. Wellington: School Publications
Branch, Department of Education. (SR)
'The Present That Mr Leonidas Got From His
Auntie.' *School Journal* Part 2, no. 1. (Poem)

1984
The Changeover: A Supernatural Romance.
London: Dent; New York: Athenaeum.
(Young adult novel)
The Birthday Burglar & *A Very Wicked Headmistress*,
illustrated by Margaret Chamberlain.
London: Dent (1984);
Boston: David Godine (1988).
Leaf Magic and Five other Favourites, illustrated
by Margaret Chamberlain. London: Dent;
Auckland: Waiatarua.
Fantail, Fantail, illustrated by Bruce Phillips.
Wellington: School Publications Branch,
Department of Education. (SR)
Going to the Beach, illustrated by Dick Frizzell.
Wellington: School Publications Branch,
Department of Education. (SR)

The Great Grumbler and the Wonder Tree,
    illustrated by Diane Perham. Wellington:
    School Publications Branch, Department
    of Education. (SR)
The Dragon's Birthday, illustrated by Philip Webb.
    Auckland: Shortland. (SR)
The Spider in the Shower, illustrated by
    Rodney McRae. Auckland: Shortland. (SR)
Ups and Downs and Other Stories, illustrated by
    Philip Webb. Auckland: Shortland. (SR)
Wibble Wobble and Other Stories.
    Auckland: Shortland. (SR)
'The Cheating Ghost.' *School Journal* Part 2, no. 4.
'The Girl Who Washed in Moonlight.'
    School Journal Part 3, no. 1.
'Christmas Shopping with the Crocodile.'
    Junior Journal No 1.

1985

The Catalogue of the Universe. London: Dent;
    New York: Atheneum. (Young adult novel)
Aliens in the Family. London: Methuen; Auckland:
    Scholastic; New York: Scholastic; London:
    Hippo (1996). (Junior novel)
Jam: A True Story, illustrated by Helen Craig.
    London: Dent; Boston: Atlantic Monthly
    Press (1986).
A Crocodile in the Garden, illustrated by Deirdre
    Gardiner. Wellington: School Publications
    Branch, Department of Education. (SR)
Horrakopotchin, illustrated by Fiona Kelly.
    Wellington: School Publications Branch,
    Department of Education. (SR)
The Adventures of a Kite, illustrated by
    David Cowe. Auckland: Shortland;
    Leeds: Arnold-Wheaton (1986). (SR)
The Cake, illustrated by David Cowe.
    Auckland: Shortland;
    Leeds: Arnold-Wheaton (1986). (SR)
The Catten, illustrated by Jo Davies.
    Auckland: Shortland;
    Leeds: Arnold-Wheaton (1986). (SR)
Clever Hamburger, illustrated byRodney McRae.
    Auckland: Shortland;
    Leeds: Arnold-Wheaton (1986). (SR)

A Very Happy Birthday, illustrated by Elizabeth
    Fuller. Auckland: Shortland (SR);
    Leeds: Arnold-Wheaton, (1986). (SR)
The Earthquake, illustrated by Dianne Perham.
    Auckland: Shortland;
    Leeds: Arnold-Wheaton (1986). (SR)
Sophie's Singing Mother, illustrated by Jo Davies.
    Auckland: Shortland; Leeds: Arnold-
    Wheaton (1986). (SR)
Out in the Big Wide World, illustrated by
    Rodney McRae. Auckland: Shortland. (SR)
Rain, illustrated by Elizabeth Fuller.
    Auckland: Shortland.
'Further Adventures of Humpty Dumpty.'
    School Journal Part 2, no. 4. (Poem)

1986

The Tricksters. London: Dent;
    New York: Margaret McElderry (1987).
    (Young adult novel)
A Lion in the Meadow, illustrated by
    Jenny Williams. London: Dent. (New edition
    with revised ending and new illustrations)
The Man Whose Mother Was a Pirate, illustrated
    by Margaret Chamberlain. London: Dent.
    (New edition, with revised text and new
    illustrations)
My Wonderful Aunt (four volumes), illustrated by
    Deirdre Gardiner. Heinemann,
    revised edition in one volume,
    Chicago: Children's Press, (1988)
The Downhill Crocodile Whizz and Other Stories,
    illustrated by Ian Newsham. London: Dent.
    (Collection)
*Mahy Magic: A Collection of the Most Magical
    Stories from the Margaret Mahy Story Books*,
    illustrated by Shirley Hughes. London: Dent.
    (Collection of 18 stories with magic themes)
    (Published as *The Boy who bounced and other
    magic tales*, London: Puffin, 1988)
Arguments, illustrated by Kelvin Hawley.
    Auckland: Shortland. (SR)
Beautiful Pig. Auckland: Shortland;
    Leeds: Arnold-Wheaton (1987). (SR)

The Fight on the Hill, illustrated by
  Jan van der Voo. Auckland: Shortland;
  Leeds: Arnold-Wheaton (1987). (SR)
An Elephant in the House, illustrated by
  Elizabeth Fuller. Auckland: Shortland. (SR)
Jacko, the Junk Shop Man, illustrated by Jo Davies.
  Auckland: Shortland. (SR)
The Long Grass of Tumbledown Road, illustrated
  by Elizabeth Fuller. Auckland: Shortland;
  Leeds: Arnold-Wheaton (1987). (SR)
The Mouse Wedding, illustrated by Elizabeth Fuller.
  Auckland: Shortland. (SR)
Mr Rooster's Dilemma, illustrated by Elizabeth
  Fuller. Auckland: Shortland. Published in
  UK as *How Mr Rooster Didn't Get Married,*
  Leeds: Arnold-Wheaton (1987). (SR)
The Robber Pig and Green Eggs, illustrated by
  Rodney McRae. Auckland: Shortland;
  Leeds: Arnold-Wheaton (1987). (SR)
The Robber Pig and the Ginger Beer, illustrated by
  Rodney McRae. Auckland: Shortland;
  Leeds: Arnold-Wheaton (1987). (SR)
Squeak in the Gate, illustrated by Jo Davies.
  Auckland: Shortland. (SR)
Tinny Tiny Tinker, illustrated by David Cowe.
  Auckland: Shortland. (SR)
Baby's Breakfast, illustrated by Madeleine Beasley.
  Auckland: Wendy Pye Publishing. (SR)
Feeling Funny, illustrated by Rodney McRae.
  Auckland: Wendy Pye. (SR)
The Garden Party, illustrated by Rodney McRae.
  Auckland: Wendy Pye. (SR)
Mr Rumfit, illustrated by Nick Price.
  Auckland: Wendy Pye. (SR)
Muppy's Ball, illustrated by Jan van der Voo.
  Auckland: Wendy Pye. (SR)
The New House Villain, illustrated by Elizabeth
  Fuller. Auckland: Wendy Pye. (SR)
A Pet to the Vet, illustrated by Philip Webb.
  Auckland: Wendy Pye. (SR)
The Pop Group, illustrated by Madeline Beasley.
  Auckland: Wendy Pye. (SR)
The Man Who Enjoyed Grumbling, illustrated by
  Wendy Hodder, Auckland: Wendy Pye.
  (SR)

Tai Taylor is Born, illustrated by Nick Price.
  Auckland: Wendy Pye. (SR)
Tai Taylor Goes to School, illustrated by Nick Price.
  Auckland: Wendy Pye. (SR)
Tai Taylor and His Education, illustrated by
  Nick Price. Auckland: Wendy Pye. (SR)
Tai Taylor and the Sweet Annie, illustrated by
  Nick Price. Auckland: Wendy Pye. (SR)
The Terrible Topsy-Turvey, Tissy-Tossy Tangle,
  illustrated by Vicki Smillie-McItoull.
  Auckland: Wendy Pye. (SR)
The Tree Doctor, illustrated by Wendy Hodder.
  Auckland: Wendy Pye. (SR)
Trouble on the Bus, illustrated by Wendy Hodder.
  Auckland: Wendy Pye. (SR)
The Trouble with Heathrow, illustrated by Rodney
  McRae. Auckland: Wendy Pye. (SR)
The Funny Funny Clown Face,
  illustrated by Miranda Whitford.
  Auckland: Wendy Pye. (SR)
The Three Wishes (with others),
  illustrated by Rodney McRae and others.
  Auckland: Shortland. (SR)
'Cuckooland.' *School Journal* Part 3, no. 2
  (Play adapted from first episode of
  TV series of the same name)

1987

Memory. London: Dent; New York:
  Margaret McElderry. (Young adult novel)
The Boy with Two Shadows, illustrated by
  Jenny Williams. London: Dent; New York:
  J.B. Lippincott. (New edition: revised text
  and new illustrations by same illustrator)
17 Kings and 42 Elephants, revised edition
  illustrated by Patricia MacCarthy.
  London: Dent; New York: Dial. (Poetry)
The Horrible Story and Others, illustrated by
  Shirley Hughes. London: Dent. (Collection
  of 21 stories, not included in *Mahy Magic,*
  from the three *Margaret Mahy Story Books*)
The Little Witch and Five Other Favourites,
  illustrated by Jenny Williams. London:
  Penguin. (Originally published as *A Lion in
  the Meadow and 5 Other Favourites,* 1976)

The Haunting of Miss Cardamom, illustrated by
Korky Paul. Auckland: Wendy Pye. (SR)
Guinea Pig Grass, illustrated by Kelvin Hawley.
Auckland: Shortland. (SR)
Iris La Bonga and the Helpful Taxi Driver,
illustrated by Vicki Smillie-McItoull.
Auckland: Wendy Pye. (SR)
The Man Who Walked on his Hands, illustrated by
Martin Bailey. Auckland: Shortland. (SR)
No Dinner for Sally, illustrated by John Tarlton.
Auckland: Shortland. (SR)
The Mad Puppet, illustrated by Jon Davis.
Auckland: Wendy Pye. (SR)
The Girl Who Washed in Moonlight, illustrated by
Robyn Belton. Auckland: Wendy Pye. (SR)
The King's Jokes, illustrated by Val Biro.
Auckland: Wendy Pye. (SR)
Feeling Funny, illustrated by Rodney McRae.
Auckland: Wendy Pye. (SR)
The Tree Doctor, illustrated by Wendy Hodder.
Auckland: Wendy Pye. (SR)

1988

The Door in the Air and Other Stories, illustrated by
Diana Catchpole. London: Dent (1988);
New York: Delacorte (1991). (Young adult
short stories)
When the King Rides By, illustrated by Bettina
Ogden. Cheltenham (UK): Stanley Thomas;
New York: Mondo (1995).
The Boy Who Bounced and Other Magic Tales,
illustrated by Shirley Hughes. London:
Penguin. (Collection originally published
as *Mahy Magic* by Dent, 1986)
The Baby-sitter, illustrated by Bryan Pollard.
Auckland: Shortland. (SR)
As Luck Would Have It, illustrated by Deirdre
Gardiner. Auckland: Shortland. (SR)
A Not-so-quiet-evening, illustrated by Glenda Jones.
Auckland: Shortland. (SR)
Sarah, the Bear and the Kangaroo, illustrated by
Elizabeth Fuller. Auckland: Shortland. (SR)
'Plans Gone Wrong.'
School Journal Part 2, no. 4. (Poem)

1989

The Blood-and-Thunder Adventure on Hurricane Peak,
illustrated by Wendy Smith.
London: Dent; New York: Margaret McElderry.
(Junior novel)
The Great White Man-Eating Shark: A Cautionary Tale,
illustrated by Jonathan Allen. London: Dent;
New York: Dial (1990).
Chocolate Porridge and Other Stories,
illustrated by Shirley Hughes.
London: Penguin. (Originally published as
The Horrible Story and Others, Dent, 1987)
The Tin Can Band and Other Poems, illustrated by
Honey De Lacey. London: Dent. (Poetry)
Trouble in the Supermarket, illustrated by
Trish Hill. Melbourne: Thomas Nelson
Australia. (Collection of nine stories, plus
biographical information and author comment)

1990

The Seven Chinese Brothers, illustrated by
Jean and Mou-sien Tseng.
London: Macmillan; New York: Scholastic.
Making Friends, illustrated by Wendy Smith.
London: Dent; New York: McElderry Books.
The Pumpkin Man and the Crafty Creeper,
illustrated by Helen Craig. London: Cape;
New York: Lothrop Lee and Shepard.
Crocodile crocodile, illustrated by Celia Canning.
Auckland: Wendy Pye. (SR)
The Little Round Husband, illustrated by Val Biro.
Auckland: Wendy Pye. (SR)
White elephants, illustrated by John Bendall-Brunello.
Auckland: Wendy Pye. (SR)
The Solar System, illustrated by Jeff Fowler.
Auckland: Wendy Pye. (SR) (Non fiction)
The Library at the End of the World: a vision musical
commissioned by the Court Theatre,
Christchurch with assistance from the 1990
Commission and the QE11 Arts Council,
libretto by Margaret Mahy,
music by Dorothy Buchanan (unpublished).

1991

Dangerous Spaces. London: Hamish Hamilton;
New York: Viking. (Junior novel)

Bubble Trouble and Other Poems and Stories,
illustrated by Tony Ross. London: Hamish
Hamilton; New York: Margaret McElderry
(with illustrations by Margaret Mahy).

Keeping House, illustrated by Wendy Smith.
London: Hamish Hamilton;
New York: Margaret McElderry.

The Queen's Goat, illustrated by
Emma Chichester Clark.
London: Hamish Hamilton; New York: Dial.

The Dentist's Promise, illustrated by Wendy Smith.
Sydney: Omnibus Books; London: Hippo
(1994).

The Dragon of an Ordinary Family, illustrated by
Helen Oxenbury. London: Heinemann; New
York: Dial. (New edition with revised text)

A Tall Story and Other Tales, illustrated by
Jan Nesbitt. London: Dent; New York:
Margaret McElderry (1992). (Collection of
11 stories previously published in the First,
Second and Third *Margaret Mahy Story Books*)

Giant Soup. Wellington: School Publications
Branch, Department of Education. (SR)

Surprising moments: the Inaugural Margaret Mahy
Award Lecture. Auckland: New Zealand
Children's Book Foundation.

1992

Underrunners. London: Hamish Hamilton;
New York: Viking (1992). (Junior novel)

A Tall Story and Other Tales,
illustrated by Jan Nesbitt. New York:
McElderry Macmillan; London: Dent.

The Horrendous Hullabaloo, illustrated by
Patricia MacCarthy. London: Hamish
Hamilton; New York: Viking.

*The Girl with the Green Ear: Stories about Magic
in Nature*, illustrated by Shirley Hughes.
New York: Alfred A. Knopf (1992).
(Collection of nine stories on nature theme
from other collections)

The Fiddle and the Gun: a Margaret Mahy collection,
illustrated by Elizabeth Fuller and others.
Auckland: Shortland.

The World in Fourteen Ninety-Two, (with Jean Fritz,
Katherine Paterson and others), illustrated by
Stefano Vitale. New York: Henry Holt.

The Great New Zealand TV Turn-off:
handbook for parents, teachers, librarians
by Sarah Clarkson, introduction by
Margaret Mahy. Wellington: New Zealand
Library Association.

1993

The Good Fortunes Gang (Cousins Quartet: Book 1),
illustrated by John Farman.
London: Doubleday; New York: Delacorte
(illustrated by Marian Young). (Junior novel)

A Fortunate Name (Cousins Quartet: Book 2),
illustrated by John Farman.
London: Doubleday; New York: Delacorte
(illustrated by Marian Young). (Junior novel)

The Three-Legged Cat, illustrated by
Jonathan Allen. London: Hamish Hamilton;
New York: Viking.

A Busy Day for a Good Grandmother, illustrated by
Margaret Chamberlain. London: Hamish
Hamilton; New York: Margaret McElderry.

Tick Tock Tales: Stories to Read Around the Clock,
illustrated by Wendy Smith.
London: Dent; New York: Margaret McElderry;
Australia: Allen & Unwin.
(Collection of stories from earlier collections)

1994

A Fortune Branches Out (Cousins Quartet: Book 3),
illustrated by John Farman.
London: Doubleday; New York: Delacorte
(illustrated by Marian Young). (Junior novel)

Tangled Fortunes (Cousins Quartet: Book 4),
illustrated by John Farman.
London: Doubleday; New York: Delacorte
(illustrated by Marian Young). (Junior novel)

The Greatest Show off Earth, illustrated by
Wendy Smith. London: Hamish Hamilton;
New York: Viking. (Junior novel)

The Rattlebang Picnic, illustrated by Steven Kellogg. New York: Dial; London: Hamish Hamilton (1995).

The Christmas Tree Tangle, illustrated by Anthony Kerins. St Leonards: Allen & Unwin; London: Hamish Hamilton; New York: Margaret McElderry.

The Dragon's Telephone, illustrated by Christine Ross. Wellington: Telecom. (Promotional book for Telecom NZ Ltd)

Shock Forest and other stories (White Wolves series). London: A & C Black.

Mr Mossop's Table (collection, various illustrators). Auckland: Wendy Pye. (SR)

'Sensible Questions', 'The Remarkable Cake', and 'The Reluctant Hero', in *The Penguin Book of Nonsense Verse*, selected and illustrated by Quentin Blake. London: Penguin.

1995

The Other Side of Silence. London: Hamish Hamilton; New York: Viking. (Young adult novel)

The Big Black Bulging Bump, illustrated by Robert Staermose. Sydney: Scholastic.

Busy Day for a Good Grandmother, illustrated by Margaret Chamberlain. London: Penguin; New York: Margaret McElderry.

Tingleberries, Tuckertubs and Telephones, illustrated by Robert Staermose. London: Hamish Hamilton; New York: Viking.

Cobwebs, Elephants and Stars, illustrated by Val Biro. Auckland: Wendy Pye. (SR)

The Greatest Binnie in the World, illustrated by Michael Martchenko. Auckland: Wendy Pye.

My Mysterious World, photographs by David Alexander. New York: Richard C. Owen. (Non-fiction, text and pictures of the author's life)

1996

The Five Sisters, illustrated by Patricia MacCarthy. London: Hamish Hamilton; New York: Viking (1997). (Novella)

Boom, Baby, Boom, Boom!, illustrated by Patricia MacCarthy. London: Hamish Hamilton; New York: Viking (1998).

Beaten by a Balloon, illustrated by Jonathan Allen. London: Hamish Hamilton; New York: Viking.

Questions Kids Ask Margaret Mahy. Auckland: Scholastic. (Non-fiction, illustrated)

1997

Operation Terror, illustrated by Ron Tiner. London: Puffin. (Junior novel)

The Horribly Haunted School, illustrated by Robert Staermose. London: Hamish Hamilton; New York: Viking 1998.

1998

A Summery Saturday Morning, illustrated by Selina Young. London: Hamish Hamilton; New York: Viking.

Don't Read This! Don't Read That! and Other Tales of the Unnatural (with Susan Cooper, Uri Orlev and others), illustrated by The Tjong Khing. Asheville, N.C.: Front Street.

Off to the Shop, photographed by Mary Walker. Auckland: Shortland. (SR)

1999

The Haunting, reissue as Puffin Modern Classic, 'Afterword' by Stephanie Nettell. London: Penguin.

A Villain's Night Out. London: Puffin. (Junior novel)

Simply Delicious! illustrated by Jonathan Allen. London: Frances Lincoln; New York: Orchard Books.

Down in the Dump with Dinsmore, illustrated by Steve Axelsen. London: Puffin; Ringwood, Vic.: Puffin.

The Dragon of an Ordinary Family, illustrated by Helen Oxenbury. London: Mammouth. (Revised edition)

What is the Solar System, illustrated by
  Jeff Fowler, reissue of *The Solar System*.
  Auckland: Wendy Pye.
'Rotten Red Riding Hood' (in *Cinderfella's Big
  Night and other fractured fairy tales*). Auckland:
  Shortland. (SR)

2000

24 Hours. London: HarperCollins, New York:
  Margaret McElderry. (Young adult novel)
Wonderful Me!, illustrated by Peter Bailey
  (reprint of *The First Margaret Mahy Story
  Book*). London: Dolphin.
Down the Dragon's Tongue,
  illustrated by Patricia MacCarthy.
  London: Frances Lincoln; New York:
  Orchard Books; Pymble NSW:
  HarperCollins.
'OhdearOhdearOhdearOhdear.' Short story in
  Storylines: the Anthology, ed. Tessa Duder.
  Auckland: Scholastic and Storylines
  Children's Literature Foundation of NZ.
A Dissolving Ghost: Essays and More.
  Wellington: Victoria University Press.
  (Essays, interviews, short stories)

2001

Mischief and Mayhem: two Margaret Mahy fantasies,
  illustrated by Helen Bacon. Auckland:
  Shortland.

2002

Alchemy. London: HarperCollins; New York:
  Margaret McElderry. (Young adult novel)
The Riddle of the Frozen Phantom.
  London: HarperCollins. (Junior novel)
Dashing Dog, illustrated by Sarah Garland.
  London: HarperCollins;
  New York: Greenwillow Books;
  London: Frances Lincoln. (Poetry)
The Great Car Clean-out, illustrated by
  Philip Webb. Wellington: Learning Media.

2003

The Changeover (reissued in Collins Modern
  Classics). London: HarperCollins.
  (Young adult novel)
Wait For Me!, illustrated by Peter Bailey
  (reprint of *The Second Margaret Mahy Story
  Book*). London: Dolphin.
The Gargling Gorilla, illustrations by Tony Ross.
  London: HarperCollins.
  (Collection of three stories)
'The Shadow Thief' in *Kids Night In!*
  edited by Jessica Adams, Juliet Partridge
  and Nick Earls. Melbourne: Penguin Books.
Me and My Dog, illustrated by Philip Webb.
  Wellington: Learning Media.

2004

Watch Me!, illustrated by Peter Bailey
  (reprint of *The Third Margaret Mahy Story
  Book*). London: Dolphin.
Shock Forest and other stories (White Wolves series).
  London: A & C Black.

2005

Maddigan's Fantasia. Auckland: HarperCollins.
  (Young adult novel linked to TV series
  of same name, produced by BBC and
  South Pacific Pictures)

Also multi-media versions of many Mahy stories and novels, e.g. audio-cassettes and adaptations for stage performance by the Court Theatre, Christchurch (*Mrs Discombobulus* 1985, *Norvin and the Shark* 2001, *The Great White Piratical Rumbustification* 2002, *A Dragon of an Ordinary Family* 2004), Canterbury Children's Theatre (*Robots, Redheads and Rascals* 1985), Tim Bray Productions (*A Lion in the Meadow, The Leaf Magic, The Witch in the Cherry Tree* 2004) and others.

Every effort has been made to ensure accuracy of this very extensive bibliography representing 45 years' writing. Principal English-language publication of each book is given for major countries (not subsequent paperback editions or reprints except where revised). The publishers welcome information on omissions or inaccuracies.

Principal publishers of Margaret Mahy's books in special editions and translations include:

UK (large editions)
> Chivers; Isis
> Educational hardcover: Longman

France
> Gallimard

Italy
> Mondadori; Ediciones Elle

Germany
> Spectrum Verlag; Sauerlander; Arena;
> Ravensburger; Neuer Finken; Jungbrunnen

Spain
> Edicones B, EDEBE; Altea;
> Grijalbo Mondadori

Spain (Catalan)
> Ediciones de la Magrana S/A

Greece
> S Patakis

Holland
> Em Queridos; Lemniscaat; Zwijsen;
> Uitgeverj Facet nv; Ploegsma; Thieme

Belgium
> de Vries-Brouwers

Denmark
> Gyldendal; Forum

Norway
> Stabenfeldt; Bogklubben Rasmus

Sweden
> Norsdedts; AWE/Gebers; Alfabeta;
> Sjostrands; Eriksson & Lindgren

Finland
> Tammi; Kustannus-Makela

Estonia
> Eesti Raamat

South Africa (Afrikaans)
> Human & Rousseau

Mexico
> Fondo de Cultura Economica

Japan
> Iwinami Shoten; Sailor Shuppan

Thailand
> Butterfly Book House

China
> Eastern Publishing Co Ltd

Principal publishers in English are:

UK
> Dent; Penguin; Hamish Hamilton;
> HarperCollins; Transworld; Frances Lincoln;
> Heinemann, Reed International; Jonathon
> Cape/Puffin

USA
> Franklin Watts; Margaret McElderry
> (Simon & Schuster); Dell; Atheneum;
> Delacorte Press; Viking Penguin; Viking
> Kestrel; Greenwillow (HarperColllins);
> Orchard Books; Godine; Dial Books

Australia and New Zealand
> Penguin Australia; HarperCollins;
> Allen & Unwin; Scholastic;
> School Publications, Department of
> Education; Shortland Publications;
> Wendy Pye Publishing Ltd

AWARDS and HONOURS

Esther Glen Medal
(NZ Library Association)
for *A Lion in the Meadow*, 1969

Esther Glen Medal (NZLA)
for *The First Margaret Mahy
Story Book*, 1973

Een Zilveren Griffell, 1978

Best Children's Books citation
for *The Haunting*, 1982

School Library Journal
Best Book citation
for *The Haunting*, 1982

Carnegie Medal
(British Library Association)
for *The Haunting*, 1982

Esther Glen Medal
(NZLA)
for *The Haunting*, 1983

Writer's Fellowship,
University of Canterbury, 1984

Carnegie Medal (BLA)
for *The Changeover: a supernatural romance*,
1984

Notable Book citation
by Association for Library Service
to Children
for *The Changeover: a supernatural romance*,
1984

Horn Book Honor List
for *The Changeover: a supernatural romance*,
1985

Children's Book of the Year citation
by American Library Association,
for *The Changeover: a supernatural romance*,
1986

Best Book for Young Adults citation (ALA)
for *The Changeover: a supernatural romance*,
1986

Esther Glen Medal (NZLIA)
for *The Changeover: a supernatural romance*,
1985

New Zealand Literary Fund
Lifetime Achievement Award, 1985

Best Books citation,
Young Adult Services of American Library
Service, for *The Tricksters*, 1987

Horn Book Honor List
for *The Catalogue of the Universe*, 1987

Ten Best Illustrated Books list,
New York Times Book Review,
for *Seventeen Kings and 42 Elephants*, 1987

Carnegie Medal (BLA) runner-up
for *Memory*, 1987

Observer Teenage Fiction Award (UK)
for *Memory*, 1987

Society of School Librarians
International Book Award
for *Memory*, 1988

Boston Globe/Horn Book award
for *Memory*, 1988

May Hill Arbuthnot Lecture
(Association for Library Service to Children),
Pittsburg, USA, 1989

International New York Film Festival,
Gold medal for TV drama *Strangers*, 1989

Inaugural recipient,
Margaret Mahy Medal and Lecture,
Children's Book Foundation of New Zealand,
1991

Order of New Zealand, 1993

Children's Book of the Year, Junior Fiction,
AIM Children's Book Awards (NZ),
for *Underrunners*, 1993

Esther Glen Medal (NZLIA)
for *Underrunners*, 1993

Honorary Doctor of Letters,
University of Canterbury, 1993

A.W. Reed Lifetime Achievement Award (NZ),
first recipient, 1999

Supreme Book of the Year
and Picture Book of the Year,
New Zealand Post Book Awards,
for *A Summery Saturday Morning*, 2000

Honour Book, Junior Fiction,
New Zealand Post Book Awards,
for *A Villain's Night Out*, 2000

Esther Glen Medal (NZLIA)
for *24 Hours*, 2001

Honour Book, Senior Fiction,
New Zealand Post Book Awards,
for *24 Hours*, 2001

Guardian Fiction Award shortlist,
for *24 Hours*, 2001

Book of the Year, Senior Fiction,
New Zealand Post Book Awards,
for *Alchemy*, 2003

Phoenix Award, Children's Literature Association
(presented in Winnipeg, Canada),
for 'the most outstanding book for children
published twenty years earlier which did not
receive a major award at the time',
for *The Catalogue of the Universe*, 2005.

In addition, most Margaret Mahy novels such
as *The Catalogue of the Universe, Memory, The
Tricksters, Dangerous Spaces* and *Underrunners*
have appeared on various American 'best
book' lists such as the Parenting's Reading
Magic List, Editor's Choice (Booklist), etc.